EDGE

WALKERS

EDGE WALKERS

Reimagining faith, church and theology

Edited by
Armen Gakavian
Karina Kreminski
Steve Taylor

At the Edges Publishing
Surry Hills, NSW, Australia

Here we meet real people – church and faith edge-walkers – telling their stories and sharing the expressions of Christian faith and church that have brought them life and enabled faithful Jesus-following. Reading *Edge-walkers* takes you beyond caricatures and misunderstandings into the hopeful faith and honest communities of these practitioners. A valuable insight for centre-church leaders and beacons of hope for those who know centre-church no longer offers life for them.
– Alan Jamieson, co-author of *In-tensional: A Way Forward for the Church*

This is not a theory book. Neither is it missiology lite. Twenty flawed saints share stories of vulnerability and delight that made me laugh out loud and cry tears of memory. They carry an autobiographical flavour, but also manage to address key concerns and challenges. What makes these packages significant is their emergence in a society still able to recall a spirit of wilderness and hothouse experimentation, despite church stagnation. These reflective innovators share theological wisdom grounded in lived experiences.
– Rev. Dr Amelia Koh-Butler, Mission Secretary, Council for World Mission

Edge-walkers is a radical call to play; to see again that the whole of our world is God-infused. Through the book's multiple lenses, we are invited into owning our questions and doubts and possibilities as nourishment for faithful living. The real value of such a collection of memoir theology is not in chapters of fixed answers, but in the encouragement of an unfinished journey with others still finding God in the surf, in Discord, around the table and in the daily questions of being human.
– Rev. Andrew Johnson, Senior Minister at Newtown Mission

This is a book written for those who grew up within Christian cultures that tend towards cultural and theological fundamentalism who are nevertheless, and for a variety of reasons, seeking to embrace more mystical, ecological and socially progressive forms of the faith. For that reason, this book will be of great help to anyone who finds themselves apparently alone and in similar territory: desiring something more and yet cautious of losing everything.
– Rev. Dr Garry Worete Deverell, trawloolway theologian and author of *Contemplating Country*

As the church in the West suffers a crisis, new spaces of creativity appear, forging community and bringing hope. This is the mantra of this book with its lay theologies, practices and hopes. Honest. Vulnerable. Explorative. Pensive. Prayerful. Between institutional church largely abandoned and personal faith almost lost lie these stories of hope in a third way, not unlike – in some ways – the stories of Desert Fathers and Mothers of old. These green shoots of faith on footpaths and in alleyways rather than in neat garden beds may well be the seeds of hope for the church's renewal.
– Dr Charles Ringma, AM, Professor Emeritus at Regent College and author of *In the Midst of Much-Doing: Cultivating a Missional Spirituality*

Edge-Walkers is inspiration for those who draw themselves into God and Christian community beyond the institutional church. This book is lived-out, grounded theology shaped around a living, revealing God in our constantly changing world. No doubt the personal life stories of the authors in this book will challenge the reader with the many difficult questions posed. It will also invite the reader to ponder the strange ways of the Spirit of God within our world and blowing on the edges of the church.
– Rev. Mark Faulkner, Saltbush Ministry Team Leader in the Uniting Church in Australia, NSW/ACT Synod

Warm and often vulnerable, the voices in this volume tell of the life that grows in the corners of community and the borders of our worldviews. They speak of a Christ who is gritty, surprising, fluid; a Christ who is present in the cracks where many of us choose not to look. Anyone searching for signs of hope for the church, this book is for you.
– Mikali Anagnostis, singer/songwriter and candidate for ministry in the Uniting Church in Australia, NSW/ACT Synod

Edge-walkers confronts an undeniable truth: Christian churches are moving away from the cultural centre. Rather than mourning this shift, the authors recognise it as an opportunity for creativity, pluralism and renewal. Through a collection of thoughtful and honest reflections, practitioners from diverse backgrounds explore what ministry looks like at the margins, offering fresh perspectives that are both hopeful and engaging.
– Rev. Assoc. Prof. Robyn Whitaker, Uniting Church Minister, Biblical Scholar, Public Theologian and author of *Even the Devil Quotes Scripture*

It is no secret that Jesus came from the margins, and the church has often served most faithfully from this place. In *Edge-walkers*, Armen, Karina and Steve gather an innovative, compassionate and articulate group of thinking practitioners seeking a shared grace across difference. I found myself in tears reading stories drawn from these richly diverse Christianities. This will resonate with those working in community development, faith-based organisations, and movements for justice.
– Dr Tanya Riches, Director, Master of Transformational Development, Eastern College Australia

Edge-walkers is an excellent embodiment of contemporary biographies as exploratory theologies. The book is a selection of courageous stories of people who have tried to hold onto their faith in Jesus while, at the same time, going to the very edge – and sometimes beyond the edge – of their faith. These stories are brave but not boastful, characterised as they are by humility, vulnerability and fragility. These accounts invite us to have the courage to join these authors on their journeys, through scary valleys of uncertainty and insecurity into sunny vistas of inclusivity and mutuality.
– Dave Andrews, member of the Waiters Union and author of
Not Religion but Love

What a rich constellation of courageous stories told from the edges – liminal spaces where faith is unravelling, re-weaving, and being lived with honesty. What stands out is the deep authenticity of these writers and the communities they have journeyed with, committed to following Jesus in the messy, uncertain work of presence, love and shared life. These stories give permission to risk, to fail, to learn and to keep moving forward with grace, shaped not by certainty but by the quiet, generative work of the Spirit. May these 'edge-walkers' awaken in us a renewed sense of curiosity and courage, as the Spirit – the One who birthed the church –forms a more inclusive and generous church, present to the world with humility and love.
– Rev. Glen Spencer, Director of Mission in the Uniting Church in Australia, NSW/ACT Synod

Acknowledgments

Publishing a book is always a collaborative effort, even more so when multiple contributors are involved. Each practitioner who wrote for this book spent countless hours contemplating, reflecting on, writing and rewriting the material that eventually became a chapter. Then we edited the stories. This involved authors and editors listening, negotiating and refining words, phrases and ideas together over several months. As the chapters were finalised and the book started to take shape, there was a deep satisfaction in seeing the stories of sleeves-rolled-up, on-the-ground edge ministries go to print.

Reading the chapters, we were struck by the uniqueness of each edge-walker's journey – a reflection of the beauty and diversity of God's people from diverse backgrounds and walks of life. But we also began to see a bigger picture – one of the Spirit of God at work in unexpected places through everyday people who love their communities. We are grateful to each practitioner for sharing their stories so vulnerably and with so much insight. Your journeys have inspired us and filled us with hope, reminding us that God *is* at work, even if we don't always see it.

There is also the collaboration that happens behind the scenes.

A generous grant from the Australian Research Theology Foundation Inc., and the gifts of several generous donors, made it possible for us to edit and prepare the book for publication.

Richard Smart from the Australian Publishers Association's advisory service provided invaluable guidance throughout the publishing journey, drawing on his decades of accumulated wisdom.

Other publishers were also generous with their advice, encouragement and resources.

Our friends, families and colleagues supported us and cheered us along the way.

Paris Giannakis generously donated his time to design the beautiful cover and spent many hours going back and forth with us to fine tune the images and text.

Our editing load was lightened by the excellent copyediting work of Alison Hill and Lesa Scholl on several of the chapters.

In the final stages of the editing process, Hanna Holford's meticulous copyediting and proofreading brought important final touches to the text. We are grateful for her dedication, patience and eye for detail.

Matthew Oswald @ Like Design shaped the manuscript into its final form, turning a simple Word document into the presentable, readable book you hold in your hands.

It's been a delight working with you all and seeing our collaborative efforts come to fruition!

This book is about the new things God is doing in our midst. We acknowledge all who came before us, both at the core and edge of the Church and everywhere in between, on whose foundations these new things have been built. We celebrate the faithfulness of God, who has been at work in every generation, renewing the Church and all of Creation.

Finally, the bulk of the work on this book was undertaken on Gadigal Land. We are grateful to the Aboriginal elders past and present who have cared for the ground we walk on and the waters that sustain us. We acknowledge that this land was never ceded and commit ourselves to truth-telling, justice and reconciliation.

Armen Gakavian, with Karina Kreminski and Steve Taylor

Contents

Introduction 1

REIMAGINING FAITH

Godspeed / Will Small 13

Mysticism / Carolyn Meers 17

Art / Michael Henderson 33

Play / Rod Pattenden 48

Trauma / Joel Hollier 62

Earthy / Jono Ingram 73

Misfits / Will Small 88

REIMAGINING CHURCH

A Prayer for a Bush Picnic / Jono Ingram 107

Pakipaki / Alimoni T. Taumoepeau, Uilisone Kiriona Mafaufau, Mosese Taufa and Seini Tokilupe Taufa 109

Neighbourhood / Christine Palmer 119

Gathering / Simon Moyle 132

Kenosis / Jennifer Trevena 149

Digital / Kelly N. S. Woods (PastoralHare) 166

Liminal / Cyrus Kung 181

REIMAGINING THEOLOGY

A Prayer for Walking the Edge / Jono Ingram 199

Decolonisation / Naomi Wolfe 201

Malagigiri / Cliff Bird 221

Making / Steve Taylor 235

Eucharist / Karyl Davison 249

Evangelism / Karina Kreminski 264

Conclusion 280

Endnotes 287

Contributors 302

Editors 308

Introduction

Beginnings

Good things come from the edges.

Edges are liminal spaces where one thing ends and new things begin. Take a look at anything in front of you right now and move your attention to the edge of that thing. You will see that the edge creates a unique perspective as it hovers between what is and what could be – what lies 'out there'. The edge carries two identities: within its DNA is the substance of what it is, yet it also reaches out and maybe even longs for what it is not. It can see another world and can move between worlds, substances and imaginations. Edges can be 'thin places' in that they connect one context to another.

Another thought that might come to you as you look at the edge of something is that it is precarious. When we place ourselves at the edge we need to artfully balance ourselves lest we lose our footing. We are on uncertain ground, and we must choose whether we stay in this unstable place or move back to certainty. Alternatively, we can choose to step out, leave the place we are in and move beyond it – to an unfamiliar place that exists outside of what is known.

The temptation to retreat is there because edges are uncomfortable. It takes courage to stay there. It's risky. It's a place of messiness and transformation. But it's when we are playing at the edges that we experience innovation, creativity and impact. The edges entice us to go deeper.

You could also picture the edge of a cliff overlooking the ocean. Think about how years and years of winds and waves shape the outline of the land. You might visit the seaside one year, trace the outline of the cliff-face, and then on a return visit the following year find that the outline has changed shape and looks quite different. The edge of that cliff is vulnerable – it must bend and bow to the elements, giving itself to and working with its context so that a new sketch emerges. Similarly, edges are always changing and transforming; they are flexible and moving, bending to and working with what lies beyond. They are open to transformation, innovation and movement.

Core and edge

You might hear today that the church is at the edges of society. Of course this is not true in every context but it is mostly true in the Western world. We have shifted away from the church being at the centre of society, integrated into the fabric of everyday social life. People used to meet in church, get married in church and look to the church for wisdom, community and authority. This happens less and less today as people find community, wisdom and spirituality or faith elsewhere.

The authors of this book don't believe this is a terrible thing. While there are many attempts today by people of the Christian faith to move back to the centre of society, we believe that the edges are where creativity, innovation and transformation occur. It is our belief that as we pay attention to what is happening at the edges of faith, church and theology and wrestle with issues at the margins, both our church and society flourish.

However, we don't want to romanticise the edges. There are plenty of communities that are at the edges of society through no choice of their own and that find themselves at a disadvantage. For them, being at the edge means marginalisation that can lead to invisibility, a lack of power and having no voice. These communities try to move to the centre so that they might be able to thrive. We acknowledge the struggle inherent in these spaces and communities and are in solidarity with them as they fight for representation.

Yet it is still worth thinking further about the core/edge dynamic. When we look at the ecology of the church and various other institutions, we can see the tension between core and edge as people struggle to work out how to coexist within the same space. While we have a bias towards the edges in this book, we believe that in a healthy ecology we need both core and edge leaders and practitioners. The core typically produces stability, familiarity and good standing in the community, and is usually resourced with property, money and expertise. The edge embraces innovation and the unknown and has fewer resources. In an ideal world the core would support and resource the edges. However, the core is often threatened by the edges, and the edges are misunderstood. And it doesn't help that the edges can be sharp! There can be a fear within the core that the system might lose its identity or stability if innovation occurs. And so the edges are often pushed out, or they leave willingly, seeing no room for them within the organisation. In this book you will read about how a range of edge practitioners have managed this tension with the core.

We want to be careful not to dichotomise core and edge too sharply, as we know this can breed a division that is unhelpful. However, not to recognise that there is a tension between core and edge is also a mistake. Most people have a little bit of core and edge in them, but usually they identify more strongly with one or the other. We have seen this in ourselves as leaders who have been in the faith context for decades. The lines between core and edge are blurred and sometimes it's hard to distinguish between the two. Other times there is a sense of being 'on the edge of inside' – this often occurs when an institutional leader finds themselves moving away from the core, or when an edge practitioner speaks into the institution. This is a difficult place to sit, as those within the institution may criticise these people for not being loyal enough and those outside may attack them for being institutionalised and too ensconced by the system!

By definition, core or 'centre' thinking is the dominant or default form of thinking in our society; its voice is prevalent and governs the way our institutions are run. *Edge-Walkers* seeks to highlight the voices and issues our world might be pushing to the side, to the detriment of the learning and growth of our church and society.

From 'Christianity' to 'Christianities'
This book came about because each of its editors is passionate about edges. We all saw ourselves as 'edge-walkers' in some way, and we knew of many others who were at the edges of their faith, church and theology, working quietly away in the background, flying under the radar. We wanted to champion their voices and showcase the brave and hard work they are doing, often unsupported. Edge-walkers are seen as

unsuccessful in the eyes of most people, as they do not measure success in the same way the core might do. Success at the edges usually comes very slowly, and the scorecard looks very different. But what we discovered as we listened to and read the stories of the brave edge-walkers in this book is that their contribution goes far beyond that of reaching successful goals or fulfilling strategies. Instead, what they bring to the ecology of faith, church and theology is innovation, play, a safe ground for experimentation and a training ground for innovative thinkers and practitioners. Even though the initiatives themselves are not lucrative, flashy or big, by their very existence they are doing something much more subversive and creative than we might expect. When we ignore or starve them out of existence, it is to the detriment of the whole ecosystem.

We want to showcase these practitioners so that the core might listen to them, understand them and support them, whether this be emotional support or financial. We encourage core institutional leaders to read this book to hear the stories, struggles and joys of each practitioner who is wrestling with the practice of faith, church and theology at the edges. We also encourage edge-walkers to read this book to discover companions who are on the same journey. Many of the practitioners who wrote for this book mentioned that they felt emotional, liberated, heard and vulnerable as they penned their stories. Writing always taps into our deepest parts and many of the contributors were moved and surprised by what they found within them as they wrote. As they wrestled with their particular topics, we, the editors, helped them to find their voices. Many of the contributors are emerging writers and we were thrilled to have played a role in their emergence. Bringing this book together was a joy for us.

This book reveals that there are emerging expressions of 'Christianities' in the West. Christianity can no longer be seen as a monolithic expression of faith (if it ever was). As these practitioners wrestle with the ways they practice faith, theology and church, new forms and expressions emerge that need to be seen and heard. These edge voices can change and are changing the landscape of faith today, contributing to the generativity of our faith. As people in the West today question spirituality and the relevance of the church, and as many Christians deconstruct and reconstruct their faith, we can find hope that our faith is not a 'one-size-fits-all'.

Being a people of faith in our time isn't about capturing the zeitgeist of the day. It isn't a pragmatic strategy where we strain to be 'relevant' to our world. We don't contextualise the gospel because of a consumerist narrative that beckons us to give people what they want or to give them more options. Nor is it a bland call to be like everyone else so that we can be likeable.

Instead, we want to encourage a generativity and diversity of ecclesial (church) communities, faith and theologies because God's realm is creative, multiform, diverse and open to possibility and imagination. The Christian Scriptures talk about the 'manifold wisdom of God' (Ephesians 3:10, NIV) revealed through the church. That word, 'manifold', means diverse, complex, rich, colourful. The picture is of an intricate tapestry.

We who follow Christ swim in a sea of miracles, mystery and complexity – that is our habitat. And our faith tradition is not dead but living, breathing and unafraid of being nimble and adaptive. God moves in and through particular people in particular places and in particular times. This means the presence and activity of God is expressed in diverse, rich and multicoloured ways in different contexts.

Gathering the stories

We gave each contributor to this book two questions to wrestle with: 'How has *practicing* faith, church or theology differently or at the edges impacted and transformed your *thinking* about faith, church and theology?' and 'How has *thinking* about faith, church or theology differently or at the edges impacted and transformed your *practice* of faith, church and theology?' We asked them to choose one word as the title of their chapter, based on a theme that emerged as they wrestled with and interrogated their lived experiences and explored the new imaginations that were taking shape. Some gravitated towards writing about doing church at the edges; others explored their personal faith; still others questioned, critiqued and interrogated normative theologies, turning them on their heads and making us question our assumptions.

We asked the contributors to write in the style of 'memoir theology', which brings together the practical, emotional, spiritual and theological through recounting lived experiences. We wanted to publish reflective and rich stories. So you will notice that the chapters are not 'academic', but personal accounts of lived experiences seen through a theological lens. By theological we simply mean thinking about the question, 'What does it look like if we bring God into this?' A future research paper, based on a thematic analysis of these stories, could provide a more academic approach and allow us to document the contribution of edge-walkers to the faith and the church.

Each of our contributors work at the edges of faith, theology or church; we chose practitioners from all three of these contexts to ensure a cross-representation of experiences. The book is organised in three parts around these three aspects, though of course faith, church and theology all speak into one another and intersect. Some of the contributors are more traditional in their practice of faith, church and theology, while others are more alternative in their approach. This means that the views of each contributor do not necessarily represent the views of other contributors, nor do they necessarily represent the views of the editors. However, what all the contributors have in common is that they are current practitioners who love their community and who desire to reimagine the church.

These practitioners' stories lead us to ask questions like: What does success look like? What are the advantages of 'failing'? What is core and what is edge in this context? What happens when the edge becomes core? Where does this new ecclesial community fit? What might be the new things God is doing here that we need to pay attention to? How do we support these edge-walkers? How do these new expressions (of faith, theology or church) interact with, impact or shape traditional forms of Christianity?

We were thrilled with the stories we read because of their honest articulation of the struggles and joys of faithfully walking with the Creator. We felt there was a good representation of diverse voices. However, we would have liked more, and we feel this is a shortcoming of this book. We did approach several other practitioners from First Nations and diverse cultural and linguistic backgrounds about writing for this book, but understandably they were not able to commit due to time and other pressures. We therefore hope to put out a second volume of stories in the future. We also understand that the format of this book, as well as the framing of the concept, might not have been suitable to some people of diverse cultural or socio-economic backgrounds. To address this, a future volume could incorporate different formats. All this to say, this book is certainly not an exhaustive list of practitioners who are edge-walkers. There are so many more stories to tell. We hope this book inspires you to look out for those stories and to showcase them as you are able.

We are deeply grateful to the contributors of this book. It has been a long journey – writing and publishing a book requires a huge commitment by writers and publishers alike. You have been our inspiration as we have read your stories. We hope this book is an encouragement to you and to others who are edge-walkers and risk-takers who traverse different worlds.

And finally, a note to those who do not identify as Christian or as people of faith. Perhaps you have never had faith, or you have had faith but moved away from the church for whatever reason. This is not a call for you to engage with the church, but an open invitation to hear these creative stories and listen to the diversity that exists within these emergent 'Christianities'. We want you to know that there is space for you if you choose. In today's world of polarisation, fear and a desperate grasp for certainty, we hope we have presented the option of a Christianity that is mysterious and complex rather than simplistic, manifold rather than homogenous, creative rather than boring, and, ultimately, generously open to all.

Karina Kreminski, with Steve Taylor and Armen Gakavian

FAITH

Godspeed

I once read that
God moves
three miles an hour

The average pace you walk

Then again,

A man told me
just yesterday

'God dwells in unapproachable light'
and if you could move at light-speed
you'd turn and see yourself coming

In truth,
I cannot tell you
what *Godspeed* actually means

But maybe

When you
find yourself *there*:

At the precipice
the edge

You must
keep walking
shuffling,
limping,
breathing

Heart in throat,
at times
you will
be tempted to turn back

But your movement
makes the path
for someone else to come

Though look more carefully
and you'll find

You're not the first
to tread this place

The edge is just the name
for whatever geography
lies beyond the reach of
yesterday's cartography

And many make the mistake
of believing the map *is* the landscape

But you realise,
(don't you realise?)
that's the part that's man-made

There's nowhere you can go
where God has not already been

So walk your soles to ground
until your feet on earth remind you

There are burning bushes everywhere

Sacred ground abounds

Even
at the precipice
the edge

The unfound.

*Note: The idea of the 'three mile an hour God' comes from
Japanese theologian Kosuke Koyama.*

Mysticism

Carolyn Meers

The Christian of the future will be a mystic, or will not
be a Christian anymore.
– Karl Rahner[1]

When Jacob awoke from his sleep, he thought, 'Surely
the LORD is in this place, and I was not aware of it.'
– Genesis 28:16, NIV

God comes to us disguised as our life.
– Paula D'Arcy[2]

A word like mysticism can come across a little 'woo-woo', a
little grandiose, reserved for those out-there saints who have
trance-like, out-of-body, near-death encounters with God. To
many people of faith, mystical experiences are perceived as
more 'new age' than deeply Christian. Yet there seems to be
a growing desire for spirituality in our world, something that
creates a connection to that which is deepest within us or that

which is beyond us. This makes sense of the growing market for things like breathwork groups, yoga retreats, forest bathing and mindfulness apps.

I write this chapter as an ordinary church girl who happened to discover the mystical tradition of Christianity. This discovery saved my faith: it led me to work towards seeing how church and mysticism could intersect. I began to understand how the contemplative practices of our faith could be incorporated into a faith community in a way that supported people longing for a kind of everyday, ordinary mysticism.

God disguised as my life

I have spent my whole life faithfully attending church. But when I think back over my formative spiritual experiences, I don't remember any of them happening within the walls of a church.

I am eight or nine years old, standing around at netball training at Jamison Park, Penrith. The sunset is an outrageous expression of red, orange, pink, fading into purple. The Western Sydney sky showing off above me feels expansive and glorious and, in that moment, I tangibly experience feeling seen and known and loved by God.

I am twenty-one years old and for the first time in my life I am facing genuine loss, grief and pain. I am heartbroken by the end of a romantic relationship. Two of my closest friends have moved away and I feel abandoned. A fellow youth leader in my church has tragically drowned in a diving accident. I am utterly confronted with the pain of life and love. A few months later I am hiking up a mountain, seething with anger and grief. At church we have been singing a song that goes something like, 'God, you are my everything'. I get to the top of the climb, look out over the wide expanse of bush and scream, 'You are not my everything!!!' That day I go toe-to-toe with God, pouring out all my rage, fear and disorientation. And in that moment, I encounter the God who can handle all my swearing and tears, accusations and despair. I encounter the Divine Presence that I do not have to perform for, but Who can hold the fullness of my wild humanity and love me in the midst of it.

I am thirty years old. I have just endured a brutal first pregnancy. At thirty-two weeks, after constant nausea and vomiting for twenty-two weeks, I am hospitalised with preeclampsia. I spend four weeks on bedrest, before they have to deliver my daughter for the sake of my health and hers. After the birth, my daughter is cared for in the NICU and they send me home without her. Every day after that I arrive at the hospital as early as I am allowed and stay there with her for as long as they let me. I am beyond exhausted. One afternoon the nurses order me home to rest, so I wander down to the beach where we live and sit on a park bench, staring blankly at the ocean. I have nothing left. No tears, no energy, no prayers, just utter exhaustion. And in that moment, almost like the wisp of a gentle breeze, I feel the Divine brush past me. Sometimes it's so hard to put words to these experiences, but I know that in that moment God is with me on my park bench, and God is with Freya, as she lies in her crib in the NICU.

I am forty-one years old. My faith has slowly been unravelling for many years. This has been at times a very painful and destabilising experience. I have lost any sense of theological certainty; things I had long felt to be 'true' no longer make sense. I'm uncertain if I can continue to have faith; God seems absent and silent. For many years, we had magpies come and land on our front deck; they would waddle up to the sliding doors and tap their beaks on the glass. I would tell my kids it was my magpie friends who had come to remind me that God's Spirit is with us. I knew they were just tapping at their own reflection, but often, while sitting at our kitchen table, working from home, the tap-tap-tap would be my little reminder of God. But even the magpies haven't been around for a long time now. I tell my husband that I think I'm done with my faith, I'm going to chuck it in. I go and sit out on our front deck with my coffee and raisin toast. I have my Bible with me and I'm going to read the Emmaus Road passage one last time. (Because isn't that what you do when you're going to end your faith? Read your Bible one last time?) This passage is about disappointment, loss and walking away with unmet expectations. In that moment I am one of the disciples, walking away from Jerusalem, saying to myself, 'I had hoped that he was the one ...' I look up and see a magpie sitting on the electric wires a few doors down. I watch as it flies and sits on the fence about three meters away from where I'm sitting. It cocks its head and looks at me; I look back at it. The magpie hops down to the table where I'm sitting. I hold out a piece of toast, it comes over and pecks it out of my hand and then flies off again. I have no idea what to do with that moment. But I have kept a hold of my faith, or it has kept a hold of me, and I'm still in the rubble, slowly rebuilding.

Ordinary mystics

A sunset, a mountain, a park bench, a magpie.

These count as mystical encounters with God. They have woken me up like Jacob was when he said, 'Surely God was in this place and I didn't know it!' They have been God, coming to me, disguised as my life.

Mysticism simply takes two things seriously: one, that God, the Divine Presence, fills the created world; and two, that we are able to experience God and know things from that experience. Mystical experiences can be bold, dynamic, obvious and impactful, but more often than not, in my experience, they are subtle, gentle, fleeting, whisper-like. Mysticism makes space for a Divine presence that 'speaks' and 'acts' while also acknowledging the presence of God known in silence and felt in absence. It invites us to take our experiences seriously, as a valid way of both knowing and connecting with God. It invites us to trust that, in humanity's long and growing relationship with God, it is only our wrestling with the mystery of Divine encounter that has helped us to make any sense of ourselves, our world and God.

Richard Rohr writes, 'We don't need to be afraid of the word "mystic". It simply means one who has moved from mere belief or belonging systems about God to actual inner experience.'[3] Mysticism trusts that God is not just 'out there' but is also deep within each and every one of us. As Paul said in Acts 17:28, 'For in him we live and move and have our being.' Mysticism is not just for cloistered nuns and holy people; everyday, ordinary mystics are people who trust that there is nowhere we can go and nothing we can do that takes us out of God's presence.

Contemplative practices equip us to pay attention. It's easy to sleepwalk through life, oblivious to the gentle and subtle movements of God around and within us. Regular practices of silence, solitude and stillness help us to notice God's presence and wake us up to the possibility of a mystical encounter in places we never imagined. Cole Arthur Riley writes, 'My faith is held together by wonder – by every defiant commitment to presence and paying attention.'[4] The Christian faith tradition is full of contemplative practices that awaken wonder in us and train us to be attentive to the Divine presence woven through our ordinary, everyday lives.

A contemplative faith

I have the privilege of leading a phenomenal and beautifully ordinary church called Central. We meet in Port Kembla, a suburb of Wollongong that is equal parts industrial eyesore and breathtaking coastal beauty. We gather on unceded Dharawal Country. The land that is now 'owned' by those privileged enough to seek ocean views, and steel industry companies, was and still is sacred to First Nations peoples.

Many of us at Central, including myself, were raised and formed by the evangelical and/or charismatic traditions of the church. The main practices we were given to sustain our faith were the 'quiet time' (devotional Bible reading and prayer), church attendance, serving (usually within the church), and speaking in tongues and tithing (for the charismatics). These things 'worked' for us ... until they didn't. We hit crises of faith with questions bigger and wider than any answers our quiet time could give us. Our lives fell apart: we experienced pain, loss and suffering, and the promise that if we followed Jesus and did life 'God's way' things would go well for us became a lie. We entered the wilderness, or the dark night of the soul, or the desert ... and we either had to go deeper into this thing called Christianity or we'd leave it all behind.

In the journey of the unravelling of my faith, I discovered mysticism and the contemplative stream of Christianity. I began reading about things I had never heard of: *Lectio Divina*, the examen, pilgrimage, silence, imaginative prayer, centring prayer, breath prayer, the daily office, spiritual direction.

I learned about the lives of the Saints, regular people who profoundly encountered God in their ordinary lives: in their shattered dreams, illness, darkness and persecution, and in creation, love, community and daily rhythms. Stumbling across contemplative Christianity felt like discovering a chest full of treasure, buried within the history of my own faith, a treasure I didn't know existed. I wanted to practice this new kind of spirituality, but I couldn't do it on my own, and so in May of 2017 we started a monthly contemplative service. We had no illusions that we would become mystics; we were just ordinary people seeking a way to open ourselves up to God's Spirit at work within and among us. At the time I think we imagined we were just trying something different, hoping it might help us out in our floundering faith. I don't think any of us realised how much it would change us.

Permission to try something new

We began our contemplative service as a six-month experiment. Using the language of 'experiment' was helpful for us, because an experiment is successful no matter what the outcome. The aim is simply to discover something new. What we would be asking in six months' time was not, 'Have we got more people attending our church?' or 'Was this successful because "x" many people showed up each month?' We were looking for life. We were going to measure lightness and ease, the sense of God's presence among us. We were hoping for honesty, authenticity and to be drawn deeper. I had thought that, if at the end of six months some of us had a few more practices in the toolbox of our spirituality, then the service would have met its goal.

Almost everything about the way we set up and structured this gathering was new and different for those of us used to church being worship and a sermon. In our classic church service, we mostly sat in rows, facing the front where the worship band and preacher stood. For our new gathering, we set up chairs in a circle around the communion table. We were going to be practicing together, all of us equals in our search for God, and the presence of Christ as bread and wine would be what we saw as we looked across the room at each other. I take my hat off to everyone at Central who was willing to give the contemplative service a try. It takes courage to show up to something different. It's vulnerable to feel seen by others in a room while attempting spiritual practices that were new (to us) and unusual. It's comforting to sing two fast and two slow songs and then listen to someone else's thoughts about God. It takes bravery to sit in the unknown, to participate and to be willing to share.

The gift of awkwardness

I was formed as a leader in charismatic church spaces, and we were trained to eliminate every trace of awkwardness in a church service. Everyone was to be welcomed with a smile, background music would fill every silence, the band would be polished, the preacher confident, crying babies were gently ushered towards soundproof rooms, our prayers were full of faith and hope. We broke every rule in our contemplative service ... except I hope we still smiled at one another.

To embrace mysticism is to get comfortable with silence. In our gatherings, times of silence became more and more common. I remember when we first tried centring prayer as a practice together. Centring prayer is a form of silent prayer where the aim is to be open to God's love for us and our love for God. Father Thomas Keating has been instrumental, along with others, in revitalising centring prayer in modern contemplative practice, and he suggests using a 'sacred word' like God, Yahweh or Love to help focus your prayer when inevitably your mind wanders.[5] We acknowledged that for many of us this was going to be difficult, because we rarely sat in silence; in fact some of us actively avoided silence. So we started with two minutes of silence and then we invited people to share what the experience was like for them. We were working to cultivate a culture of honesty where the 'right answer' was just the truth, not the answer you were 'supposed' to give. One person said the silence felt warm, comfortable and familiar. Someone else shared that they spent the entire two minutes trying to come up with a good sacred word. A third person said they started off okay and then unintentionally began planning their dinners for the week and only remembered they were supposed to be praying when the timer went off. And then another person spoke up and said, 'I hated that, it was awful ...' We all genuinely laughed. For some the silence was life-giving, for others it was difficult but something they wanted to lean into, for yet others we just suggested they use the time to take a nap. We were learning to embrace that not everything works for everyone, and that's ok.

Most of us attending this contemplative service and leaning into new spiritual practices were used to feeling 'successful' at Christianity. We were still attending church, we knew how to tick the box of prayer and Bible reading, but in our attempts at contemplative practice we were being humbled. We were encountering the God who was simply pleased with our feeble attempts at prayer and connection, and who didn't require anything of us except our showing up. We were learning to embrace failure as a legitimate way of being present to God, and we were slowly learning how to embrace awkwardness in our gatherings.

A confessing community

After a few years of running our contemplative service we had crafted a familiar rhythm. We'd begin with a welcome and a grounding or presence prayer. We would then do two spiritual practices, sometimes based on a theme, sometimes connected to the writing or wisdom of a particular saint, mystic or spiritual teacher, and we would always finish with communion.

But ever since starting these services I had been wrestling with the loss of confession as a life-giving spiritual practice. In the Scriptures we are encouraged to be a confessing people, but the Christianity I was experiencing seemed to have forgotten how to tell the truth about ourselves as individuals and as a collective. There was no place for confession in our gatherings, and looking like you had it all together was celebrated and encouraged.

I wondered what confession would have to look like as a practice to help create an authentic, real, trusting community. I didn't want people to feel guilt or shame, but neither did I want a kind of performative confession as a 'box-ticking' exercise. I wanted to create a community that could tell the truth and was safe enough to bear all our brokenness – a space where we could each confess the truth of our lives – both the precious and beautiful and the messy and painful and hard.

We eventually added a practice of confession to the beginning of our contemplative service. Not necessarily the confession of sin, but the confession of what is true and real for us. We would put a confession prompt up on the screen and, with the person next to you, you would be invited to answer honestly. There would always be a blessing for us to speak over one another to finish.

Some examples of our confession prompts and blessings have been:

> **Confession:** *How* did you come to church this morning?
> **Blessing:** You are welcome here today, just as you are. May the loving kindness and mercy of God meet you in every place of need this morning.

> **Confession:** When in the last week have you resisted mercy towards yourself or another? This may have been in word, thought or action.
> **Blessing:** May the God of unfailing love and great compassion reveal to you Their tender mercy which is always at work in your life.

> **Confession:** What is your natural orientation towards time? Do you spend energy looking backwards to the past with either regret or nostalgia? Or energy looking to the future with either anxiety or hope for the next exciting thing?
> **Blessing:** May you know the peace that comes from living in this present and holy moment, being here, now, and not captured by the past or the future.

Our confession was an act of truth-telling that we hoped would be an expression of freedom and that would remind us of the mercy and love of God. There were two things at work: the willingness to be vulnerable and authentic with another person, and the willingness to listen to another person share something real and true; to be present to that person and not try to fix them or give them advice, but simply to speak words of blessing over them.

This practice of confession is changing us. We are learning to listen more deeply to one another and to ourselves. We have been surprised by the things that have come out of our own mouths and the mouths of others. We are becoming a more beautiful, rich and hope-filled community. We are also growing the capacity to be humble as a community. To be able to confess when the collective 'we' has made mistakes, we have been building the muscles for communal lament. This was especially necessary in our journey of becoming LGBTQIA+ affirming and being able to respond collectively to things like the failed referendum on the Indigenous Voice to Parliament and the horrors in Gaza. As a community we are letting go of the need to be right and embracing the gift of being real.

Trusting the Wild Spirit of God

I had no control over the personal mystical experiences I shared at the start of this chapter; they just happened. I am learning to trust in the wild Spirit of God that is constantly, through all things in this world, seeking to meet us, bless us, love us. Contemplative practices awaken us to be more aware of Divine Presence in our lives, and this is what we are trying to cultivate in our contemplative service. Faithful spiritual practice prepares us to notice the subtle, delicate and patient ways the Spirit moves in and around us. Then, occasionally, we get bowled over by a more tangible, unignorable encounter with God – like a mystical encounter with a magpie.

Over the years that we have been running our contemplative service, we have occasionally had people with absolutely no

Christian background come along because they randomly, in the midst of their ordinary life, had a mystical encounter with Something they named as the Christian God. They were looking for somewhere to make sense of what they had experienced or a community they could connect with as they continued their journey with this wild Spirit.

We have wrestled with what discipleship looks like in a practice-based contemplative church. What does it look like to trust the Spirit to continue the work They began in people? If people come into the church because of a mystical encounter, do we then load them up with doctrine? Can we trust the space we're creating to form people into Christlikeness? This has been a huge challenge for me as a leader. Again, I was formed in a leadership culture that told me it was my job to make sure people ticked the boxes of correct belief and appropriate moral behaviour. In other words, discipleship was often seen as a form of indoctrination. But perhaps true discipleship is about equipping people for a robust spiritual life – preparing them for a life-long adventure of following Jesus, one that will likely include hardships, doubt, wilderness, loss, strange encounters, love and lots and lots of mundane ordinary time. In this wrestle of what to do, I remind myself that what we are trying to cultivate at Central is not new; it's ancient. The monastic tradition has a long history of trusting the Spirit, life in community and spiritual practice to form people.

Widening Circles

What happens when you expand? By that I don't mean when your church grows; rather, as poet Rainer Maria Rilke writes:

> I live my life in widening circles

that read out across the world...
I circle around God, around the primordial tower...
and I still don't know: am I a falcon,
a storm, or a great song?[6]

Embracing contemplative practice had the unintended consequence of widening our circles of influence and belief. Through our contemplative service and practice we were exposing ourselves to Celtic Christianity and the writings of the Desert Fathers and Mothers, being given language for God and the spiritual life by Teresa of Avila and St John of the Cross, learning about Divine Love from Julian of Norwich, trying to embrace a spirituality of descent as outlined by Meister Eckhart and learning to see God in creation through the writings of Hildegard of Bingen and Teilhard de Chardin. St Ignatius of Loyola was liberating our imaginations, St Benedict was teaching us to work and pray, we were singing Taizé and we were learning how to practice the presence of God like Brother Lawrence. We were definitely circling around God. Divine Love was the centre that was holding us and we were feasting on the treasures of Christianity across time and culture. But there were unexpected consequences to expanding beyond Evangelicalism.

This widening worldview and experience and knowledge of God was leaking into the rest of our church. Our sermons were richer, contained more diverse thinking and offered more perspectives through which to read the Bible. We were discovering that there is more than one way to read the Scriptures, to view the world and to follow Jesus. From our more restricted Christian upbringings we were expanding. For each of us, I think this expansion was equal parts uncomfortable and exciting, but for me it was also lonely. As a leader of a quite unusual church, I didn't feel like I belonged anywhere. When I shared what we were doing with other pastors in networks I was connected to, I was regularly met with blank stares and silence. Locally I didn't have many points of connection within the church world. This was often not helped by being a woman and being more progressive in what is largely a conservative church landscape. My experience is that it's lonely in ministry when you're doing church differently. I had to look for encouragement and connection elsewhere: in friendship with others on a similar page, in non-church based contemplative communities, in books and podcasts. By far the greatest sustaining energy in my journey of doing church differently has been the community of Central Church, the people I gather with week in and week out, who love me well, who hold me in my humanness and who willingly come with me as I lead us somewhere new.

Our contemplative service that started as an experiment in 2017 is still going strong. We still meet monthly and it's still giving life to those of us who show up. In 2021 at Central we created Wild Church and added it to our monthly rhythm. Wild Church is another contemplative style gathering wrapped around liturgy, silence, reflection, wandering and communion, but held outdoors in the cathedral of God's creation. We also still have classic church services; there's definitely a place for singing and sermons in our rhythm of being the people of God. Slowly we are cultivating a practice-based faith community and hopefully we are becoming everyday mystics as we continue to open up to the wild and untameable Spirit who meets us in both small and profound ways.

I don't claim to know what Karl Rahner meant when he

wrote that the Christian of the future would be a mystic or would not be a Christian anymore. But I know the truth of that statement in the story of my own life and in the lives of others in my church. Deep in the heart of our Christian tradition lies another way open to those who seek it: the mystical and contemplative path. A way characterised by silence and stillness, a spirituality that attunes itself to the subtle movements of the Spirit deep within us and in our world, and a space where it's possible to encounter the Divine Presence in everyone and everything.

Art

Michael Henderson

My work centres on creative spaces where the Trinity – God, Jesus and Spirit – can draw people to Themselves through beauty, vulnerability and shared human experience. This work is grounded in my experience with Them, my knowledge of Them and, increasingly, my imagination of Them – especially when They take me well past my own imagination for what is possible. I have found that in these open spaces provided by the creative work, genuine, generous and open faith conversations between God and us can take place.

In Australia, where faith conversations are already fraught, my enthusiastic efforts that had been effective in my earlier years of faith began to fall flat. I watched eyes glaze over as I explained theology. Some became hostile when I dominated conversations by trying to tell them everything I knew. Relationships grew distant as abstract debates replaced personal dialogue. People walked away from me more convinced than ever that Christianity was rigid ideology, and I walked away increasingly hesitant to share what mattered deeply to me.

I was trying to drag people towards an encounter with the divine through persuasion and intellectual force, but all I created was resistance. I wasn't listening – not to God's leading, not to the people I was speaking with, not even to my own authentic voice as a person or as an artist.

I was walking a dual life. With faith, I was all doctrine and teaching. With art, I was open and creative. Art was in my DNA before I came to faith at twenty, and when faith became part of my life, I always understood it as a reflection of being made in the image of our endlessly creative God. However, I struggled with how to bring the two lives together – how to create authentic encounters rather than forced arguments, and how to listen as deeply in my faith conversations as I did in my creative process.

Epiphany in the wilderness

In 1998 I created my animation *Life After Birth*, and accidentally found something different. Instead of arguing with people about life and death and faith, I wrestled with my own journey through art. Without realising it, I had begun listening in three directions simultaneously: to my own authentic questions about identity and mortality, to what God was revealing in my journey and to the audience who might encounter this work. This threefold listening created an encounter – an interaction between my story, the viewer's story and the divine story.

I won a NSW Film and Television Office grant – one of eight selected from 9,000 applications – and gained support from SBS Independent Television. But more importantly, the conversations felt alive rather than adversarial. When I showed the film at festivals, people spoke about life and death and faith in ways I had not encountered before.

Yet I didn't understand what I'd stumbled onto. The animation still showed my desire to be clever and argument-based. It also, however, revealed a tiny stream in the wasteland, showing me how I could speak authentically of faith and invite the broader community into dialogue. This was my first glimpse of creating spaces where blessing – calling forth what could be – and prophecy – future hope and restoration – could emerge from encounter, even if I wasn't ready to embrace it fully.[1]

I went to Bible college in search of answers. When I finished, I became a church pastor. The demands of ministry and family slowly pulled me away from creating art. I found myself teaching about art rather than making it, talking about faith rather than living it creatively. I was 'doing faith' instead of experiencing God.

This was my wilderness – professionally successful but spiritually and creatively disoriented. I had all the right answers but none of the right questions. Worse still, I drifted back to arguing rather than sharing, proving rather than listening, convincing rather than exploring. I had stopped listening in all three directions – to God's movement, to actual people, to my own authentic voice. The artist in me withered while the arguer grew desperate.

Everything changed when I hit my own faith crisis. My abstract God disappeared, and suddenly I found myself desperately trying to find Him. In that vulnerable space, I rediscovered art as a language for understanding my own life, joy, sorrow and identity.

In that desperate place, I began listening again. I listened to the silence where God had been and discovered presence. I listened to my own breaking heart and found truths my theology never could. And I started learning to listen to human need around me – not to fix it, but to honour it.

What I needed was to rediscover the real, present, active God who could do immeasurably more than all I could ask or imagine (Ephesians 3:20) – a God who was able to do real things in our world. When I understood how much God, Jesus and Spirit were working in my life and in the world around me, I understood the invitation to join Them in wonder and mystery. Now I could see a path forward, one where I could experience and join in the new things They were already doing (Isaiah 43:18-20). I embraced the open invitation to wonder with Them, to see possibilities where I hadn't seen them before and to follow Them into these possibilities. This was the foundation for creating art that offered genuine encounter, authentic blessing and living prophecy – and it began with learning to listen.

Art transformed and transformed through art

Two voices became pivotal in my transformation. Krista Tippett's *Speaking of Faith* showed me that conversations about the sacred could be life-giving rather than life-draining – that faith conversations could welcome different beliefs, speak of common ground and honestly share where we differed without putting others down.[2] Her humble approach of asking good questions of ourselves before we ask them of others revolutionised my understanding of engagement. She taught me how to create space for encounter rather than demand agreement and, fundamentally, she taught me how to listen – to the divine mystery at work in all our lives, to the person across from me and to my own authentic questions.

Miroslav Volf's *A Public Faith* introduced me to the

revolutionary idea of sharing values rather than winning arguments – listening with genuine curiosity, asking questions that invited wonder rather than demanded answers and walking with people as we shared our points of connection and difference. Volf wrote, 'I want to make Christian communities more comfortable with being just one of many players, so that from whatever place they find themselves – on the margins, at the centre, or anywhere in between – they can promote human flourishing and the common good.'[3] This was the language of blessing, not conquest. It was about listening to what flourishing meant – for communities, for individuals, for myself – and creating work that honoured those values.

I began to understand healing and faith as paradoxical, most effective when they incorporate what is broken rather than denying it. I learnt from people I once thought were opposed to me and my faith. I learnt about aspects of God from people who openly declared they were still searching for God: aspects like the beauty and struggle of love when relationship is complex or damaged. I heard God's voice, speaking to me in an increasing number of places and through an increasing number of people. As Tippett writes about narrative theology, 'everyone has relevant observations to make about the nature of God and ultimate things – the raw material of our lives is stuff of which we construct our sensibility of meaning and purpose in this life.'[4] Everyone had something to contribute to the encounter, if only I would listen.

My art and missional practices now took on an intentional inclusion of my authentic life – of all my struggles and joys. It was more than just airing my dirty laundry; it was directly connected to what I could share about my life and insights and how I could invite others into conversation. I was learning to create encounters, offer blessings and speak prophecy through open invitation rather than certain declarations, and this required developing a discipline of listening in the three directions of myself, God and others.

Over the next eleven years, I became someone my previous self would barely have recognised. Instead of cornering people with doctrine, I began creating what I call 'in-between spaces' – physical and emotional territories where people could explore faith with as little human comment or judgment as possible. Spaces where there was an expectation that God, Jesus and Spirit would speak if we got out of the way. These were spaces designed for encounter with the divine, saturated with blessing, pregnant with prophecy.

Each work began with listening: listening to how God was moving in my life and in the world, listening to the specific people or community I hoped would encounter the work and listening to my own deepest values around identity and human flourishing. This threefold listening, connected to encounter with the divine, and to blessing and prophecy, became the foundation for everything I created.

My art transformed from clever arguments to vulnerable confessions. There is a profound difference between hearing someone say, 'this is *the* truth', and hearing someone say, 'this is *my* truth'. You can't disagree with my experience and, having invited you in, I can't disagree with yours. Now I was having actual conversations full of mystery and complexity and life, where I shared my faith in a way that invited conversation. Those viewing my art were shedding light on my experiences as much as I was on theirs.

Rather than telling people about a distant deity, I began sharing my intimate experiences of life with God. Instead of presenting conclusions, I offered invitations to explore. I have had many people enter my exhibition space simply because the poster out front offered: 'This work tells stories of losing and regaining faith'. I shared. They responded. We talked. We listened. And I allowed my world, God's world and their world to open as I did.

Three commitments and three practices

As mentioned, through this journey I developed three core commitments that became my framework for creating spaces in my creative work and that guided me in my dialogue with people in each of my works. These were:

> **Create an encounter.** I wanted to provide a space for interaction between my life story, the viewer's/community's story and the Trinity's ongoing story. This sounds super lofty, but my goal was to create a space where someone could encounter the sublime. Not an argument, not a story, but a space where God could draw people in through beauty and our shared human experience.
>
> **Gift a blessing.** The created work needed to be more than a pretty picture. Artistic beauty is important, but I wanted to express my awareness of God and invoke in the viewer something of God's presence and His beauty, tenderness, peace, faith, worship, healing. This blessing needs to speak of what is already present *and* call forth what could be. It doesn't force but invites.
>
> **Offer a prophecy.** I wanted to offer something of future hope and restoration. Restoration with God, regeneration and revelation in our communities, and

wisdom for our time, people and place. Not prediction or teaching, but an invitation to explore this hope and restoration with me and with God. A space where God can speak and ask, 'I am always doing a new thing, even in places that feel desperate: Can you see it? Will you join in?'

To fulfil these three commitments authentically, I needed a listening practice, where I could pay attention to God, the people and the community around me. In this space I wanted God, the community and I to actively share, listen and refine. The threefold listening practice I committed to was:

> **Listen to the Divine.** What are God, Jesus and Spirit already doing in this moment, in this place, with this person or in this community? Where is the divine movement I can join rather than manufacture? What do I sense is on Their heart in this very moment? Where are They leading?
>
> **Listen to a person or community.** Who am I listening to? What are their stories, struggles, hopes, questions and longings? What can honour their journey and story? What do they reveal, hide, cheer and cry over?
>
> **Listen to my own values.** My work has a focus on identity and flourishing, and by extension on what gets in the way of these. So I ask myself, how do I connect with what God, Jesus and the Spirit are revealing, and with what I have heard from a person or a community? How do I embody these values in the work itself, while I listen to God and a person or a community?

This dialogue of threefold listening became inseparable from my three creative commitments. I became convinced that I couldn't create authentic encounters without listening to the divine movement of God. I couldn't gift genuine blessing without listening to people's hearts and honouring my own values around identity and flourishing. I couldn't offer a living prophecy without listening to where God was leading me and what the community was ready to hear.

The Adelaide Fringe Festival and Saint Francis Xavier's Cathedral, 2017

My art installation at the 2017 Adelaide Fringe Festival was where all of this came together for me. Before creating my work for the Festival, I spent months listening – to what God was showing me about my faith journey, to the festival community of artists and seekers who might stop outside a cathedral, to the leadership within the Catholic Archdiocese of Adelaide and to my own values.

The work was a series of sixteen drawings, making up one long image that was twenty-two metres long and installed in Saint Francis Xavier's Cathedral. For four days, I stood inside the installation as over 1,500 people encountered my personal testimony and art – not as a theologian with answers, but as a fellow traveller with questions and hope. I had over 300 meaningful faith conversations where we discussed God and faith for more than five minutes. Many returned again and again. Some brought friends. But these numbers only tell part of the story.

Some wanted to talk about the two figures either side of Jesus – Peter and Judas – as they saw themselves in these disciples' confused expressions. This was encounter: their story meeting the Trinity's story through my art. Others wanted to talk about the relationship angst in the Adam and Eve drawing and share their own struggles. This was blessing: creating space where people felt safe to bring their brokenness. I had listened to my own values around authentic relationship, and that listening created permission for others to share.

But by far the image with the most connections was my depiction of Jeremiah – an old man, tired but determined. This surprised me, as it wasn't beautiful in the traditional sense. When I explained that I drew myself as I feared I might end up – longing for hope but seeing no real change – they were in. This was prophecy: speaking honestly about despair while holding space for hope. This image emerged from listening: to my deepest fears about identity, to the divine promise that God is always doing a new thing even when we can't see it and to a community that needed someone to name their weariness before they could imagine hope.

There were others who asked if I could exhibit this piece in a neutral space, away from a cathedral building with the baggage that came with entering a religious space. We talked about their struggles and I offered to walk through the exhibit with them, helping them to explore who God was in that moment. I became a safe person – creating an encounter, offering blessing rather than judgement, embodying prophecy rather than pronouncing it. I believe this happened because I was continuing to listen in real time – to where God was moving in their wounded stories and to my own values. In that respect, the art may have started the conversation, but then it dropped away.

***Shorelines*, to commemorate the one-hundred-year anniversary of the World War One armistice in 2018**

It is one thing to hold this posture with faith-based organisations like the Catholic Church, but it is another to do it with multiple secular organisations. Could I bring this same posture of creating an encounter with God, gifting blessing and offering prophecy, using disciplined listening to create a meaningful work in a public space?

The answer was yes, although at multiple times on the eight-month journey I didn't think so. The listening was extensive. I held ongoing dialogues with the State RSL, with the Tasmanian State Government, with community groups, with historians and with my own exploration of a divine story of sacrifice, death and resurrection. This was a steep learning curve: I had to balance all these views and perspectives over eight months of dialogue, while also keeping a vision for a creative work that could hold space for faith, invitation and exploration.

The final work, *Shorelines*, commemorated the one-hundred-year anniversary of the World War One armistice. It covered the entire front lawn of the Tasmanian Parliament. Fifteen thousand individual boats, representing all the people who served from Tasmania, created small waves across the lawn that people could walk through. Many were brought to tears. The work invited conversations around sacrifice, service and the going and returning of soldiers, both physical and spiritual.

***Breathe, Shine and Seek to Mend:* Hobart Baptist Church and the Dark Mofo Festival, 2019**

Now I had become bold. In 2019, I proposed to Hobart Baptist Church that I exhibit a work at the much-opposed Dark Mofo

Festival, an infamous festival with a reputation for extreme and anti-Christian vibes. While some Christians were aggressively against the idea, I wanted to share my values with the festival.

My practice was maturing. I listened to what God was revealing to me about the church's complicity in abuse – the divine grief over institutions that buried truth. I listened to the Dark Mofo leaders and community leaders and a Royal Commission and heard them associate Christianity with hypocrisy and betrayal. And I listened to my own values – I believed in accountability over defensiveness, in naming darkness and allowing it to reveal our God, not hidden in the darkness but able to meet people there.

The work I installed in the church, *Breathe, Shine and Seek to Mend*, was a five-metre-high crucifixion figure, wrapped in hessian like a dead body being disposed of, and strapped to a framework cross.

Each evening during the Dark Mofo Festival people could enter the church and sit in the pews and contemplate this enormous and imposing figure that loomed large over them. This was encounter in its rawest form – not comfortable, not beautiful, but honest. It was a challenge for everyone who entered – as much for those close to God as it was for those who considered themselves far away.

In this space, I met a middle-aged businessman. He asked why I had created the work and I shared how I am prone to covering Jesus up so that I can ignore him. I then asked him what he saw. He began to weep in the back pews and immediately asked me if he could untie and unwrap Jesus. He felt that he had wrapped and hidden Jesus from himself, and he needed to find a way to see Jesus again. The image so confronted him that he came to faith moments later in that back pew.

This is what happens when you create genuine encounters for people to explore. I had listened to the divine heart breaking over abuse done in Jesus' name, to a community's need to see Christians confront our own failures and to my own values that authentic faith must include lament. That threefold listening created space for the divine to move and offered prophecy – speaking truth in a way that calls forth transformation. The work was covered in the local paper's Guide to the Dark Mofo Festival, even though it wasn't officially a part of the Festival!

How Lonely Lies this Land, Once so Full of People, and the Tasmanian Government, 2022

In 2019, a year after *The Uluru Statement from the Heart* had been written and shared, I started to gain a vision for a non-Indigenous response. As I was creating my final work, which was a series of five-metre-high sculptures, I found myself on a long detour as a group of Tasmanian Leaders came together to write what became known as *A Non-Indigenous Response to the Uluru Statement from the Heart.*

Very early on my dialogue with the original statement from Indigenous Leaders and with God centred on three words: Remember, Welcome and Courage. My posture also was clear – I wanted to follow the leadership shown by our Indigenous Leaders. And I wanted to embrace 1 Corinthians 13 and offer genuine, practical love, not just empty offers of money, wisdom and celebratory cymbals.

The listening was profound. I listened to the divine call for justice and reconciliation, to the Indigenous community's stories and invitation to walk together, to the desire for right remembering, to the genuine offer of welcome, to the need to hold courage as we walk together on this long journey and to my own values. Each word came to embody the three commitments. Remembering created encounter, bringing Indigenous and non-Indigenous stories into honest heart-felt dialogue. Welcome offered blessing – speaking peace and honouring identity. Courage embodied prophecy – pointing towards the new thing God is always creating.

When I started to speak with leaders across our State – from political leaders and human rights lawyers to the National Reconciliation Council Annual Conference – it led to a leadership group, chaired by the then Governor of Tasmania, drafting the non-Indigenous response. This was completed in 2021 and read to leaders within the Tasmanian Aboriginal community. The response was joyful tears.

A year later, I started a new dialogue with three churches – C3 Hobart, St Georges Anglican and Hobart Baptist Church – and asked them to join me in celebrating this theme. The resulting sculpture series, *How Lonely Lies this Land, Once so Full of People*, consisted of three five-metre-high sculptures, with one installed in each church, again called Remember, Welcome and Courage.

These weren't sculptures designed to drag people with force towards correct thinking. They provided spaces for God to draw people through beauty, multicultural vulnerability and shared national and state experience – through encounter, blessing and prophecy, all made possible through listening to the divine, to community and to own my deepest values.

From mind to heart

The journey from mind to heart to creative practice has taken twenty-six years and counting. Nowadays I'm rarely the Christian who needs to be right or wise; I'm the one who's comfortable with mystery, wonder and curiosity for where God might show up. I've learned that the most powerful apologetic isn't an argument – it's a shared authentic and honest personal encounter, one that invites others to join in. I've learned that listening and good questions and genuine dialogue are more powerful than speaking and good answers.

This approach has created thousands of meaningful faith conversations across Australia. The old me tried to drag people into faith through intellectual force. The new me creates spaces where God can draw people through beauty, vulnerability and shared human experience. The difference isn't just methodological – it's transformational, both for those who encounter the art and for the artist who creates it.

I believe by following this approach we can rediscover ancient Christian practices that valued wonder in spiritual formation. It offers an alternative to the intellectual arguments that have dominated contemporary faith conversations. It's about becoming authentically fully human to point others towards the divine. It's about creating encounter, gifting blessing and offering prophecy in a world desperate for all three. And it's about learning to listen – to God, to community, to ourselves – as the foundation for everything we create.

Play

Rod Pattenden

Doing church is serious business. We strain forward to see God's kingdom. We survey the chaos of our lives, looking urgently for the signs of God's grace. We step forward, while walking among the messy threads of other human lives, holding them with tender care. We yearn to see our hopes realised, our visions enacted and our plans fulfilled. There is an expectation that our work will shine like light in the midst of darkness. This striving for such a brilliant future leaves us with a multitude of exceedingly large expectations. This task requires the best, if not all, of us.

It is a task and a vision that matters not just for our personal sense of belief, or even our ambitions, but for the big picture of the witness of the church in the world and its impact for all of eternity. I'm sure at times you feel like I do, that we carry the very future in our own small and humble hands. It's a job description that brings about stress, if not anxiety, and at times even an ongoing sense of failure. It is an impossible horizon that leads, for some, to spiritual and emotional exhaustion or even burnout.

The expectations are high and the conditions of our contemporary culture make it even more challenging. Social structures are becoming more fluid and human beings are pulling away from being organised, regulated and socialised. People are wary of social contracts that do not directly enhance their lives. In short, the task of doing church at this moment in history is fraught with anxiety and stress, weighed down by an uncertain future. This apparent crisis has created conditions where some look for answers in fundamentalist certainty or return to tried-and-true ways of doing things that served previous generations, creating a church that looks like a cultural anachronism or a cult shaped by nostalgia.

I am going to offer an antidote that could be summed up in the simple phrase: In a crisis, play!

You might consider this to be frivolous, peripheral or of little use to your personal calling, but it might be the advice that changes your future or at least serves to lighten the life tasks that have been placed in your lap. It was this simple advice that saved my own life.

Play is a pathway

I have suffered from extended periods of zealous seriousness. During those times I tried to get everything right, lining things up in neat patterns, reading the latest insights and analyses. I was wisely guided by tradition yet utterly hip and user-friendly, fashionable, stylishly relevant and, most importantly, all things to all people. I suffered from stress with an added dose of boredom. I feared change, was averse to risk and evaded any sense of adventure!

The saving grace of play met me in the midst of a midlife

crisis. I am now a recovering workaholic and serious person, having let go of the fixation on an endpoint in history where my own and God's perfection meet. I can say quite plainly that what saved me was not giving in to the pressure to attend the latest conference, or developing specific skills, or having better time-management techniques or the correct reading of contemporary culture, but play. It was by recovering imagination and the ability to improvise that I was able to land safely on my feet. Right at the point when I thought it was all going to collapse around me, I discovered the joy and physicality of InterPlay.

I was thirty-nine and feeling bored and depressed with life and who I had become. Work was challenging; I was involved in a dynamic inner-city ministry that was asking important questions about faith and culture in a shifting world. The people and questions were engaging, but I felt like my internal operating system needed a whole new mechanism for how to deal with who I was in the middle of this chaos and change.

There was no single answer that unlocked things like a magic key, no inspiring insight or wise words, just the realisation that I was boring and was doing the same things over and over in the same way. I needed to learn some new skills or, more profoundly, to improvise and trust my intuition and imagination. I needed to learn to play on a very big stage and to trust that if I fell over, I would be able to get back up again, learn from my mistakes and greet every moment trusting that I would find the gesture, move or step that was needed. Ministry became more effective when I developed the ability to live in my imagination and to play with all my skills and energy, trusting that an answer would arrive at the moment I needed it.

InterPlay arrived like a splash of cold water on that hottest day in summer. I had invited the leaders of InterPlay to come to Australia from San Francisco for workshops.[1] InterPlay is a form of improvisational theatre where adults learn to play again. There is playful movement on your own, and then in pairs; there is hand dancing, laughter, surprises, poetry with made-up words, songs, sighs and voice. Untapped resources come bubbling up, and you trust in the moment with its chaos, hope and physicality.

The four days of workshops I had organised for others turned out to be what I was most deeply searching for. I recovered a sense of myself as a playful body. It was hilarious. It was wonderfully ecstatic, dangerous and delightful. What would my faith community think now? A middle-aged man rolling around the floor of my own church building, just happy being myself in this moment. It was profoundly disturbing, yet thoroughly familiar and utterly humanising. I discovered that I could dance, I could make up stories in the moment, I could sing, express and live with my deepest hopes and desires as companions to the present moment. It opened me up to myself and to others. I found a deep sense of self-compassion and joyful tolerance of the diversity and quirkiness of those around me.

At a crucial time of depression and loss of direction, the seeming chaos of improvisation helped me to land. Serious play is sneaky, seductive and a powerful agent of change and hope. It activates inner resourcefulness, memory and resilience. As I trusted the process of improvisation, I found the steps I needed to find my way out of the mess and to create a more graceful future. Play can be understood as a spiritual practice that activates imagination and hope, creating something in the present moment that moves you towards outcomes that are world-building.[2] It allowed me the freedom to wonder, keeping me away from the rush to find an answer and/or find sure knowledge. Wonder allows fluid and surprising answers to emerge and for innovation to occur. It allows you to be more tolerant within complex systems, to let go, to not know, to wait for creative outcomes to arise out of the surplus of choice. Improvise, innovate, approximate, try again and the solutions do arrive. Just trust in the process. How terrifying could that be?

I found this most profoundly in storytelling. I am a genuinely shy person, unsure about the value of what I think and have to say. Speaking in public does not come easy, as I am a keen observer of any mistakes or missteps I might make. I prepare a clear script ahead of time. Learning to improvise showed me that, even as I stumbled through speaking, I had a rich reservoir of stories embedded in my history. As I opened up to this trove of memories, experiences and wisdom, I found I always had something to say that was wise, funny and delightful to others. My sermons became more humorous and engaging, as well as more vulnerable and down to earth. I got over myself and my professional expectations and found deep enjoyment in recounting my life as a subject of the love of God. Telling the stories of my life has provided a rich vein of wisdom that has made me gentler with myself and helped me see the grace of God in others. We are all rich with story. It is a great gift to find such treasure in one's own narrative, as a humble form of salvation history.

It might be too forward of me at this stage to recommend you attend an InterPlay workshop. It might be too challenging for the meek and too exhausting for the humble. But if we take play seriously as a spiritual practice, we might wonder where else in our lives we get the opportunity to learn the skills of improvisation to deal with complex, layered thinking, or where we escape the limits of linear time to find moments where all of our brain is awake and aware. This is where thoughts leap across the divide between logic and imagination, where we can become comfortable with complexity and learn to trust in the creative process of embodied thinking.

Play is the highest form of research. It underlies the thinking processes that sustain all the arts and sciences. It is a fundamental part of our daily problem-solving and choice-making. Playing is a skill that can be enhanced through regular practice, encouraging your brain to think in the wider, more holistic ways that play ignites. It may be as simple as spending regular time with children, playing with Lego, telling stories or taking your dog for a walk, or more advanced activities like hand dancing or rolling on the floor. I am suggesting that these are tasks deserving of serious research by over-serious Christians who might want to live more fully in the image of God.

Innovation

Play makes us human. It is one of the defining characteristics of humans that we develop and learn through facing new situations and discovering new solutions. D. W. Winnicott, a well-known psychiatrist who specialises in educational theory and the study of human development, observed the learning patterns of infants and explained healthy human development through the processes of play. Winnicott drew attention to how a child uses play to explore their world, and in turn to find a sense of self not as a solitary being, but in relation to the world around them. Play creates culture; it fills the void left by the parent figure, helping the child to find its individuality and sense of independence. It allows a child to experience the delight of discovery and to name its world and inhabit it as a separate individual. Winnicott said, 'It is in playing and only in playing that the individual child or adult is able to be creative and to use the whole personality, and it is only in being creative that the individual discovers the self.'[3] In this way, we learn to play and relate to our immediate world. We play at first by ourselves and then learn to play with others, creating community through mutuality and difference. Play is not an idle activity to fill in time – it is person-forming and world-building.

While play is as natural as breathing, many adults feel great anxiety when they are asked to perform in contexts where they don't know the rules or where they might feel awkward or show a lack of skill. Alongside play comes the yawning fear of failure. Fear of failure is a huge black hole full of anxiety, even dread, that inhibits innovation and risk-taking.

Leaders in the church tend to be people who manage systems well and keep the status quo. People who have the capacity for risk tend to be entrepreneurial and will often work better outside of structures and organisations. How do we develop leadership in fresh expressions of the church that balance organisational structure with the play of innovation and experimentation? Organisations like to manage the boundaries and to know the edges; entrepreneurs push the edges and allow innovation in. How does a community tolerate change? There will always be moments of uncertainty on the journey. How does the terror of change transform into excitement about new solutions? Resilience in community life only comes from the wisdom gained through failure and discovery. Thank heavens for prophets and change agents who are able to help the rest of us play seriously through those transitions marked by uncertainty, and to find the grace of God.

There is no shortcut for leaders who want to learn about innovation. Just find a private space where you can get used to the uncomfortable feelings of failure and play long enough to arrive at a moment where you get over yourself. My daily practice is through visual forms. At meetings I doodle, and at home I get to paint. I practice the art of failure and erasure every day and have excruciating moments where I get to choose between options. I try to practice evading easy solutions. I feel the temptation of shortcuts. I struggle and work hard, sometimes with poor results or none. At other times I am visited by exhilarating moments of discovery. Find a space or form in your life where you are allowed to fail often, so you get over your ego, your polished persona, your trinkets of self-esteem; so you get on with it and seriously play and sift through enough solutions to find what fits the best. If that doesn't work, I recommend you put on a piece of music and move 'til you feel the ground under your feet. That ground is all you need to know embodied delight. God is this ground upon which our fumbling steps find grace and wisdom.

Physicality of grace

Play gets under your skin, into your fingertips and, eventually, out through your toes. It is full-bodied and enlivening. The brain sparks best when our bodies are moving, whether it's through competition or solo. It could be through walking, team sports or moments alone, where exhilaration and exhaustion cross a finishing line that gives a sense of deep satisfaction. Christianity is a fundamentally embodied religion. This is exemplified in the incarnation, where God becomes human in the form of a vulnerable child. Our faith involves being a body through birth, growth, death, resurrection, pain and ecstasy. Bodies love to dance, move, work together and know the support and love of others through touch and gentle support. The grace of God is not just a theological concept or religious doctrine; it is something we carry in our human bodies. It is there in the moments when we feel the warm sun on our backs, have a hot shower or bath, feel the sweat of exercise or engage in regular tasks like cooking, cleaning and ordering our domestic spaces. Western traditions of theology have erred on the side of making faith an intellectual exercise. Yet faith is also about our behaviour, customs and the material physicality of our existence, as we know pain, struggle, ecstasy and love.

The Christian faith is a this-worldly and material religious tradition. Yet we are often ambivalent about embracing the flesh as an expression of the goodness of God. An example of this comes from the life of St Simeon Stylites, a saint of the early church, who spent thirty-six years lashed to the top of a wooden platform so he could dedicate his life to prayer without any earthly distractions.[4] Although he was fed each day by faithful monks, his body gradually became deformed due to the ropes that held him in place wearing through his muscles and bones. The saint would lovingly remove the weevils and grubs from the deep grooves that developed, yet he allowed himself to decay under the task of this painful form of devotion. This saint reminds us of all those people who have made a virtue of punishing the flesh, as if there is something essentially wrong with what God has created. Surely it is more orthodox to affirm that within the life of the body we seek to celebrate a sensuous connection with the divine and in our flesh see God. This affirms physical action as a form of devotion, thankfulness, creation and play. This is good for us, good for others and good for the creation around us. For me, dancing was it. Being in my body in the moment, my right brain and left brain having a snappy conversation, being body/spirit/mind all in one breath! Being at one with myself, and with all that connects me to the world I inhabit, and with God. Such is the gift of faith.

But there is more at work in the Western tradition than just a distrust of the body. There has been an implicit hierarchy of preference toward male identity over female experience, rationality and logic over feeling and intuition, and human culture over the natural world. Is it possible to know God through the sensuous engagement of the body in forms of prayer and devotion, ethics and behaviours, community and life patterns?

There is much to be learned from the insights of feminist and queer studies about how we understand the human experience of the grace of God. Isherwood and Stuart's seminal book *Body Theology* was the first work that helped me appreciate this broader context of understanding that I am a 'cultured' person who has been trained in how I exercise and perform masculinity and gender. These roles come with constraints and limitations on my freedom to express myself as being made in the image of God. 'Body Theology holds out the hope of healing the cruel rupture that patriarchal thinking has introduced into theology; it attempts to put the body, mind and emotions back together in order to see anew the glory and goodness of all of creation.'[5] These sorts of observations point to the expectations around men and women as they perform their roles, and the subtle differences in power and opportunity that come with such social practices.

I want to think holistically about my body, and its delightful ability to play with the life I have been given, as a gift that is open to the future and always in formation. I realise that at this point I am touching on a whole set of ideas around the social construction of the self that fuels debates in the church about same-sex marriage, gender roles and who gets to lead or to be a priest. But for this moment I want to affirm the words of the distinguished theologian Elizabeth A. Johnson: 'About the Creator Spirit this can be said: loves bodies, loves to dance. The whole complex, material universe is pervaded and signed by her graceful vigour.'[6] It is a careful, delightful challenge to live in and through my body as the best way to express and experience grace, forgiveness, hope and delight, pain and ecstasy, and to see God in my flesh. As another early Church Father, St Irenaeus, said in 185 AD, the glory of God is a person fully alive.

Healthy systems and an ecology of play

The church is not a system defined by perfection or operational efficiency. It is a complex organism with many parts that is involved in a dance of leading and following, failure and discovery, delight and readjustment. Such a body needs to play. People need to enjoy themselves and to find their purpose, otherwise they may choose to resist or opt out of the group process. This is more urgent if such a body is seeking to change, innovate and meet new challenges. Leadership needs to arise from all those involved, as there will be a rich reservoir of experience to offer in the face of new challenges. It is not helpful if those in leadership need to manage everything, as there will be moments when they simply do not know what to do. Someone in the community will have an idea, an experience or some wisdom that might move the community forward. To move forward is to try things out, to tolerate failure, to readjust and try again, and to allow for new solutions or ways of doing things. New challenges require new solutions, otherwise communities stagnate out of the double fear of the future and what they see as the terrifying threat of making a mistake.

Fresh expressions of gathered community require this dynamic and are best done in the spirit of play. The joy and the buzz found in playfulness is not summarised in the score at the end of the game. It is the mix of pleasure, struggle and exhilaration of the process that is more important. The journey is as much fun as the destination. Otherwise it is just a very long journey accompanied by the drone of voices from the back seat, repeating the words, 'Are we there yet?' Play in community allows for leadership to come from all its component parts. Like the new young women whose complaint about putting out the seats in nice, neat rows for our evening service led to the idea of a café-style church, which then ran successfully for three years. Or the throwaway comment by a well-known jazz musician on the strange experience of playing in a church that led to the long-running Angelic Jazz series of concerts in inner-city Sydney. Or the comment about putting kids first that led first to a messy church, then an all-age worship event that was so much fun it eventually took over the main morning worship service. Change comes in from the edge. Such voices, gestures and often timid offerings need an environment of permission-giving in order to be played with and trialled, through failure and success, to eventually renew a community's centre.

One of the practices of InterPlay is a simple hand dance, where two people learn to lead and follow. Participants learn about their leadership style and their capacity to give leadership and receive the leadership of others. With more experienced players one can make up a movement piece with individuals offering stillness, leading or following. Ideas come from all quarters, and people find the pleasure of being part of something bigger than themselves without losing any sense of orientation or connection to place. It is a made-in-the-moment performance and an utterly amazing experience for the viewer. They see that bodies know innately how to play together, provide support, offer their uniqueness and yet find cohesion and wholeness. We are a communal species with great wisdom about how to play together in safe and mutually empowering ways. This is a physical enactment of the body of Christ at its best. Things develop when everyone's involved, creating opportunities to lead and follow to the mutual benefit of those involved and for the common good. It's such a beautiful thing to witness, and an even more wonderful thing to be a part of.

Incubating the new

In terms of being and growing the church, at this time in history there is no other way forward than through innovation. There are no scripts for maintaining the past or ensuring the present. Play is a key skill that can bring resilience and hope to leaders as well as to communities who see themselves on this journey of discovery. Leaders can encourage a spirit of discovery and surprise, knowing that answers and pathways will be found not in cleverness, but in and through the body of Christ. They can find play as a spiritual practice and enhance their capacity to take risks, learning to live with fluid states of being and trusting that solutions will emerge in the process of creating.

If you find yourself in a leadership role, then I recommend you pursue practices that enhance your capacity to play in and with your life. You can dance, move, sing, do opera in the shower, paint, doodle, create, find a team or do a solo, and in so doing find exhilaration rather than procrastination, expression rather than depression, uniqueness rather than blandness. You can exercise your difference through balancing the centre by being on the edge. Be out of breath, but never out of ideas! And then be part of a community of faith that values your uniqueness and idiosyncrasies. Find your strengths and enhance them. Know what it is to be loud so you can know the wisdom of moderation. Fail often so you taste the sweetness of success. Finally, be part of a community of faith that lives out its calling as a learning community where playful wisdom is incubated and celebrated. Play well with others. Know the grace of God.

Trauma

Joel Hollier

The day I stopped giving money to my church was the day my archbishop announced they were giving one million dollars to advocate against same-gender marriage. My marriage. By God's grace, I have not given a single cent to that denomination since then.

The day I stopped attending my (ostensibly more progressive) church was the day I was taken off the prayer roster. I'd already been removed from the preaching roster, the service-leading roster and the music team. My husband and I had hung on, believing we could make a change. And by God's grace, we had. We'd raised a small army of queers within that church who worshipped boldly. When we left, that small army disappeared from that church overnight, finding their spiritual homes elsewhere.

'Stay away from church' were not words I ever thought I would become familiar with. And yet here we are. If you are queer, attending a church is considered a risk factor. Your typical congregation is more likely to push you *away* from

God than draw you *in*. This great bastion of *faith*, *hope* and *love* has been shown for what it is, and right on cue, the people of Australia are calling bull. Here's my hot take: This 'love' is anything but. This 'hope' is grotesque. This 'faith' is rotten, and the institutions that prop it up are a blasphemous affront to the gospel of Jesus.

Those are fighting words, so let me tell you where I am coming from: I believe the message of Jesus is liberative, expansive, hopeful and eternal. I am convinced that God's Spirit is moving, enlivening and enchanting. I have seen healing, and I have witnessed hope dawn.

I am also speaking through the lens of significant hurt. My journey is, at times, one of ostracism and exclusion. But it pales compared to the stories I have heard. As an academic, I have dedicated years to understanding the impact of religious trauma on vulnerable communities, and as a pastor, I've had a front row seat to the show. The stories playing on repeat are harrowing.

Predictably, my research has shown that LGBTQIA+ people, women and people with disabilities all report significantly higher rates of harm in religious spaces, and all groups report that this harm has dramatically shaped their spiritual journeys.[1]

All of this has played out against the backdrop of declining trust in the church. Sixty-seven percent of Australians reported the church's stance on homosexuality blocks them from engaging with Christianity.[2] Meanwhile, ninety percent said their perception of Christianity is negatively influenced by the church's history of abuse.[3] The *Royal Commission into Institutional Responses to Child Sexual Abuse* heard from 4,000 survivors across 1,691 religious settings. It should never have taken a Royal Commission to uncover the horrific abuses perpetrated against children and covered up by clergy.

The church has, in my opinion, forfeited any right to act as moral arbiter of society. And yet, bizarrely, it continues to do so with alarming ferocity. As an experiment, I asked ChatGPT, 'Who poses a greater risk to children: pastors or drag queens?' I had assumed AI would hedge its bets, but I was wrong.

> The contrast between the two groups is often fuelled by culture wars and media narratives rather than evidence. Drag performers are often unfairly targeted in moral panics, while abuse in religious institutions has been substantiated and investigated. ... Based on available evidence, pastors (particularly those in institutions with a history of cover-up or lack of oversight) have historically posed a greater documented risk to children than drag queens.

The reputational damage the church has experienced will take generations to repair, if it ever can be repaired. Perhaps it is true that Christianity, in its current iteration, has expired. Meanwhile in the rubble of the exodus we are left asking, 'How are we supposed to understand the God who gave rise to this movement?' Is it possible to reimagine God after religious trauma?

Starting something new

It was my umpteenth conversation with yet another person who had seen their world implode after coming out as gay. Once again, I was hearing someone lament the fact they had no church to call home. They told me outright they didn't need another counsellor, psychologist or therapist. What they needed was a faith community.

Reflecting on this conversation later, I turned to my husband and said, 'I think we need to start a church.' As the world roiled with a global pandemic, we gathered a group of friends and began meeting in a living room, then on Zoom, then back in the living room. We prayed together, cried together, shared our chasms of doubt and gently reminded one another of the reason we called ourselves 'Christian' in the first place.

'How do you, just, start a church?' someone asked me a while later.

The answer, at least in my low church Protestant tradition, was quite straight forward. 'You just start it, I guess.' It's a team effort, and once two or more are gathered, it begins.

Those early meetings were sacred. There in those holy gatherings we could peel back the layers of disguise to say, 'See my scars.' As though discovering Jesus' resurrected body all over again, we discovered these scars could be divine. 'Place your hand on my side,' said Jesus to the doubter, and we echoed Jesus' words. The story of the resurrection is a story of scars. With all our teeming questions and wild uncertainties, something new was born.

Each of us had tired of the constraints of the institutions we had grown up in. Some of us had been in ministry and had been shown the back door. Some were working in Christian schools, others were returned missionaries. All had skin in the game.

We knew that some key things needed to be central. Firstly, we needed to create space for diversity on its many axes. Our gathered community ran the gamut of traditions, but as we discussed who we wanted to be, three themes emerged: we would walk towards Jesus, we would seek to build authentic community and we would strive to enact justice in our world. Slowly, an affirmation of beliefs emerged, beginning with:

> We affirm the breadth of the Christian faith – the Church is the community of all those who confess that Jesus Christ is Lord and Saviour. As such, there is within it a breadth of perspectives and expressions of understanding around aspects of faith and doctrine. This is natural and to be expected given the diversity of cultures, persons and traditions.

Out of necessity, the hurt that had drawn us together was demanding we open our eyes to something bigger. Richard Rohr reflects that 'the best criticism of the bad is the practice of the better', and this is what began to emerge.[4]

Secondly, we needed to be trauma-informed (whatever that meant). The term 'religious trauma' was only just beginning to gather steam across the world. Language was being developed that gave hooks for us to hang our conceptual baggage on. We needed to be upfront as we recognised 'church hurt' and 'spiritual harm', and we needed to be honest with the fact that we didn't have all the answers. Drawing on broader concepts of trauma-informed care, we understood our community needed to centre choice, agency, and collaboration. But these are easier said than done.

Of course, our little gathering was also deeply flawed. Put a group of hurt people together and what else could one expect? We clashed. Research shows religious harm has a significant impact on people's ability to relate to other people in healthy ways. It also has a significant impact on everyday functioning.[5] Trauma will always make itself known. So we attempted (sometimes successfully) to build rhythms of rupture and repair.

It was messy, but it was also deeply attractive, and people began to find a home in that space. It quickly became apparent that we were not only rediscovering new (though often ancient) ways of *doing* church, we were also having to carve out fresh ways of *knowing God* within the church. While religious harm impacts our human relationships, it also radically reshapes how we conceptualise the divine. Just as Jesus cried, 'My God, my God, why have you forsaken me?' so too did we learn to wrestle with a God who we believed had forsaken us.

Re-knowing God

As we started New City Church, two contradictory things became apparent. Firstly, people were craving something new – emergent, different, counter-cultural, revolutionary. They wanted a space where they could distance themselves from the harms they had experienced. Secondly, people were craving something familiar – predictable, stable, normal, mundane. They wanted a community that looked and smelled like the spaces that had once felt like home, just without the exclusion.

These two irreconcilable realities acted as stark reminders of the hurt we had all been through. Complicating matters, it wasn't as though there was one part of the community that wanted the latter, while another part wanted the former. We could sense the swirling mess of contradictions within ourselves. We each individually carried this tension, to greater and lesser extents. So we had to ask ourselves: How do we build a community where prayer is both a trigger and a balm? How do we read the Bible when its words of wonder have been weaponised? How do we sing songs that proclaim 'God is for us' when the artists who penned the lyrics are advocating against us? How do I co-pastor a church when the idea of church itself makes me shudder?

Every spiritual rhythm I had relied upon to retain a sense of grounding had been distorted by the stories I'd come across. I couldn't shake the feeling that the source of harm was also the source of healing and that, somehow, we would need to weather the storm together. This tension inevitably shaped how I began to see God. How could it not?

We were committed as a community to 'doing theology' in conversation. I was being asked to imagine God through a new lens, which was jarring to someone with my fundamentalist formation. After being fearfully and wonderfully made in my mother's womb, I was propelled into the young, restless and reformed movement. I dutifully upheld Evangelicalism (of the fundamentalist flavour) as the only authoritatively inspired branch of true Christianity. Everything else sat on a spectrum of heresy. Having been shaped in this conservative certainty, I found new ways of understanding the divine destabilising and disorienting.

I've never been one to throw the baby out with the bathwater, so the challenge of discerning what to reject, what to redeem, what to reimagine and what to keep proved fraught for me. No one can say I went down without a fight. In fact, no one can say I 'went down', period. Doing church among hurt people meant staring down terms like 'fallen away', 'backsliding' and 'apostasy'. There were days when I would have described myself as a bitter agnostic, and days when the mysteries of God felt enthralling. At times I raged against God, and at times I felt myself carried in the Spirit with wonder. Perhaps that is the nature of doing theology in community.

It is almost certainly the nature of doing theology post-harm.

When American Christian author Rachel Held-Evans passed away, I picked up one of her books again and read her justification for holding on to God. She was a person who understood how harsh the church could be. 'The story of Jesus is still the story I'm willing to risk being wrong about', she said. I wept, because try as I might, I too simply couldn't let go of the story of Jesus.

As a community, we tried to create multiple spaces where people could engage in theology in ways that were healthy for them. Some people started a community group that used poetry and art to approach the divine. We had exegetical Bible studies for those inclined, and spiritual harm support groups for others. We held storytelling nights and fireside chats. Our Sunday gatherings started with a variety of structures but gradually took on more predictable forms. Along the way people left because we were too liberal, too conservative, not 'Spirit-led' enough, too charismatic, too prayerful, not prayerful enough, too discussion-based, too reliant on sermons, overly sensitive to people's trauma and careless with people's hurts. Sometimes it felt like we were the last station in people's journey away from faith. Sometimes it felt hard to pinpoint something we did right. And yet, this little band of hurting people became wounded healers for the people who came to call New City home. We began finding the God of the margins.

Painting a better picture

As the years rolled on, I found myself becoming more comfortable with the shifting sands of doubt and questions. This community, through its trauma and pain, was demonstrating for me what it looked like to pursue the sacred with authentic resolve. In myself, I began to take a certain comfort in the mystery they held. Inexplicably, I fell in love all over again with the God they followed. The refrain that echoed through conversations was simple to articulate but difficult to swallow: 'It's time to take God out of the box.' The boundaries I had drawn around God were beginning to dissolve, and God was taking on a more expansive form. This is one of the great gifts of LGBTQIA+ people to the church: by our very existence we transcend boundaries and binaries. In my experience, LGBTQIA+ Christians consistently understand God to be bigger. And as my God grew, so too did my theology:

My Christology (theology of Christ) took on a deeper, more human form. Drawing from liberation theologies, I saw with fresh eyes a Jesus who was siding with the poor and oppressed. I read the gospels more seriously than I ever had before. Trauma theology taught me to see Jesus' hurt as validating and honouring survivors rather than blaming them.

My soteriology (theology of salvation) began transcending its 'get out of hell free' status and began to incorporate the here and now. Being 'saved' was so much more than an afterlife promise. I saw Jesus' saving work among the people I was serving alongside.

My ecclesiology (theology of church) both relaxed and extended. I lost all interest in the pedantic politicking of denominations and dogma and began seeing the Church as it transcended space and time: God's people, wandering and hopeful. I saw the need for structure as a means of keeping us accountable while retaining our autonomy and agency.

Along the way, some of us felt the need to gather more voices from the margins. Having had our picture of God expanded, we knew that we were only scratching the surface.

We also craved a deeper, more collaborative support network. The beautifully progressive voices in Australia are often siloed and disjointed. Our movement is not strong on organising and gathering.

From this spark, the Future Church Conference was born. We put out the call for people who wanted to engage in forward-thinking conversations about how we could do church. We were overwhelmed by the response. Pastors, chaplains, lay leaders and clergy came together from across Australia to ask questions like, 'Can we decolonise the church?', 'What could LGBTQIA+ inclusion look like?' and 'What does intersectionality teach us about being God's people?' Together we have explored gender equality, solidarity with the poor, anti-racism, disability inclusion, non-violence and trauma-informed care. Behind each of these pressing social issues, we recognised the rich theological wells we were drawing from.

I expected to walk away from these conferences with an urgent sense of the task at hand. Inclusion takes work. There is a hunger for change. What I hadn't anticipated was the way my understanding of God would continue to expand. As we spoke about some of society's deepest wounds, I sensed that our spirits were in step with *the* Spirit.

Pushing forward

One always hopes the lessons of history will shape change. One dreams of an Australian church where past harms are honoured and the journey to healing is actively pursued. One also is wise not to hold one's breath while dreaming. As I write this, several churches and pastors across NSW and ACT are being unceremoniously booted out of their denomination for daring to imagine a more expansive God. And our theological colleges are cracking down on 'dissent'.

But I for one am choosing to remain stubbornly optimistic.

Twenty years ago, the idea of 'religious trauma' barely registered a peep. A year ago, I was asked to write a chapter on that very topic and how it has influenced my theology. That's progress. Writing that chapter (which you have just read) has left me feeling raw, vulnerable and hopeful. I have spent time reflecting on how far I personally have come and what an honour it has been to walk alongside New City Church.

I do not stand here pretending to be thankful for the harm I have experienced or the trauma I have seen in my community. But most certainly I am thankful that, through it, I have had my image of God expanded.

I am praying for a world in which, one day, I can enthusiastically give money to a denomination again. Wouldn't that be a lovely?

Earthy

Jono Ingram

I find myself outside, a lot.

I surf. I love the feeling of cool saltwater on my skin in the early morning. I love the exertion of paddling hard, jumping to my feet and tracking the wave down the line, the salt spray flying across my face.

I garden. From helping Dad plant strawberries as a four-year-old to now where I teach people to grow food and restore native ecosystems, I find a strange pleasure in getting dirt under my fingernails until they are permanently black.

I run. Most weekends I'm out early, running trails in the mountains. The sweat ends up pouring off your body after a few hours of running up the rocky gorges, even in the depths of a Melbourne winter. My legs burn as I push up yet another hill. Then, as I crest the top, I often find myself standing still, heart pounding, breathing heavily, but taking time to gaze out over the valley below and watch yellow-tailed black cockatoos and wedge-tailed eagles glide around over the treetops.

Experiencing life connected to the earth, to nature and to

the seasons is key to who I am. And yet, so many of my church experiences have pulled me away from creation – treating it as secondary, or even something to be cautious of.

Head-room only

Some of my earliest childhood memories of church are of sitting in a seat, sliding up and down, fiddling with the little plastic knobs on the legs of the chairs. The expectation to sit still in church was really hard. I hardly recall a church service I haven't walked out of midway to 'go to the toilet'. As an adult, even as a pastor, this trait has never left me. I was, and still am, a fidgeter. For me, church is all just so passive. So still. So … indoors.

Whenever I sat in churches my mind was pretty much the only part of me I felt I was allowed to use. When our bodies came into the conversation, Christian leaders told me what *not* to do with it. Don't drink, don't smoke, don't swear and for God's sake don't have sex. It seemed that the most I was allowed to do with my body in a church service was to stand up and sing.

By extension, I didn't feel like other parts of my life or the world were all that important to God. Nature and the earth? I mean it was nice and 'the heavens declare the glory of the Lord' (Psalm 19:1, NIV), but unless the declaration of God's glory led to someone's conversion or to our own deeper understanding of some doctrine, it wasn't worth much time. And if you took church outside into the bush, you might be accused of being some kind of pagan nature worshipper. church and Christian spirituality, I figured, were better kept inside – indoors, in your head and in your heart.

Thankfully, both Mum and Dad would often talk in ways

that suggested that things like gardening or eating or walking in the bush were spiritual activities, or at the very least to be thought of as important to God in some way. But that's not the vibe I got from church and other Christians.

In my late high school years, a couple of friends and I went to big Pentecostal conferences in the city, led Bible studies, played in the church worship band and even had a crack at preaching. But I think the time where I felt the most community, where we had the deepest conversations about life and faith, was when the three of us were sitting around a fire. On weekends we'd meet at Luke's farm with our swags, light a fire, have a couple of cheeky beers or a scotch, and talk for hours into the night – about life, our hopes, our fears and where we saw God in all of this. There was something different about experiencing faith and community like this. Something real, something tangible, something grounded.

Getting out of my head (and into the earth)

As a young adult, I engaged in Christian youth work in a public housing estate, doing ministry with people who were sleeping rough or at risk of homelessness. It was in these places that I started to see the real grittiness of where heaven and earth overlap.

Around this time, I met Jon Owen and Ash Barker, who were working with Urban Neighbours of Hope in Springvale (Victoria, Australia) and Klong Toei (Bangkok, Thailand). These guys were living with their families in some of the roughest neighbourhoods, taking seriously Jesus' command to 'love your neighbour'. For them, faith was about moving into the neighbourhood, living alongside people and doing normal stuff.

I was intrigued. I wanted my spirituality to be like this.

Not long after, I came across Shane Claiborne's book *The Irresistible Revolution* (2006). Again, I was captivated. In the introduction, he writes: 'There is a movement bubbling up that goes beyond cynicism and celebrates a new way of living, a generation that stops complaining about the church it sees and becomes the church it dreams of.'[1] This was what I wanted – to shift my energy away from frustration, and even anger, and direct it towards being the church I dreamed of. Here was a guy who moved into the worst neighbourhood in Philadelphia and spent his time planting veggie gardens, running homework clubs, throwing neighbourhood block parties, fixing houses for homeless people to live in and starting social enterprises. And it wasn't *despite* his faith, but *because of* it.

I decided that church-based ministry was not for me. I felt I was better off being a schoolteacher and just living in a neighbourhood, committing deeply to God and to people. I studied primary education while my wife and I explored some options for this kind of life. But our plans for this didn't look like they would work out. I ended up circling right back around and taking on a pastoral ministry role for the next seven years – the sole pastor of a rural Victorian church, while teaching in a school part-time.

We enjoyed this time immensely and learnt a lot from our small country town about community life and taking care of one another. Yet I was longing for something more, so I did everything I could to get the church outside the four walls.

It took nearly six years, but I eventually had people eating meals with others, being randomly generous with no strings attached, learning what it might look like to simply love our neighbours and do good, regardless of whether people believed what we believed or not. We hosted parties where we blocked off the street and had tables lined up down the road. We had Happy Hour on the front porch with people bringing their own drinks and chatting the afternoon away. We had firepits and bonfire nights where people could just come and be themselves – no agenda, no gospel talk, no guest speaker, just food and drinks and friendship. I even had our church research launching a social enterprise – a market garden on a disused lawn bowls site. 'Practising resurrection,' I had said, quoting Shane Claiborne.[2] We explored how we might employ people to grow food and do something for the common good of our town.

However, I got pushback from people in the church about some of this stuff. The market garden project didn't come off, and I began to realise I was travelling much faster down a road than my church was. At times, it felt like I was trying to drag a freight train behind me. I had started in pastoral ministry with the naivety of a twenty-three-year-old, thinking I could change the church, but seven years later I was much less sure. It still needed to be done, don't get me wrong, but I no longer felt I was the right person for it.

An earthy spirituality

During this time, I found myself trying to find a new set of spiritual practices. Evangelical Christianity encouraged daily habits of reading the Bible and prayer, going to church, singing worship songs and listening to sermons. But I wanted something different. I wanted practices that were more grounded in day-to-day life as I experienced it.

Reading *The Irresistible Revolution* took me down the rabbit hole of discovering the contemplative tradition, monasticism and *new* monasticism. I read books by Chris Haw and Jonathan Wilson-Hartgrove, and old monastic books like *The Rule of Saint Benedict*.[3] I researched the stories of Saint Anthony and the desert fathers. I discovered Father Richard Rohr, and Dorothy Day, and Australian practitioners like Jarrod McKenna, Simon Moyle and the Community of Transfiguration. I found a whole tradition that saw tangible things like commitment to place, practising non-violence, sharing resources and living in community as spiritual practices as being of equal importance to Evangelicalism's daily Bible reading and prayer.

Of course, the monastics also had much to say about Bible reading and prayer. It's what they called 'contemplation and action', or what Saint Benedict would call *ora et labora* – 'prayer and work'. We see the needs in the places where we live – we see crime and violence, we see pain and suffering, we see inaction on climate change and the ice caps melting – and so we pray. My Evangelical past would want me to pray for its healing and wholeness, to pray away the pain, to pray for God to intervene and miraculously save us. Sometimes this is appropriate, but my experience is that things are often much slower, messier. Contemplation invites me into the grittiness and to stay a while, to slow down and hold space.

These contemplative practices don't require me to feel a particular way, or even to believe particular things. It's more open-ended, inviting questions and even doubt. In the examen practices from Saint Ignatius, participants are asked to reflect openly on the good and the bad, the joy and the pain, of each day. We're invited to sit with this even if it is uncomfortable, not to try to solve it or explain the discomfort away. These practices invite me to be open and sensitive to what my body is feeling and telling me.

However, contemplatives are also called to act, or as Shane Claiborne would say, to 'become the answers to our prayers'.[4] We sit in contemplation, we hold space for one another and for God, and then out of this, we discover ways to join with God as we fight against injustice and form communities of love and inclusion. This is the physical, tangible kind of spirituality I always craved.

It was here that I first truly understood the idea that Christian eschatology (the theology of last things) is fundamentally physical. Our hope is earthy. My Evangelical childhood taught me that heaven was immaterial and located away from the earth. I began to imagine: What if our hope is for a *world*, the *earth*, indeed for the whole *cosmos*, renewed, redeemed and restored? What if we began to include all of nature in our eschatological vision? 'Your Kingdom come, Your will be done, on earth as it is in heaven' took on a whole new meaning as something grounded in ordinary, physical life. 'Kingdom work' could include caring for creation – the rivers and birds and animals – not just for people's souls. With the current threat of global climate change, a community of Christians devoted to heralding in this coming Kingdom is more required than ever.

An earthy vocation

I remember struggling with the idea of leaving traditional vocational ministry. Even though I was excited by this change, it made me question my definitions of 'calling' and 'ministry'. I wasn't sure I even wanted to continue to use these words or if they even had a place outside of church-based ministry. I recall re-reading *The Irresistible Revolution*. Up until this point, since I was a pastor in a church, it was easy to draw a line between my paid work and some kind of calling from God, but in his book, Claiborne writes:

> I've come to see that this is the difference between a career that is just about paying the bills, and a vocation that is about seeking first the kingdom of God. A vocation is when we take our passion and connect it to the world's pain. Then we do what we are gifted at, and it alleviates the suffering of others... More important than whether you are going to be a doctor or a lawyer is what kind of doctor or lawyer you are going to be.[5]

Eight years on, I feel I have finally found my vocation. I operate an environmental not-for-profit I founded in 2019 in the northwestern suburbs of Melbourne. I was frustrated by the church's slowness to tackle climate change, so I am trying to *be the change* I wish to see in the world, with or without the church.

I am biased, but for what it's worth I think what our organisation does is beautiful. Eat Grow Garden is an edible and native landscaping enterprise. The profits generated from landscaping are fed back into our environmental educational programs and community activities.

Our community garden provides educational workshops, while also engaging the community in growing produce to address food insecurity. We educate people about biodiversity loss, particularly as it relates to Melbourne's grasslands where urbanisation is slowing destroying the remaining one percent of native grasslands we have left. We take schools and community members onto grassland and wetland sites to learn about these issues and engage in our revegetation programs.

A couple of years ago, we held our annual native revegetation day on National Tree Day. Around 180 community volunteers came and planted 3,000 native grasses and saltbush in Aintree Reserve. About six months later, I received a message from one of the volunteers, a young fourteen-year-old girl who lived locally. She said how much she enjoyed the planting and how she was now involved in a sustainability group at her school. She had gone back to school and told others about the community planting day, insisting that her school become involved in the school program I was organising.

When I spoke to the Assistant Principal about it, she said, 'Oh yes. She has been *very* vocal about this and very insistent that we get involved. She was really impacted by her day volunteering.' Her school has now engaged in more planting days than any other school in the past two years and is always the first school to book in again each year.

This work, obviously, looks very different to my old pastoral ministry role. I had one person from our old church say to me, 'So you've definitely left the ministry then'. And I guess I have. But I feel like I have taken on vocational work that is just as crucial if we are to truly see the Kingdom of God on earth as it is in heaven.

In search of thin spaces

Particularly since leaving the traditional church, I have been able to explore my spirituality in wild places. I have always felt a calmness on top of mountains and I have always had this strange, deep (spiritual) connection to red gum trees on the banks of an inland river. Celtic Christianity call these 'thin spaces', where heaven and earth meet.

When I left pastoral ministry, I sought out these 'thin

spaces'. I didn't attend church on a Sunday morning anymore, so I went into the bush or down to the beach. I originally felt guilty about this, constantly being pulled back into the idea that I should be centring my spirituality around a church service. But I knew in my head that these daily, ordinary activities were spiritual.

I knew God was with me as I surfed. I sense God in the breeze when running up a mountain. I understood more tangibly the presence of Christ while sipping a cup of coffee and sitting in the morning sunshine. I knew the majesty of the Creator when watching a sunrise. And I often felt closer to God on the summit of a mountain than I ever did in a Church service.

But something was still lacking. I wanted to mark these moments as sacred. I wanted to ground these everyday practices, these experiences in nature; to locate them and name them within my spirituality. And so I did this through writing.

> Our bodies warm, as we sit in the
> soft flickering glow of
> hot coals and flame.
> Sparks fly upwards as
> timber crackles and pops as it burns,
> and all my stress, and anxiety
> of a week that's now past, melts
> as we simply sit and bask
> in the fire's glow.
>
> We sit here,
> drink in hand,

> roasting marshmallows,
> chatting and laughing loudly, then
> quietly watching the flames as
> they dance in praise to the
> One Who Made Them.
> Draw us into your Love, O God,
> and deliver us from fear. Amen.[6]

The stuff we do day-to-day, the things that ground us, these things matter. These things make us who we are. These things help us to encounter the Living God, the presence of God among us.

Table Church

Naturally, the kind of church and Christianity my children now experience is very different to what I grew up with. Rather than gathering with people in a church in rows, singing songs and listening to sermons, running Bible studies and evangelistic programs, we find ourselves gathered around a kitchen table, a park bench, a collection of beach towels or a firepit. Table Church is a small gathering of less than twenty people that enables us to engage some contemplative practices that inform our acts of love in the world. Let me describe for you what it is like.

It's Friday night. My wife and I have just spent the last thirty minutes rushing around, preparing food and doing a quick tidy-up of the lounge room. Our kitchen table has a large white candle placed in the middle with a wooden, hand-carved Celtic cross leaning up against it. A mason jar of homegrown flowers sits on one side of the candle and a framed lino print icon of Jesus drinking a mug of coffee is placed on the other side.

There is a knock on the door and people begin to arrive, letting themselves in while carrying bottles of wine and bowls or plates of food. Most of it is homemade, and then there is always the weekly takeaway bag of Red Rooster and white rice added to the mix. The kitchen counter becomes the dumping place for all the food, and people pick up a wine, a gin and tonic, a glass of kombucha or a home-brewed beer.

The kids immediately find one another. Some go straight outside to find our pet rabbit or to jump on the trampoline. Others float upstairs to sit, messaging on their phones and chatting about school.

The conversations are about our week, updating each other on news or asking how that job interview went or the community theatre rehearsals are going. Eventually everyone is here, and the food has finished cooking or being reheated.

A small bell rings – or sometimes it's just the clinking of a spoon on a glass, or the shrill cry of one of the children yelling, 'Come and gather around the Table!' People begin to meander to the table, sitting or standing as the paper copies of the Table Church Liturgies are passed out.

'Come and gather around the table', the host begins.

'It is good to be here', comes the chorus of replies.

After we acknowledge the stolen, unceded Aboriginal land on which we are gathering, a few lines are read indicating the kind of community we desire to be together.

'You can come as you are, not as you think you should be', we say together.

'You can participate as you choose.'

'You are welcome to make a cup of tea.'

This last one is sometimes the most poignant. We are very aware that many of us bring trauma into this space, not least spiritual trauma, and so we acknowledge that we need to make space for people to get up and disengage whenever they need to. To make a cup of tea. To go for a walk. Even to leave early. No judgement here. You are welcome to engage as you are and as you can, or as you can't.

The liturgy continues with descriptions of 'tables laden with good things', reminding us to be aware of the smells and textures and flavours as we eat. We declare we are making space for the presence of Christ among us, and we recite prayers that remind us to be people of love and justice and goodness. We light the Christ Candle in the middle of the table, 'the presence of Christ, the Light of the World', and then we share in communion.

Now here you can imagine that we bring out those tiny cubes of stale white bread. Oh, no! We grab a slice of pizza from the table in front of us, or a loaf of garlic bread, or a handful of corn chips – this is our bread! This entire meal is how we will remember Jesus Christ, his life, his death, his resurrection. And then we grab our cups of juice, our wine glasses, our cans of beer, and we raise them up and toast – 'To Jesus! Cheers!'[7]

There are sounds of glasses clinking, and the repeats of 'cheers', especially from our smallest guests who absolutely love this part of the liturgy. And then we feast. We grab plates and load them up, and we sit and eat, knowing that this meal is as much an act of worship as it is an act of rebellion, an act of justice, an act of defiance, an act of hospitality, an act of love.

The conversation flows as we eat. Sometimes it's laughter, while other weeks, due to things happening in our lives, it is more serious and solemn. Whatever the moment requires, this is how we will respond to each other around the Table.

After eating, we often sit down with all our kids and engage in some kind of tactile activity. It might be making a collage of endangered animals from flowers in the garden. Or reenacting this week's Bible story using teddy bears and Barbie dolls. Sometimes it's quieter and the prayer candles come out. We speak about things we are grateful for before lighting a tea light in the Christ Candle.

And then the kids usually disappear – back to the trampoline or their phones. And the adults have a more in-depth conversation. No one preaches. No one prepares a study. Everyone's opinion is valid. We read or listen to something and then ask, 'So what did you think about that?' We invite questions and doubt, and appreciate it when people challenge our long-held beliefs. We constantly look to be more expansive in the ways in which we are called to love and welcome and include others, or how we can work for justice and goodness in our neighbourhoods and in the world.

We finish our night with prayer – just words, or names, or the occasional story – as we light a tea light in the Christ Candle and place it on the coffee table next to the picture of Jesus drinking coffee from a mug.

'Lord, hear our prayers. Amen.'

Grounded

The story of Christian spirituality is a story that begins and ends in a garden – a garden God creates and tenderly places humankind into, and a garden that overtakes the city at the renewal of all things. This, I believe, is an invitation to experience God, our faith and our Christian community in a real, grounded, tangible way. It's an invitation into an earthy kind of spirituality.

Our lives are deeply connected with one another and with

this planet. The way we eat, the way we drink, the things we do with our hands – these things matter. They make a difference in the world we're living in, whether we are aware of that or not. But we can choose to live mindfully.

We can choose to be aware of the presence of God in meals with friends, the first rays of a sunrise and the flames dancing in a firepit. We can choose to discover our God-given gifts and passion, and to connect it with the world's pain in our vocation. We can choose to centre our spiritual gatherings around earthy practices, with food and drink that is good for you and the planet. Our spirituality can become tangible and grounded in our ordinary, daily life. We just need to allow ourselves to slow down and to shift into a more mindful, earthy, spiritual existence.

Misfits

Will Small

Geese have flocks.

Fish have schools.

Crows have murders.

What's the collective noun for a group of misfits?

We'll come back to that ...

But first

Let's get this out of the way:

On the one hand, I'm aware of the absolute audacity of daring to identify as a 'misfit' when I – straight, white, cis-gendered, heterosexual, able-bodied, happily married and monogamous father of three with a couple of expensive degrees and a mortgage in suburbia – tick every box of privilege I can think of.

On the other hand, if the last few years have taught me anything, it's that *all kinds of people* from *all kinds of walks of life* can find something of their story in the phrase 'spiritual misfit'.

From the queer Christian who came out to her church community with fear and trembling and received rejection in exchange for her courageous vulnerability. To the new dad questioning how God could possibly be portrayed as a father demanding blood sacrifice, when the lived experience of holding an infant immediately dispels the notion that any father worthy of being called 'good' could ever be so violent and callous. To the pastor losing sleep the night before the sermon, wondering if they can voice their doubts without losing their job.

Apparently – I've been discovering – there are misfits everywhere.

Some of my own story

I grew up completely immersed in the waters of Christianity – in an Australian context, but with a significant infusion of American evangelical influences. Watching VHS tapes of a big blue character called *Psalty the Singing Book*. Listening to *Adventures in Odyssey*, a children's radio serial. Reading *Breakaway*, a magazine by Focus on the Family for teen boys (the girls got *Brio*). Inspired by DC Talk, my first email address was jesusfreakwill@hotmail.com. I learned to touch type trying to evangelise my friends over MSN Messenger.

There were many beautiful and life-giving aspects of the faith I grew up with. I remain deeply grateful to my parents, who have always instilled in me a deep sense of God's love and compassion – as well as role-modelling the flexibility to ask difficult questions of God, particularly when life cracks open rigid theological frameworks.

Because sure enough, cracks do come.

For me, this cracking open primarily happened during my mid-twenties. I now know this is an entirely appropriate developmental stage – both cognitively and spiritually – for this to take place. At the time, though, it was disorienting, feeling as though the solid ground underfoot was shaking.

My eldest son was born when I was twenty-five years old and barely boasting a fully developed pre-frontal cortex. Two months later I commenced my first pastoral role at a Baptist church. The timing of these two events created some significant shifts in the tectonic plates of my worldview. Becoming a parent is its own process of unravelling. The mix of sleep deprivation, increased responsibility and the existential weight of nurturing a brand new human being can certainly rock your confidence in how life works. At the same time, a pastoral role often seems to go hand-in-hand with an *expectation* of confidence. You can internalise the idea that people assume you know how everything works.

Our first son (and his two subsequent brothers) suffered from severe gastro-oesophageal reflux as a bub. He spent a large percentage of his days and nights screaming in pain. I vividly remember holding him at 2 am, walking around the house as he cried like a banshee. I felt so tired and frayed. I prayed desperately, *God, would you just stop this kid from f**king crying?*

Anyone who has held an inconsolable baby at 2 am knows this is a relatable prayer. And yet I remember these thoughts popping into my head in that moment:

But if you answer this prayer, that would just raise more questions for me. Like why didn't you heal the young Dad in our community who just passed away from cancer? Or what about kids overseas dodging landmines or malnutrition? The world feels so unjust in so many ways. So as much as I want you to miraculously intervene and allow me to get some mother-fudging sleep, I'm not sure my faith could handle that right now.

That little window of cognitive dissonance began to open up more often and more intensely.

There were many times over the next few years when I would lie in bed late on a Saturday night, contemplating a sermon I was going to preach the next day. Things I had always believed with great certainty were changing. I was no longer sure God actually gave some of those violent commandments of conquest in the Hebrew Scriptures. I felt like 'salvation', as we typically understood it, seemed like a cosmic poker machine – being 'saved' appeared to largely come down to luck (where you were born, how your parents treated you, what kind of experience you had of Christianity). I began to question whether hell was really a place of eternal suffering. I started flirting with the idea that a truly good God would only be one that could bring healing and wholeness to *every* body and soul that arrived on this harsh and beautiful planet.

While this was all happening, Australia was engaging in a very messy public discourse about same-sex marriage. I was witnessing conservative Christians make an enormous fuss about the genitals represented in other people's relationships, yet I was also meeting an increasing number of queer Christians who were thoroughly queer and thoroughly Christian. This too was creating fundamental shifts in my framework for understanding the world.

I can write about all this now in a few paragraphs, but in reality my journey of evolving faith simmered away over many years (and continues to do so).

Changing the tyres

As life raised increasingly difficult questions for me, I found my theology profoundly shifting. In his book *Faith After Doubt*, Brian McLaren refers to this stage of faith as 'Perplexity'.[1] It follows 'Simplicity' and 'Complexity' and *can* (but doesn't always) lead to 'Harmony'.

The questions I was wrestling with weren't just intellectual curiosities – they were reshaping some of my core understandings of God, salvation, Scripture and the very purpose of faith communities.

In recent years one of the ways I have conceptualised this process is to think about a car getting a flat tyre. Imagine not knowing the tyres could be changed. Imagine thinking the original tyres had to last for the lifespan of the car. Imagine abandoning the whole car over a damaged tyre. And yet I wonder how many of us have grown up without ever learning that the 'tyres' of our faith need changing. I wonder how many of us were given the impression that faith was a static and fixed object to carry, unchanging, from the beginning to the end of our lives. If you aren't taught that faith is *supposed* to evolve – to die and resurrect, over and again – it can feel like the end of the road, when you might just be discovering a new one.

I suppose I was lucky – as I was losing certain theological conceptions, I was simultaneously discovering a far broader 'tasting menu' of the tradition. Writers like Bradley Jersak, Rachel Held Evans and Pete Enns were introducing me to different ways of reading Scripture that did not demand a violent, tribalistic, bloodthirsty God.[2] Nadia Bolz Weber and Brian Zahnd were showing me new ways to receive the gifts of tradition that did not stifle the Spirit's ongoing movement.[3] Kristin Kobes Du Mez and David Gushee would help me put the American Evangelicalism that had so infused my childhood and teen years into a historical context.[4] Others like Phyllis Tickle and Brian McLaren would help me to think more about the larger shifts happening today, within a longer story of cultural evolution and human development.[5]

These voices were vital guides: part of the support mechanisms I now realise were allowing me to continue in ministry and to ultimately seek out new expressions of Christian community.

The shift happening in me wasn't just academic. It affected how I preached, how I prayed, how I parented. I found myself less interested in providing answers and more committed to creating spaces where questions could breathe. My understanding of God was expanding from a cosmic rule-enforcer to the ground of all being, the love at the heart of reality that holds all things together.

Perhaps most significantly, my understanding of salvation was transforming. Rather than seeing it primarily as an individual transaction securing afterlife benefits, I began to understand salvation as healing and wholeness – both personal and communal, both now and in the age to come. This reframing made sense of Jesus' ministry, which seemed far more concerned with restoring people to community and wholeness in the present than with checking boxes for eternity that were based on giving ascent to certain mental propositions.

These shifts I was undergoing often placed me in a strange 'in-between' place.

Many of my friends were leaving or had already left the Church for the very same reasons I would have, had I not found some of the thinkers, writers and pastors mentioned above.

Within the Church I was finding myself increasingly

strained, aware that my theological views were increasingly on the fringes of the community and denomination I was part of and could easily jeopardise my employment.

This was my 'misfit' experience. But rather than signalling the end of my engagement with either of these tension points, it became the motivation to seek out the sacred space 'in between'. The intersection of faith and doubt. The conversation between tradition and progress. The 'sacred fringe'.

I hoped I could bridge the gap between those who no longer wanted the Church in their lives and those in the Church who genuinely did want to incarnate a more hospitable and expansive form of Christianity.

I wondered if it would be possible to create a space where this could all come together. A place where beautiful ways of thinking about divinity could sit alongside doubt, questions and uncertainty.

Could we create a different kind of church?
For the excluded ones.
The confused ones.
The holding-on-by-a-thread ones.
The misfits?

A Meeting Ground for Misfits

So, we gave it a crack.
We shared the idea. We invited people to join us.
We called it Meeting Ground.

We kept it simple. Gatherings in homes (or on Zoom during COVID lockdowns!). Occasional singing. Coffee, always. Food, often. Some poems by Mary Oliver, quotes from Richard Rohr.

Space for questions and conversation.

Perhaps most significantly, we decided to orient the shape of our community around a set of stated values rather than a program.

These values were (and still are):

Inclusion
Hospitality
Learning Jesus
Justice
Community Beyond Us

We experimented. At times we did more. At other times less. We discovered over time our own eclectic rhythm:

Two Sunday mornings a month in homes.
One Sunday morning in nature.
One week each month off, as a reminder that weekends can mean more than church – and vice versa.

Ultimately, we sought to prioritise connection and creating a space of curiosity and friendship, while gently re-engaging some of the wisdom within the larger tradition(s) of Christianity.

Some people came. Others left.
Now, six years later, we're still at it.
Doubting. Believing. Asking. Seeking.

People are welcome to come as they are, with whatever skerrick of faith they have left in the tank. For some people, it's been their last stop on the way out of church. For others, it's made a gentle return to church feel possible. For many of us, it's been a healing place and a way to approach our spirituality without any pressure to perform.

I don't think what we do is anything remarkable.
In many ways, it's rather ordinary.
But maybe that's the best thing about it.

In a polarised, distracted, competitive world … could a small, local community with a shared rhythm and a non-judgmental posture be its own kind of miracle?

What about all the other misfits out there?
About two years in we faced a tension. Part of what was beautiful about our community was its smallness. We loved meeting in homes and didn't want to change that. At the same time, we felt like we were tapping into a bigger conversation – one that extended far beyond our living rooms. How could we expand what was happening in our one humble, flesh and blood community to include others out there who might be asking similar questions?

Thus began the *Spiritual Misfits* podcast. It started with a conversation with my friend Bronte, a social worker. One conversation led to another, and since then it's grown well beyond 'our living rooms'. I think of it as the public work of our small community. On any given week as twenty to thirty of us meet in a home on the Central Coast of New South Wales, many hundreds of others listen in and continue the conversation where they are – all around Australia as well as across the world.[6] It has led to many beautiful connections, a growing network of people exploring faith, community and healing in a multiplicity of ways.

At this point I've interviewed well north of one hundred people who articulate some version of 'misfittery' – and if there's a common thread between them all, it's this:

At some point, something within their personal identity and deeply held values felt out of alignment with the religious status quo of the environments they found themselves in. Misfitting is as much about the environment people find themselves in as it is about who they are as an individual.

This does not automatically equate to a rejection of those environments or the larger religious project of Christianity. In fact, there's an argument to be made that all healthy spiritual seekers will, at some point, inevitably face the contradictions and dissonances that exist between their interior reality and their small patch of the world. I almost wonder at this point if I can trust any religious leader or person claiming to follow the life and teachings of Jesus if they have never felt some version of this experience. Life is so riddled with contradictions, inequity, hypocrisy and absurdity that I wonder if 'misfitting' is just what happens when you're paying attention.

The 'OG' misfit

Indeed, the man from Nazareth himself could hardly be a better ringleader for misfits, given his own constant and eventually somewhat catastrophic clashes with the religious elite of his time and place.

Is there a better descriptor for Jesus than *spiritual misfit*?

At a cursory glance:

- Challenging religious authorities seemed like a favourite pastime for him (from sabbath laws to temple practices to the hypocrisy of the top dogs, Jesus had plenty of beef with business as usual).

- He kept unsavoury company and was 'guilty by association' (friend list included tax collectors, sex workers, Samaritans and lepers).
- His teaching methods were unconventional and revolutionary (using subversive parables as a go-to communication tactic, including women in his inner fold at a time when this was unheard of, and focusing on internal transformation over outward compliance).
- His message was radical (e.g. love your enemies, consider gouging out your eye).
- Given that Jesus apparently spent so much effort tearing down religious walls and identity markers, one must wonder: how have we done such an effective job reconstructing them 'in God's name'?

Why have we tried to place a God who broke every social, cultural and religious box back into them?

Perhaps the Incarnation itself might be viewed as the grandest act of 'misfitting'. If we are using this term to refer to some kind of dissonance between the interior world of an individual and the exterior environment they find themselves in, then the idea of the divine, cosmic Creator becoming enfleshed in the vulnerable skin of a human being could certainly be understood as an extreme example of 'misfitting'.

What is interesting though is that, in this story, God's response to this vast distance and seeming 'dissonance' is to move *closer*. God stands in solidarity with the human experience rather than seeking to liberate us from it.

If God knows what it is like to 'misfit', how might this

reshape our approach to those who find themselves on the edges and margins? How might it influence the way we shape and structure churches and faith communities? How might we, like Christ, show solidarity with the misfits of this world, embedding ourselves more deeply into our local communities and embracing them in love?

From isolation to belonging

If a key characteristic of the misfit experience is internal dissonance, one of the frequent outcomes is a sense of isolation and loneliness.

Am I the only one asking this question?

Am I the only one seeing this differently?

If I voice *this* – in front of my family, my church, my circle – will I be rejected?

Sadly, a sense of isolation seems to be an inevitable result of 'misfitting'.

In these moments what comes under threat is our sense of *belonging*.

Do I have a place here anymore? Can I still be my honest self here?

I wonder if the great tension of 'misfitting' could be summarised as a crisis of belonging.

On the other hand, I wonder if one way to understand the very heart of Christ is to remind all of Creation about the truer and deeper sense of existence in which 'everything belongs', as Father Richard Rohr puts it.[7]

A couple of years ago I was invited to share some of my poetry and stories at a church in my local area. This church is no stranger to 'misfitting'. After going on their own journey to become fully affirming of sexually and gender diverse folks, they found themselves in the crosshairs of conservative churches determined to remove from their state association any churches and pastors rethinking questions around sexuality and gender.[8] That's its own long story, but suffice to say this is a beautiful community of people who know what it's like to feel like they don't 'fit'.

On my visit to share with their community that Sunday morning this question came up: *What's the collective noun for a group of misfits?*

Looking around the room in that moment I felt a strong sense of connection, of kinship, of warm community with these people. Without really thinking about it, I wondered out loud: *Could this be a 'belonging' of misfits?*

It was one of those phrases that just rolled off the tongue. Now, though, I think it's become something more than that. An ethos. A mission.

My answer to the question I opened this chapter with.

Yes, people *feel* like misfits. At some point, many of us experience a dissonance between our evolving sense of self and the frameworks we inherit.

But what if there's *actually* room for everyone?

What if belonging is the very thing Jesus offered people?

What if we could create 'belongings of misfits' everywhere?

I suppose these days this is one of the questions to which I'm trying to live out an answer.

A work in progress

I don't want to give a false impression and pretend it's easy or straightforward.

Six years into any community is long enough to have tasted some losses. There have certainly been times when I've questioned all of it.

Could we have done something differently for the people who came and left? Should we be more active in inviting people in?

Are we too Christian? Not Christian enough?

Are we even a 'real church'?

At the end of the day though, I think we've stumbled upon something beautiful.

On any given week at Meeting Ground, you'll walk in the front door of someone's home and be welcomed. As you walk through the house you'll see children – sometimes banging a drum in the corner, at other times building a Lego tower together. Someone else enters the house – someone in their sixties who has had a lifetime of trying to figure out faith and God and life, but here they are, just showing up, like they always have.

Coffees are made with love for all who want them. After about forty-five minutes we'll gather in a circle, moving furniture, finding space. We acknowledge the Country we meet on, becoming mindful of the place we are and its vast history that significantly predates all of us.

Then there might be a reading, followed by a question. Conversation ensues. One week we asked, 'What does love taste like, look like, smell like?' and listened to answers from people of all ages and stages of life. Another week we explored what it means to be a 'trauma-informed' community.

Sometimes there are very vulnerable things shared in our gatherings. Other times it is light and fun. Often we wonder: how can we, as a small community of people, in a world that feels very chaotic and overwhelming, bring a little love into the week ahead of us?

It can be hard to measure how well we're answering that question. But the fact that we loop back to it often makes me feel like we're doing something right.

Everything changes, and that's ok

As I reflect on my own evolving journey, and the way Meeting Ground has shifted over its six-year journey, I'm reminded that life, faith and community are always in flux. And perhaps another one of the shifts I've been through is to embrace that flux rather than resist it.

I can't tell you what any of this will look like in another six years – nor do I feel the need to. Where my confidence is limited, I try to have a healthy curiosity.

As I look to the future, both for Meeting Ground and for the broader conversation about 'spiritual misfits', I carry a blend of hope and questions.

I wonder if we're witnessing not just individual experiences of misfitting but a larger cultural shift in how people relate to religious institutions and traditions. The rise of the 'nones' and 'dones' (people with no religious affiliation and people who have left the church) suggests that traditional models of church are increasingly failing to connect with many segments of the population. Yet the hunger for meaning, community and transcendence remains.

I wonder if communities like Meeting Ground aren't just temporary balms for wounded believers but early experiments in what faith communities could look like in the future – smaller, more flexible, less institutional and more focused on relational connection than doctrinal uniformity.

I'm also curious about how the theology that emerges from these 'belongings of misfits' might reshape broader Christian thought. When people who have experienced marginalisation within religious spaces begin to articulate their understanding of God, Scripture and community, new insights emerge that can enrich the whole tradition. Voices from the edges often see things easily missed from the centre.

For Meeting Ground specifically, I hope we continue to evolve in response to the needs and insights of our community. I hope we remain small enough to be intimate while committed to fostering and participating in a larger conversation, so that we don't become insular or self-referential.

Most of all, I hope we continue to create space where people can bring their whole selves – their doubts and beliefs, their wounds and hopes, their questions and insights. Because ultimately, that's what I believe the God of the Incarnation offers us: not certainty or perfection, but an affirmation that we belong as we are, where we are, in a world that is both aching and beloved.

In these times of polarisation and isolation, perhaps this is the most radical thing we can offer – not answers, but presence. Not perfection, but belonging. Not a fixed destination, but solidarity on the road.

A belonging of misfits, moving together toward wholeness.

A closing prayer of mine — make it yours if you'd like.[9]

God,

Orient my life
in the direction of the Good
like a compass pointing north

May the magnetic forces within me
tune into the true and the beautiful

I often feel as though
there is no map for the paths I walk
(sometimes not even a path)
yet always there are guides
and clues
and the wisdom of things

And I know
feeling alone doesn't mean I am
feeling lost doesn't mean I am
and I choose to trust that
in the landscape of love
there's no way that doesn't eventually
lead back to home.

CHURCH

A Prayer for a Bush Picnic / Jono Ingram

Here, nestled among the trees,
sitting on an old log or rock,
the breeze whispering to us
and the sun warming our faces;
be near to us O God.

It is good for us to eat outside,
to make our table upon the grass,
with dirt still on our hands,
for it is here that we are reminded
that our own lives are not separate
from the lives of forest and rivers,
oceans and mountains.

May this bush picnic,
with birds and kangaroos
as guests at our grassy table,

draw us more fully into the Good Life,
the simplicity of good food and good drink,
as we choose today
to walk lightly and in harmony
with all of Your creatures. Amen.

From 'Dirt Church Liturgy'. Originally published at https://jcingram.wordpress.com/2024/09/02/a-prayer-for-a-bush-picnic/. Republished with permission.

Pakipaki

Alimoni T. Taumoepeau,
Uilisone Kiriona
Mafaufau, Mosese Taufa
and Seini Tokilupe Taufa

Pakipaki: Transforming lives

Alimoni T. Taumoepeau

The word for communion in Tongan is *pakipaki*, which means 'breaking', for holy communion refers to breaking bread. *Pakipaki* is a useful way of describing what happened when Jesus approached the disciples on the road to Emmaus and engaged with them about the Scriptures. As they entered the village, the disciples invited Jesus to eat with them. At the table, Jesus 'took bread, gave thanks, broke (*pakipaki*) it and began to give it to them. Then their eyes were opened and they recognized him, and he disappeared from their sight. They asked each other, "Were not our hearts burning within us while he talked with us on the road and opened the Scriptures to us?"' (Luke 24:30-32, NIV).

Pakipaki can happen in many different types of gatherings. A Methodist minister, Rev. Sau Faupula, started a small group gathering called *ha'ofanga* ('sharing together') in Tonga, and it soon spread to every Methodist church in the country. Others in Tonga then began to use the word *akolotu* ('learn to pray') to describe these gatherings. These were ways of bringing people together to learn about *lotu* ('worship' or 'prayer') and creating a space to *pakipaki*. They gave people the opportunity to learn about God through Scripture reading and reflection and to build confidence to pray.

Traditionally, Tongans enjoyed different types of social gatherings. One of these is the *kava* club, named after a traditional Tongan drink. In these gatherings, there are often people from all walks of life: the educated and uneducated, the religious and non-religious. In the Australian town of Griffith in the early 1990s, there was a medical doctor by the name of Dr Viliami Tangi who was a lay preacher at the Uniting Church. In a *kava* gathering, he introduced the *lotu* once a week, and everyone was invited to *pakipaki*. Today, in various Tongan and other Pacific Island churches in Griffith and throughout Australia, the men still gather for *kava*. They open up the Scriptures, usually the lectionary reading for the week, and share how each one understands Scripture in their own way. It's a lowkey, informal event. No interpretation of the text is given; everyone can *vahevahe* ('share') what they hear from the text. Each person is respected for their opinion and ideas.

Eventually, this form of gathering spread to every Tongan *kava* club around the world. The practice of *pakipaki* became a source of quiet evangelistic fire, resulting in individual transformation not limited to any church or non-church context.

Across the world, some of the men who have joined the *pakipaki* have become local preachers, lay leaders, community leaders and evangelists in their own right, while others have changed for the good of their family and society, or have gone from never reading the Bible to reading it daily. Many participants have never before had the opportunity to connect Scripture to their daily living, and some have never been in a space where their voice, opinion or story has been heard.

Transformation happens when people are given the opportunity to engage with the Bible in ways they can understand, and to have a say and to learn from others' perspectives and experiences. *Pakipaki* no longer only applies to those who drink *kava*, but to those who gather for conversations about their faith and life journey over a coffee in all types of gatherings. This is one way of responding to Jesus' Great Commission to 'go into all the world and make disciples ...' (Matthew 20:19). *Pakipaki* has become a tool and model for discipleship in Tonga and in Pacific Island communities around the world.

What is pakipaki?
Uilisone Kiriona Mafaufau
Pakipaki refers to a biblical concept that traces its origins to Jesus himself. It is the Tongan translation of the word 'broke', which describes the moment Jesus broke the bread and gave it to his followers to distribute to the crowd of five thousand (Matthew 14:19, Mark 6:41, cf. Luke 9:16). Likewise, *vahevahe* ('sharing') describes the way the early Christians shared and distributed their wealth in order that everyone's needs would be met (Acts 2:43-47). Jesus also broke/*pakipaki* bread on the night he was betrayed, when he instituted the Lord's Supper after celebrating Passover with his disciples (Matthew 26:26, Mark 14:22, Luke 22:19). He took the bread, blessed and broke/*pakipaki* it, gave it to his disciples and said, 'Take, eat; this is my body.' Paul claims he received the same directive from Jesus

to continue this practice of breaking bread (1 Corinthians 11:24). Luke records how Jesus again took bread, blessed and broke/*pakipaki* it and gave it to his two disciples who walked to Emmaus on the evening of the day of the resurrection (Luke 24:30). He also mentions that it was customary for the early Christians to meet on the first day of the week to break/*pakipaki* bread (Acts 20:7). This breaking of bread was their celebration of the Lord's Supper, in which they also 'ate their food with glad and generous hearts, praising God and having the goodwill of the people' (Acts 2:46, NRSV).

I want to highlight just a few important aspects of Jesus' breaking of bread that are essential for the practice of *pakipaki*. Firstly, apart from the feeding of the five thousand, all the above-mentioned incidences of breaking bread were conducted in the presence of Jesus' faithful disciples. These disciples had been nurtured and invited to understand and accept the significance of Jesus' broken body in their lives. Therefore, *pakipaki* is a gathering of believers who see themselves as Jesus' disciples and members of his broken body. Jesus, in the celebration of the Eucharist, invites his followers to eat the broken pieces of the one loaf of bread, which is emblematic of his broken body being shared by all of them. Similarly, *pakipaki* invites each participant to share his/her own views as part of the divided but one witness to the Word of God. It is very important for all *pakipaki* participants to understand that their gathering, which revolves around the sharing of and learning from the Word of God, is different from all other gatherings.

Secondly, the feeding of the five thousand with the bread and fish occurred in a context where people were physically hungry. Here, the act of breaking bread/*pakipaki* highlighted Jesus' commitment to the holistic care and nourishment of the body, mind and spirit of his followers. As already mentioned, the early Christians are known to have often broken bread in their homes and eaten their food 'with glad and generous hearts'. Therefore, practice of *pakipaki* participants sharing their gifts of confectionary and other foods during or after their sessions is closely aligned with the biblical idea of breaking bread together as an act of holistic care.

Thirdly, a key feature of the *pakipaki* is singing and praying, which again was one of the practices of the early Christians. Paul encouraged the Ephesians to 'sing psalms and hymns and spiritual songs among yourselves, singing and making melody to the Lord in your hearts' (Ephesians 5:19, NRSV). He also wrote to the Colossians, saying, 'Let the word of Christ dwell in you richly; teach and admonish one another in all wisdom and with gratitude in your hearts sing psalms, hymns, and spiritual songs to God. And whatever you do, in word or deed, do everything in the name of the Lord Jesus, giving thanks to God the Father through him' (Colossians 3:16, NRSV). This is Paul's blueprint for *pakipaki*.

Finally, Jesus' breaking of bread was always preceded by a blessing. The blessing of the Eucharist (both the bread and the cup) is the invocation and acknowledgement of the power of the Holy Spirit that transforms the simple loaf of bread into the blessed broken body of Christ. Blessing the *pakipaki* before it commences is essential because it reflects the blessing and inspiration of the Spirit who is at work in all the participants, and the call to respect one another as image-bearers of God.

While the informal nature of *pakipaki* is evident in impromptu jokes, laughter, singing, stories, prayers and so on, its participants must never lose awareness of the divine volition for them to care for, nurture and respect the concerns and needs of other participants. *Pakipaki* is taking the body of Jesus, the Word of God, and breaking it up among the participants, so that they may be nourished to live in the power of the Word.

Give me *pakipaki* for Jesus anytime!

Pakipaki at Auburn Uniting Church
Mosese Taufa

Pakipaki is a form of *talanoa* – a traditional form of gathering for 'story, storytelling and conversation' – but with the purpose of sharing the Word of God.[1] *Pakipaki* is open to people of any culture, age and gender and can occur anywhere and at any time. *Pakipaki* did not originate with the church, but is an attempt by *faikava* people (people who gathered to drink *kava*) to *talanoa* – to share God's word and to explore how it can be applied to our lives.

We have witnessed how *pakipaki* has transformed the lives of people who are now key leaders in our parish, Auburn Uniting Church.

We offer *pakipaki* as a safe space for people in the community to gather and to have fellowship with one another. There is a *pakipaki* for men every Monday night and for women every Thursday morning. Interestingly, the women tend to refer to their time of sharing God's Word as *vahevahe* ('sharing'), a word that is deeply connected to motherhood. When a baby is conceived in the mother's womb, the mother *vahevahe* (shares) food with her baby.

Both the *pakipaki* and *vahevahe* always finish up with a time of prayer for our families, our church activities, our community and the world. We receive prayer requests from our friends who attend the *pakipaki* and *vahevahe,* as well as from people from all over the world. These gatherings are the powerhouse of our parish.

Our youth also have *pakipaki* time, which they call 'Bible Sharing Time'. They usually do this during special seasons like Advent and Lent. Last time they had their Bible Sharing Time, the parents who brought their children ended up joining in. This is always an exciting time for our youth. It is their time to foster their faith, socialise and have fun.

During the COVID lockdowns, physical gathering was not possible and we missed seeing one another. But with the help of technology, *pakipaki* was held on Zoom and Facebook Messenger. It was a safe space where people could join in or opt out whenever they liked. The invitation was sent out to our friends and, amazingly, many people made an effort to be part of the Zoom *pakipaki*. Some even joined us from other parts of the world, depending on their availability.

In the *pakipaki*, people are not forced to speak or to share. This is a one of the ways we help those who join the *pakipaki* for the first time to feel welcome. Newcomers are usually quiet for a few weeks before they start to speak out and become part of the conversation. It is always a privilege to see people you don't really know finding the confidence to open up and share their own experiences and stories in the group.

Someone once shared a story from the early 1990s that highlighted the impact of *pakipaki* on those who attend. There was a man who loved alcohol and did not like drinking *kava*. Over time he joined the *kava* gathering and listened with interest to people sharing (*pakipaki*) the Word of God. At first he didn't speak, but after a while he began to open up. He also started to attend church more regularly with his family. Eventually, he committed to church activities and showed a growing interest in the Bible. In the late 1990s, he became a worship leader and then a local lay preacher. He earned the respect of the congregation and later became the chairperson of the church council for over ten years.

In his simple act of *pakipaki* and *vahevahe*, Jesus invites, encourages, nurtures and empowers us to do likewise. Today, we see around us how life is becoming more difficult for so many. People are going without food and shelter and are ending up on the streets. This reminds me of how the first Christian community lived. Many poor people joined them, but soon they were no longer poor because people shared (*vahevahe*) all they had (Acts 2:43-47, 4:32-35) and practiced *pakipaki* daily. I believe the world would be a better place with more *pakipaki* and *vahevahe*.

Women's pakipaki

Seini Siseliana Tokilupe Taufa

Once a week, in my local church, a group of women come together for women's *pakipaki* – a time of fellowship and sharing from the Bible. One person is allocated to lead and facilitate the sharing. We sit around the table and each of us brings our Bible and hymn book. The sharing is based on the lectionary readings for the week. There are usually four readings. Each passage of Scripture is read and then we open it up to anyone who wants to share from the Bible. The women may also choose to sing a song after sharing. At the end, we all pray aloud together, with singing in the background. This is a common spiritual practice that Tongan women actively participate in, both in Tonga and in the diaspora.

The *pakipaki* is a time when the women of our church take a break from their daily activities and gather together with a purpose. It is a time of sharing God's story of love, grace, peace and hope. The space allows us to reflect on what God's story truly means for us and for our personal stories of faith. In our engagement with the Scriptures we are nourished, nurtured and sustained spiritually, cultivating a deep connection with God and one other, strengthening our faith and relationships and being transformed. I witness this in my ninety-year-old mother who always looks forward to this time of fellowship with other women and who prepares for it. The Word of God is her dwelling place, her inspiration, her strength, her source of guidance and wisdom – it is her life – and the *pakipaki* is a place to nurture this devotion.

The Tongan word for sharing is *vahevahe*. Sharing (*vahevahe*) is about giving (*foaki*) and receiving (*ma'u/tali*). It is an act of generosity, acceptance, welcoming and hospitality. *Vahevahe* can also mean to divide or partition. The word is used more often by the women to describe their gathering as it has a distinctive, softer tone than *pakipaki*, which is used by the men. *Vahevahe* is amiable, conveying a sense of warmth. It is gentle, expressing a sense of caring and loving kindness. There is sincerity, honesty and authenticity in *vahevahe*.

The act of *foaki* and *ma'u/tali* is very much a central theme in the Bible. It is deeply rooted in the biblical narrative and woven into the tapestry of the Old and New Testaments. The ebb and flow of *foaki* and *maú/tali* creates a space for relationship to be created, strengthened and sustained. It brings to light God's abundant provision and the fact that we are the recipients of God's act of *vahevahe*. This is evident through creation, communities and families, and is an expression of God's care, faithfulness and generosity. God's ultimate provision is Jesus Christ who took the bread, blessed it, broke (*pakipaki*) it and gave (*foaki*) it to them, saying, 'Do this in remembrance of me' (Luke 22:19). Similarly, when Jesus fed the five thousand, he took the bread and the fish, blessed it and then broke (*pakipaki*) the bread and gave (*'oange,* another word for *foaki*) it to the disciples to then give (*foaki*) to the people.

The concept of *vahevahe* is deeply rooted and embedded in God's love and desire to reach all people. *Vahevahe* is the visible outpouring of love that flows out from the act of *pakipaki*. It has universal impact, reaching out beyond those who are gathered. *Vahevahe* reflects the heart of God for all creation, all the way to the ends of the earth.

Neighbourhood

Christine Palmer

> I am inclined to think that all effective ministry, regardless of context must be incarnational.
> – Noel Castellanos[1]

At the end of 2023 I found myself scrolling through Facebook, looking at images of colleagues in their liturgical gear at various church ceremonies and activities. They'd be standing with arms outstretched over bread and wine, or delivering a sermon to a congregation sitting in rows, listening intently. Meanwhile here I was, mixing up playdough, collecting groceries for donations for a local community organisation, having coffee with a distressed and overwhelmed mum, advocating for a new high school in our fast-growing suburb and curating material for an online spirituality group. I found myself struggling to relate to the ministry my colleagues were engaged in. It no longer felt comfortable or connected to where I was and what I was experiencing. It made me realise that a significant shift had taken place in my practice of ministry and my understanding of mission.

I'd grown up in the church and been involved in multiple ministries: teaching Sunday school, going on summer Beach Missions, coordinating camps for underprivileged children, leading worship, supporting my husband in a church plant in the early years of our marriage, doing paid pastoral care work and preaching. Ministry as a layperson in the church had always been part of my life. Then I'd felt God call me to ordained ministry, and in 2014 the church affirmed this call by ordaining me as a Minister of the Word in the Uniting Church. I had always felt my gifting lay in serving and equipping the church to be the people of God in the world. However, there was a growing passion within my heart for how the church was called to be part of its local community and to engage in relevant ways, living out Christ's ministry of reconciliation and renewal within its neighbourhood.

A growing call to neighbourhood ministry

In my first placement I was drawn to a church that was interested in and part of its community. We revitalised a program that reached those living with disabilities and their families. We got to know the people using our facilities and did one or two projects with them. We worked in partnership with another church to host a playgroup for the community in our facility.

This desire for the church to meet people where they were and to engage with its neighbourhood led me to do more reading in this area. I also completed the Mission Shaped Ministry course, which was developed in the UK to equip people to plant and sustain fresh expressions of church (doing church differently for those who are not yet part of the church). The emphasis of the course is on joining in with what God is doing in the neighbourhood, building relationships, listening, loving your neighbours, sharing the Good News of Jesus and letting church take a shape that is relevant to the context of the community.[2] The more I explored and learnt about fresh expressions, the more it resonated with me. I went on to do the SENT course, a one-year program at Morling College that equips people to start new churches and emphasises similar themes. Both these courses are grounded in the theology of *Missio Dei* – the mission of God – and incarnational ministry – immersion in the local context in the same way that Jesus, or the Word, 'became flesh and blood, and moved into the neighbourhood'.[3] Just as Jesus was sent into the world, so too the church is a sent people, called to be part of God's activity in the world and in our neighbourhoods or, as missiologist David Bosch so beautifully puts it, 'to participate in the movement of God's love toward people'.[4]

As I reflected on the ministry I was involved in, I realised that while we as a church were seeking to engage with our community – and doing it well for a small, ageing congregation – our focus was still on the church and its structures. It was about programs and being attractive, drawing people to the church rather than going out into the neighbourhood. It was Sunday-centric, with a lot of our activity and time devoted to making a Sunday service happen and keeping the church going. So I encouraged the church to begin to think about our neighbourhood and how we might engage more deeply with it.

Around this time, I heard about the Sydney South-West Project. The Parramatta Nepean Presbytery of the Uniting Church wanted to create a presence within the growth area of South-West Sydney using a fresh expressions model of ministry, which was to be innovative and to grow contextually appropriate expressions of church. I felt God was calling me to this ministry, so I put in an expression of interest to be part of the project, and the church affirmed my call to this ministry.

Moving into the neighbourhood

In July 2019 I literally moved with my family into the neighbourhood. Jorge Acevedo suggests that the incarnational life of Jesus should shape the life and ministry of those who follow him.[5] So as I unpacked our boxes, I set about getting to know our neighbours and exploring what it might mean to embody God's love in my local community. We introduced ourselves to our neighbours and invited them over for meals or coffee. We got to know them in our everyday encounters. I joined the local Facebook pages, interacted and took note of the issues that arose. I looked at my community's profile online to get a statistical snapshot of my neighbourhood. I found a hairdresser with a home salon in our suburb, located a local dog groomer and ordered cakes from a local baker with a home business. I frequented the local café, took notice of where people gathered, joined in local activities and began to attend the local council Community Interagency meetings.

I tried to do everything locally to build relationships and to understand my community, to hear what mattered, to discover who lived here and to become part of my neighbourhood. Incarnational ministry is focused on meeting people where they are, and if I was going to share life and share Jesus with our neighbours, I needed to grapple with what the Good News looked like in our neighbourhood. As Brad Brisco suggests, we need to engage in the lives of others, and this missional incarnational living enables us to see and hear where God's Spirit is moving and to join in with it.[6]

Listening, loving and serving the neighbourhood

Ministry for me became about being present in the community, listening and building relationships. As I did this, one of the things I noticed was mums of new babies inviting others to meet up with them at the park. These new mothers were looking for community and connection, people to share this life stage with. Good news for them was to know that they were not alone. I began to wonder if we needed a playgroup in this new area, one where connections could be made. But being a new suburb, we had no facilities. Could we do a playgroup at the park?

Just as I was about to investigate this idea, I heard about a mum in the community who was starting an outdoor gathering for mothers. I approached her and said I had the same idea. As she'd already started, I asked how I could help and join in. She said she would love administrative support – someone to organise the gatherings. This mum was so busy she didn't end up making it to the gatherings, but the playgroup in the park grew as I and another volunteer faithfully turned up, week after week, to serve the community and to build not just relationships but friendships. We now have three playgroups a week, with an average attendance of fifty people, at various parks in our area, as well as an online playgroup Facebook community of over 2,000 families.

We've been able to connect families with a range of services they need, as well as connect families with one another. When I see them making friends and sharing tips, services and supports with one another, I see part of God's reconciliation and renewal taking place; God's love embodied in caring for each other and building a healthy community.

One friend from the playgroup introduced us to her family

members, a husband and wife who had recently moved to the area. The husband had recently become a Christian and his wife was interested in exploring Christianity. Since my friend from the playgroup knew I was a Christian, she asked if I would meet with her relatives. My husband and I began to meet with her family members, building a friendship and exploring the Christian faith together with them. Over time, the wife decided to follow Jesus and be baptised. We have continued to meet regularly and do Bible study together. Since then, they have shared their faith with another family, which has led to that family's baptism.

The COVID lockdowns proved to be a particularly challenging time. We had been in the neighbourhood for only nine months when the first one hit, and had to wrestle with how we could continue to get to know our neighbours when we couldn't be out and about in our community. I had to learn to trust that God was still at work, so I continued to try to be present and build relationships. I just had to do it a different way. I got to know people online in our local community Facebook pages by lending equipment to people when requests popped up, joining with others to organise online trivia nights and participating in a Zoom meditation group. I collected groceries for those struggling due to losing jobs in the lockdown. I invited people in our neighbourhood, via our local community Facebook page, to drop off groceries to my door. We would chat and connect outside while remaining physically distanced, and then I'd drop off all the groceries to a local organisation that prepared and distributed the hampers. As lockdowns relaxed and small gatherings were allowed again, we worked with members of our community to create events that brought the community together in safe ways, like an outdoor Christmas scavenger hunt in the suburb for families. Members of the community helped create clues and posters to look for around the community, while local businesses and some local residents donated items to go into a Christmas bag for the children when they completed the scavenger hunt. There was not a sense of the church needing to 'own' these activities or events, but rather a feeling of doing it all together.

Conversations in the neighbourhood

While living and working alongside those in our neighbourhood, we've made friends, shared meals and been part of people's lives. I've been invited to bless special occasions and perform a wedding. It is in these various spaces and relationships that conversations about life naturally occur – at the playgroups, online, on a walk or during meals. I get to hear about what matters to people and what gives them meaning, and to have spiritual conversations. In response to what we've heard, we've created spaces for exploring faith and spirituality, experimenting with various gatherings. Some of these groups have worked, some haven't. Sometimes they have evolved over seasons.

The Facebook group Deep Breath emerged to fulfil the desire for spirituality and self-nurturing that we were hearing about as we talked to people. Each day, some form of content is posted for people to engage with. It might be a quote, a poem, a journal prompt, a question or a mindfulness activity. At various times I offer in-person gatherings for those who want to meet over coffee and chat about particular issues.

We've also experimented with a mums' meditation group during the week. Some mums expressed how hard it was to go to church with their children. They said they were so busy looking after their children at church that they couldn't engage with what was going on. So we tried meeting at our house. We read the Scriptures and discussed what we were hearing and what God might be saying to us. We made sure that the space we created was child friendly, and we could stop if necessary to attend to the children so the mums didn't miss out. We had mums come along to this group who would refer to themselves as a Christian and others who were curious and wanted to learn more about Christian faith.

The group ended up morphing into a Sunday breakfast, with partners coming along as well. We've also invited others from our neighbourhood with whom we've connected and who have expressed an interest in Christian faith, and they have joined us for Sunday breakfast. It's become a place to discuss and ask questions about God and the Bible. The only rules are to be curious and non-judgemental, and that it's okay to ask any question. The focus isn't on doctrine or having the right belief, but on creating an open, safe and welcoming environment and trusting that God is working in each of our lives. Each time we meet, my husband and I are encouraged by people's engagement and learning and the rich conversations that happen around the table.

All these stories remind me of how when we listen to our community, build relationships and look for what God is doing and join in, we see God at work in the lives of those around us. We can respond and be part of what God is doing.

Fresh Expressions

Michael Moynagh refers to this process as the Fresh Expressions Relationship-first Model.[7] He suggests that when we become part of our neighbourhood and community – when we listen, build relationships and serve the community – there is space to share Jesus, and church can take place in whatever form works for that context. I've tried to follow this framework as I've approached ministry in my neighbourhood. Moynagh reminds us that this is a 'framework, not a straitjacket', emphasising that all our work should be based on attentively listening to the Spirit of God and participating in God's reconciliation and renewal of our communities, and that this is going to look different in every neighbourhood.[8]

Letting go and trusting

Ian Mobsby suggests that if we are to join in this ministry of reconciliation that God calls us to, it is going to require a 'more contemplative, incarnational way of living – one that listens, heals, and restores'.[9] I've found this to be true, as this way of doing ministry means letting go of control, relying on God and being responsive to the Spirit, instead of relying on resources and programs. I've had to develop deeper contemplative spiritual practices and different ways of listening to God that help me to see where the Spirt of God is at work. I've had to lean into these spiritual contemplative practices when ministry has been difficult, and they continue to help stretch me and grow me in the area of trusting and depending on God.

One story that I return to time and again is the story in the Gospel of Luke where Jesus sends the seventy disciples out into the villages (Luke 10:1–11). The disciples must trust and depend on God, as they are sent with few resources. Jesus warns them it won't be easy. They will need to start where they are, build relationships, find people to work with, experiment and be willing to move on when things don't work. This passage has been foundational for me in the ministry here and reminds me that it is God who sends us into our communities and neighbourhoods to build relationships and to be present. I'm reminded not to trust in programs or resources, but instead to depend on God.

Challenges

Doing church differently has been challenging, especially when some of the wider church operate on a different set of metrics and struggle to understand what you're doing. While many are keen to support what I am doing, there are often questions like: How is your congregation going? Where does your church meet? Where is your church? How many people come to your church? What programs are you running? These kinds of questions highlight the framework, expectations and metrics that many people in the church work within. Good ministry equals Sunday worship gatherings, numbers, lots of programs and busyness. I've felt the pressure and frustration of these expectations and metrics. I have had to develop a new set of metrics based on what it means to be present and to embody God's love in our neighbourhood: How many relationships are being developed? How are we being part of God's Good News in our neighbourhood? Where are we seeing transformation take place? Are people actively engaged in discipleship? There has also been the challenge of navigating safety and legal compliance to ensure the ministry is accountable while being responsive, flexible, informal and embedded in the community.

When I first moved into the neighbourhood there were a few others who were part of the ministry project, but this shifted after a year and a half, and my husband and I were left on our own. At times it felt lonely. The church was unsure of how best to support what we were doing. Early on it became important to find a community of people who got what I was doing and was wrestling with the same challenges and questions. I joined some peer coaching groups for those exploring doing church differently and became part of a national fresh expressions practitioners' group.

More recently, I have found individual coaching to be extremely helpful. Reading books, listening to podcasts and attending workshops and conferences has kept me engaged and informed about how the church beyond my own denomination and country are also navigating neighbourhood ministry. During the initial years of the ministry, having a supervisor with an understanding of incarnational ministry and fresh expressions was essential, as it provided a supportive environment where I could address challenges and receive encouragement. This guidance also helped me to navigate the transitions happening in my ministry and theology.

Lost bearings

Karina Kreminski writes about the 'discombobulation' we can experience when we step out of the church and participate in God's mission in the neighbourhood.[10] She writes that:

> To do this work of contextualisation is sacrificial, deeply risky and transformative. We end up in places we have not been and become people we might not have predicted we would be. This is kenosis and it can make us feel like we have lost our bearings.[11]

That's what I felt a couple of years ago as I found myself staring at Facebook, struggling to connect with the images of ministry and church I was seeing. I felt like I had lost my bearings, as ministry in my neighbourhood was so very different; so different that it caused me to question if I was fulfilling my ordination vows. I found myself going back to those vows and to the list of duties for a Minister of the Word in the Uniting Church Regulations, only to find that they are consistent with the theology of *Missio Dei*, incarnational ministry and the way I was practising ministry. I was encouraged to see several duties listed that involve the minister engaging with the community, equipping others for ministry in the neighbourhood, pioneering new expressions of the gospel, bearing witness to the gospel and proclaiming the Good News beyond the community of faith.[12] I realised that I was fulfilling my vows and duties in ways that reflected the relationships and context of the neighbourhood I was in. Since this crisis, I have been able to reflect on the shift that has taken place within me and in my practice of ministry as I've sought to embody God's love in my neighbourhood.

It has been a shift from programs to relationships; from being a host, where we are in charge, to being a guest and allowing ourselves to be welcomed into spaces, joining in with what is already happening. It has been a shift from control to trust, from a focus on doctrine and belief to engagement, exploration and belonging; from a focus on the church to a focus on the mission of God in the neighbourhood. Now I preside over coffee and croissants around our breakfast table, prepare two-minute video messages, curate a spirituality page, write a reflection on life for our playgroup families, have conversations over puzzles and playdough, and explore and experiment, creating other spaces where people can gather and explore faith. I am much more comfortable with not having answers or a program, as I am more interested in going on a journey with people where they are at, responding to their questions and curiosity and welcoming everyone to the table. When programs do develop, it's because they have come out of listening and responding to my neighbours. I'm not concerned about whether it's our program; I'm more interested in how what we are doing contributes to God's mission of reconciliation and renewal in our neighbourhood. The Spirit of God continues to transform and challenge me about what it means to be a faithful presence in my neighbourhood. This intentional ministry of presence takes time. Building relationships of trust is slow, steady work.

Future presence in the neighbourhood

Losing one's bearings and feeling disoriented can be an unsettling experience, yet it also allows you to recalibrate. It has enabled me to reflect on ministry; anchoring me in the theology and practice of incarnational ministry in the neighbourhood and allowing the incarnational life of Jesus to shape my own life and ministry. It has shifted my posture from 'doing' to one of intentionally being; to listening to our community, building relationships and looking for what God is doing and joining in. My prayer is that as the ministry here continues to develop and grow, incarnational ministry will continue to shape what takes place as the church seeks to embody God's love in the neighbourhood. May we continue to look for and join in with God's work of transformation through shared, loving relationships and presence in our neighbourhood. We hope that this will be the measure of the church here in this neighbourhood, for as Tim Soerens states so simply, 'presence trumps performance every single time'.[13]

Gathering

Simon Moyle

When the guru sat down to worship each evening, the ashram cat would get in the way and distract the worshipers. So he ordered that the cat be tied during evening worship.

After the guru died the cat continued to be tied during evening worship. And when the cat died, another cat was brought to the ashram so that it could be duly tied during evening worship.

Centuries later learned treatises were written by the guru's disciples on the religious and liturgical significance of tying up a cat while worship is performed.
– Anthony De Mello, *The Song of the Bird*[1]

In 2002, my wife and I moved into Whitley College, a residence for students of Melbourne University. My role was to be a live-in chaplain to the 130 students, mostly from rural Victoria and New South Wales. Over the next two years we formed a deep connection with these young people, most of whom were from no faith background but were wrestling with the big questions of life. We began to wonder what 'church' might look like for these folks who would never darken the door of a traditional expression of church.

Three years later we started inspiral, a 'new missional community' to these students as they moved out of college into the wider neighbourhood. We began meeting in our home in the inner-city suburb of Brunswick and worked on building a recognisably Christian culture more natural to these folks than mainstream evangelicalism. By this time I was running trainings in nonviolent activism, which dovetailed neatly both with the ways this new community understood Jesus' life and teachings and their desire to respond to pressing contemporary issues like climate change and war. Just as we all needed training in how to be effective agents of social change, we also needed training to be the kind of counter-cultural community that embodies Christ's upside-down Kingdom. In a world of war, we needed to learn peacemaking; in a world where the poor and homeless are rejected, we needed to learn hospitality; in a world of ecological crisis, we had to learn to care for God's good earth. That meant meeting regularly to learn those skills together and being formed through participation in practices, not merely intellectual education.

Having come across the story of the ashram cat, we started wondering: how much of contemporary church culture and practice are similar vestiges of a bygone era? What habits and skills, old or new, are most efficient or effective in forming a Kingdom culture of making disciples? Ideally the discipleship rationale for our practices would be self-explanatory, but if the culture or practices were going to be weird for newcomers, we wanted to be able to explain what practical purpose the weirdness served. Particularly given that most of the folks who were part of our initial crew had never been enculturated into church practice, there were no expectations of what should be done. For those of us who grew up in church culture it can be hard to tell what really matters until it's gone. Hence we decided to start with a clean slate, throwing out all of the practices that had been part of the gathered church's experience across the West, and only to add them (or other things) back in if they served a recognisably formative purpose. What follows is the fruit of twenty years of experimentation, trial and error, and creative play.

Rhythms

One of the first things we realised was that we needed some counter-cultural formation around time, or we risked simply being formed by the culture around us by default. We adopted the rhythms of the church year in order to be steeped in a different mode of time – essentially to live the gospel story repeatedly every year and to allow it to form us. We also adopted the Revised Common Lectionary, a three-year cycle of Scripture readings from the First Testament, the Psalms, the Gospels and the Epistles. This would ensure the discipline of tackling texts that we might otherwise be tempted to avoid and that would connect us with a broader community of churches around the world who follow the same pattern, even as we engaged it in our own ways.

We met in the living room of our home. This was initially just a practical option, but we soon realised there was theological importance to this. Firstly, the space we gather in is primarily a place of hospitality, where all are intentionally welcomed not to a generic building but to specific people's own space. The heart of our practice is having residents host gatherings rather than having an empty building that people visit once a week. Secondly, it emphasises the lived and grounded nature of our faith – that it is the home where the rubber of our faith hits the road. As a result, even if we had the option to meet elsewhere, we would have chosen homes.

In 2010 we joined with Emmaus Baptist Community, formerly North Carlton Baptist Church, one of the founding churches of the Baptist Union in Victoria. Started in 1883 in North Carlton, by 2007 the church had bought two adjoining houses and land on Nicholson Street in Coburg and changed their name to Emmaus Baptist Community. Their vision of a community centre, a workshop, a vegetable garden and an Oratory (prayer space), in addition to the housing, largely coincided with inspiral's, but with only a small handful of people left they were running out of steam to finish the project. With inspiral lacking funds to acquire property for a permanent base, it was a God-given match. The resulting merger was renamed GraceTree. We continue to meet in the main house, hosted by the residents.

Space, bodies and senses

In declaring creation 'good' and by becoming human in Jesus, God made all materiality holy. For this reason our gatherings try to take our embodiedness seriously.

What you face when sitting in church tends to form you in terms of what you expect about the nature of God. For this reason, we sit in a circle. This way there is no front or stage, and therefore no expert, no one above or below, and no one person who mediates God's presence to us – everyone can see everyone, and only together are we the Body of Christ. To see one another is to see God both in ourselves and in those like us, but also in what is other to us, whether culturally, in age, gender, etc.

Physical objects are always used as part of our gathering, and these vary with the church season. Sometimes they introduce the themes of the season, other times they are passed around to remind us what to pray for – a box of band-aids to remember those who are sick or hurting, a compass for our leaders, a world globe for the care of the earth.

In the beginning of the gathering, as we invoke the Trinity, we physically make the sign of the cross over ourselves. This reminds us that not only are we bodily people, but that God is the Lord of our bodies. We touch our heads as a reminder of our intellect (mind), our stomach as a reminder of our emotions (heart) and our right shoulder and left shoulder to symbolise strength. Our thumb, pointer finger and middle finger are held together as a symbol of the unified Trinity, and the remaining two fingers are held together as a reminder of Christ's dual nature as both divine and human.

We intentionally engage the five senses every week in our gatherings – from the smell of incense in the Oratory to touching objects as they are passed. Taste is engaged both through the Eucharist and the lunch we share together each time we gather. For sight we have many visual focuses – from the candle in our midst as a visual focus on God, along with the Eucharist bread and wine (and a spiral at Lent and Advent), to the icon in the Oratory. Cloths coloured for the church season are draped over the coffee table in our midst and adorn the Oratory. Our hearing is engaged in listening to one another and in singing songs together.

Intergenerational gathering

In the early years of combining inspiral with Emmaus, I was challenged by proponents of intergenerational worship (gatherings with all ages together) to see it as an issue of justice. There are no other demographics we would happily segregate from our gatherings – can we imagine, for example, having a special separate session every week for the over 70s? Or for disabled folks? Even the suggestion is offensive – instead, we do whatever we can to ensure such folks are welcomed and accommodated. So why would we not do this with children?

Intergenerational gathering requires changing our thinking from church being primarily education to primarily formational – about becoming the kind of people God calls us to be. What we learn, then, is how to be together – to be the *church* – in ways that meet the needs of all ages and bears with one another's needs. We learn patience, we learn to love one another, we learn that the young are willing to ask questions older folks don't have the courage to ask. In our culture, adults tend to retreat into their intellect; intergenerational gathering challenges this as it means playing games, making Bible stories from playdough and allowing ourselves to be interrupted by blue-tongued lizards walking past the window. It means embracing parts of ourselves we have learned to be ashamed of – our impatience, our dancing, our lack of drawing ability. It means relativising whatever our agenda was coming in (including the leaders!) to what is actually important – the people and their experience of God, which may well come in unexpected forms.

Liturgy

A formal liturgy was not part of my tradition in the conservative evangelical Baptist spaces in which I was raised. To say the same form of words week in, week out was thought of as vain repetition, rendering those words meaningless. Only novelty could keep the ideas and experiences fresh. Nonetheless, we humans are creatures of habit – even in my non-liturgical church, everyone knew the pat phrases and verbal tics of whoever was leading the service or presiding over communion.

In contrast, a set liturgy has freed us from the need to make it up as we go. Careful thought and creative expression have enabled us to be formed in 'how to speak Christian', as theologian Stanley Hauerwas puts it – that is, how to rightly speak the truth in ways that inspire meaningful imagination, without having to constantly reach for novel ways of articulating ourselves.

It is also formative – the word 'liturgy' comes from the Greek *leitourgia*, meaning 'the work of the people', and is therefore something for which we are all responsible. Some parts of the liturgy we read together, while the rest of it is read by individual members of the gathering, who simply take it in turns to read the next part. This means all voices are heard and valued, both in the cacophony of the collective and the clarity of the individual.

As the words are the same over a given church season, those who are illiterate or pre-literate can often learn it and participate.

Our liturgy sheets are printed in a font designed to be read more easily by folks with dyslexia. They are intentionally created as visually beautiful objects, with a seasonally appropriate icon on the front cover and multiple images throughout.

Our liturgies change with the church season, but all include the following elements, each of which has specifically formative purposes.

A *Trinitarian invocation*

We start by acknowledging the One we have learned to know as Triune: Father, Son and Holy Spirit. This invocation centres us on who it is that has called us together, as God is always prior to us and our presence together is a response to God's call. It is a reminder that God is not merely a generic God, but the one true God of Christian worship. The words we use to invoke the Triune God change seasonally, shaping how we approach gathering and worship over that time. Typically, images will come from Scripture, local native creatures or landforms, or from our direct experience; ideally all three. For example, our Advent invocation is:

> Stop what you're doing! And be still;
> wait patiently on the One who comes to you
> as the Hopeful whisper as you wake in the dawn light,
> as the Peace in stressful moments,
> as the Joy of a cool change on a hot summer day.
> Stay awake, watch, and listen;
> Love is coming to put all wrong things right.

This picks up the themes of Advent and names them as aspects of the Trinity, bound together as one by love.

The only appropriate response to having named this God is for us to be silent. We therefore pause briefly in quiet awe immediately afterwards.

Acknowledgement *of country*

We are settlers on Wurundjeri country, and situating ourselves in this way at the beginning of our gatherings helps us to acknowledge ourselves as guests and learners here. This is essential to living truthfully and justly, speaking truth not only about God, but about ourselves.

Wurundjeri people recognise seven seasons instead of the European four, each characterised by the movement and changes in the stars, plants and native creatures. Naming these changes as they're happening helps us to notice, honour and protect them. At the same time, naming the Creator Spirit they know as Bunjil ensures that we acknowledge and seek to learn from their experience of the creation of this place, rather than imposing one from elsewhere.

We have been fortunate to learn, from a number of Aboriginal and Torres Strait Islander Christian friends and wise people over the years, about how to live well in this place in a way that honours them as the First Peoples and brings their experience of Indigenous theology into our own practice. As people who gather on land near a creek known as Merri Merri ('very rocky' in the Woiwurrung language), it grounds us in the ways this place is different to all others.

Songs

When we first started inspiral we decided group singing was culturally odd, and therefore not for us. It was only as we deepened our involvement in antiwar activism that we revisited this. After all, activists of all faiths and none were happy to join in with 'Down by the Riverside' or 'You're the Voice' at our protests and demonstrations. In fact, the more we looked, the more we realised that every successful social change movement in history has involved singing – or at least chanting – as part of their gathered expression of their politics and worldview. Singing bonds a group together, uniting us around a common message and even common breath. Why would the church, this Kingdom movement for social, political and spiritual change, be any different?

We started with movement songs like 'We Shall Overcome' and 'Freedom' and expanded from there. Musically we have always been limited by my basic guitar skills, but this helps us keep it simple. More recently we have started writing our own songs, grounded in the experiences of this place and its people.

We sing the same set of songs for the whole church season (except Ordinary Time and Epiphany), themed to that season, which helps us increase our confidence in singing together over the weeks.

Scripture readings

The stories of Scripture are the primary stories to shape our lives. As I mentioned earlier, having the story of Jesus' life, death, resurrection and return play out over the course of each year means it sinks into our beings and shapes our realities, sometimes without us realising it. While the proclamation usually only focuses on one of the weekly lectionary readings, we read aloud at least three of the four so that we are exposed to different parts of Scripture, even if it just washes over us.

We ask for folks to volunteer to read these out to everyone, balancing voices of gender and age, and sometimes including reading in people's native languages other than English. At times we act them out, if it involves a story, to get a sense of the relationships between bodies and place, of movements and so on; or we might build it out of playdough or Duplo blocks.

We stand for the reading from the gospel, because while all Scripture is important, it is Jesus who is the Living Word. After the reading from the gospel, we respond:

> May Your Word dwell deeply within us
> And bear much fruit to Your glory

This is an acknowledgement that while the Bible tells us about Jesus, He is alive and working in and through us and all creation. His presence is in – but not limited to – the words on the page.

Proclamation of good news

For a number of years we were sceptical about monologues, especially given their rarity in our culture, people's resistance to them as a mode of communication and the potential for setting up elitist dynamics. Instead, we opted mostly for discussion.

Over time, however, our experience has been that discussion without preparation can simply be a pooling of ignorance. Understanding Scripture requires work and preparation, as this gives us some grasp of context, background, culture, allusions etc. Discussion based on this deeper understanding usually results in much richer outcomes.

As a result, we have settled on this time being a balance between the two – certainly an important time of announcing and proclaiming good news, specifically the good news of Jesus Christ, but also for wrestling honestly with it. The talk itself is always interruptible and usually features facilitated discussion questions before, after or throughout.

The good news we focus on varies even within the same passage over different years, but it is always centred on what Jesus makes possible. Often we will ask a number of questions about the reading for discussion before or after hearing from whoever has prepared the talk, asking the kinds of questions that the person preparing it has typically wrestled with:

What did you notice?
What did you struggle with?
Where is God in this passage?
Where is power?
What is good news here?

The talk itself is a maximum of ten to fifteen minutes long and aimed at all ages – not a children's talk specifically, but something they can at least understand.

A practical activity

We humans are bodily creatures, and we learn and engage not only with our minds but with our whole selves. Hence, in response to the proclamation of the good news, we engage together in an activity designed for all-age participation – not just for the kids, but with the expectation that they can be involved. It could be a game we play, or a craft activity or a task to complete together. For example, we might have to find items from nature of all different colours to make a rainbow, or have a relay race of 'living water' from the water fountain to fill buckets, or build as tall a tower as we can out of Duplo blocks to illustrate how far God's love extends. The activities are designed for practical learning and reflection – to give some experience of what we have been wrestling with together rather than simply communicating ideas or information. It is important that this time is fun, and also one where we interact with one another so that relationships and trust are deepened. Afterwards we will usually share any feelings or insights we might have had, usually accompanied by laughter.

Confession

Over the years we've wrestled with how to do confession in a way that rightly reflects God's extravagant grace and therefore helps produce genuine repentance and transformation, rather than merely shame, guilt or fear. Shame, guilt and fear are poor motivators for change, and usually lead to inner resistance and deficit-based thinking about ourselves. The traditional practice of confession preceding the announcement of absolution can reinforce this logic, and make it appear as though our confession *enables* God's forgiveness. Instead, we have learned to reverse this logic by starting with the announcement of absolution and placing our confession in the context of God's preceding grace. As our liturgy puts it, 'Confession does not enable God's forgiveness; rather God's forgiveness enables our confession.' God's forgiveness being a foregone conclusion means we are freed from the need to hide our brokenness and sin, and our repentance is a response of gratitude for the fresh start we have been afforded.

Eucharist

We share the Eucharist weekly, passing the elements around the circle. Everyone is welcome at this table – it is not our table, but the Lord's, and if he saw fit to include even those he knew would betray and deny Him, then we are not in a position to exclude anyone. We also want the children to know Jesus welcomes them and feeds them - and they often return for seconds or even thirds, showing a hunger and thirst for Jesus that we adults would do well to emulate. We serve one other, passing the bread and grape juice to one another and addressing each other by name as we say, 'The body/blood of Christ, given for you.'

Community news

Community news is often the highlight of our time together. An average week would have people sharing health news for themselves or loved ones, a story from school or a recent birthday party, or something noteworthy happening at work. Space is given for whatever people feel moved to share, and as a result achievements are celebrated, griefs are shared and our journeys are known.

Intercessory prayer

Community news leads naturally into a time of intercession, when the concerns and joys God has placed on our hearts are given voice. After each prayer is prayed, the person says, 'Lord, in your mercy', and we all respond, 'Hear our prayer', to add our own 'Amen' to it. This can involve lighting tapers for those who cannot voice their prayer, or writing our concerns on strips of paper to become a chain to decorate the room in Advent, or passing objects around to remind us of things to pray for.

Contemplative prayer

Our prayer time continues with a time of quiet contemplation. While there are other brief moments of quiet throughout the gathering time, this is a more extensive time to listen for the still, small voice within. For this time we make our way from our main gathering space into the Oratory, a separate space dedicated for quietness. This shift in space helps us make the mental shift being asked of us. The emphasis is not so much on quietness as stillness – and for this we encourage folks of all ages to find a position they can keep their body in that is relaxed but alert.

We're often asked how young children go with a period of quiet stillness. The reality is that many adults struggle with this as much as the kids! But actually, the discipline of doing this, particularly together, helps shape all of us, even those who find it difficult.

Ideally, in terms of the logical flow of the gathering, my preference would be for this to happen between the readings and the proclamation of good news; but for practical reasons, since it means changing spaces, it happens as the last thing. We have ten minutes of silence, with a bell to signal the beginning and end of that time. We also ring the bell after three minutes, at which point those who are feeling wriggly or like they've had enough can feel free to leave.

Benediction

You are a child of the Most High God
Creator of heaven and earth.
Walk lightly and humbly in creation,
Showing love to all those God draws near.
May the Father's love flow through you like the
Birrarung,
Christ's grace be planted deeply within you like the
Manna Gum,
and the Holy Spirit protect you like a nesting
magpie.
May you lose yourself in the wonder of the ancient
stars,
and find yourself in the One who made you from
the soil. Amen.

Our benediction intentionally picks up on and expresses commonalities between Christian and Wurundjeri worldviews, to ground us more deeply in this place and in our story. For example, Birrarung is the Wurundjeri word for the Yarra River, which meanders slowly through the heart of what they and Bunurong/Boonwurrung people know as Naarm, the country now often called Melbourne. Wurundjeri refers to the grub that lives in the Manna Gum, a native tree with a particularly deep taproot that anchors it to country, drawing water and nutrients. And one rendering of the Wurundjeri creation story has the Creator Spirit Bunjil creating Kulin (people) from the mud of the Birrarung, which we hold alongside the Judeo-Christian creation stories of people made from the dust of the ground.

Grace

Before we transition to sharing a meal together, in recognition of all the good things God has given us in our lives – even in the hard times – we go around the circle and each say something for which we are thankful. In this way we get to know what is bringing each of us joy at the moment, make sure everyone has a voice and encourage a posture of gratitude towards God.

Lunch

We share a meal together because this is the way we show the hospitality of God to one another. N.T. Wright reminds us that, 'When Jesus wanted to explain to his followers what his forthcoming death was all about, he did not give them a theory, a model, a metaphor, or any other such thing; he gave them a meal.'[2] Similarly, we have found that being responsible for one another through this practice is one of the greatest gifts we can give; it is as sacred as any other part of our gathering. It is also one of the ways we can share economically – as John Howard Yoder reminds us, 'The "common purse" of the Jerusalem church was not a purse: It was a common table.'[3]

While all of this may sound rigid, in practice it gives structure and shape to what could otherwise be a much more chaotic and messy time. It is chaotic and messy anyway (some days more than others), but we're committed to persevering through it.

It's worth noting that we have attempted things that haven't worked or that are works in progress. Confession is one aspect of our practice that has morphed over time; other aspects have been dropped as they weren't serving the purpose intended.

We continue to experiment, listen to folks' experience of God through our gatherings, watch the development in our lives collectively and individually, and pass on the reasoning for why we do the things we do. In this way, we hope that our practices continue to bear fruit as we grow and change together into the likeness of Christ, while avoiding creating any new ashram cats. It's the collective practices of a community that tell you most clearly what it considers valuable and what it believes, but ultimately the proof lies in the lives we live as a result of being formed by those practices.

Kenosis

Jennifer Trevena

Questions for reimagining the church

I had an unexpected encounter in 2017 when I was working as a student pastor on Sydney's North Shore. A frail elderly lady was preparing to step onto a pedestrian crossing on a busy road. Her walk was unsteady and weak, yet she was well-dressed in an elegant formal outfit, complete with a regal-looking hat.

I couldn't help but keep watching her until she finished crossing safely. When the next light turned to green, I ran to her and asked if I could help with anything – perhaps even a lift home. She gratefully accepted my offer, and I drove her to her house in a neighbouring suburb.

We started to talk and she told me she had sensed I was a Christian, which was why she trusted my offer of help. She was a devout Christian believer and had served as a missionary in India when she was young. She was devoted to prayer and had a strong gift of spiritual discernment and encouragement, but she no longer attended a traditional church. Instead, she explained, her ministry was on the city streets – reaching out to people experiencing homelessness and others God brought to her. She said, 'Every time I go out, the Lord connects me with His people. And today, He brought me to you!'

I thought to myself, *If she were part of our church community, many of our elderly members could be greatly encouraged.* So I invited her to join us, but she gently repeated, 'My church is on the street – with the homeless and with the people God sends me.' She said church was not just about going on Sundays to sing and then return home.

Her view of church seemed unusual to me at the time and even made me question her faith, but I could understand her perspective. Her focus was on practical worship and mission. Even though I had a lot of questions about her understanding of faith and church, I could not deny her relationship with Jesus as a true disciple. Although she was old and frail, barely able to walk, she did not waver in her firm commitment to going to the city to visit those experiencing homelessness, to meet with God's people and to encourage them, to share the Word and to have fellowship with them. These actions were her sincere and genuine expression of church. Her ministry exemplified a self-sacrificial and self-emptying, or *kenotic*, approach to ministry – a concept to which I will return later in this chapter.

After that encounter I started to ask myself: *Could this really be called church? Or is it merely an unusual expression of it? Why does she refuse to join the traditional church and instead choose to embody her own expression of what it means to be the church?* For me, trained in a traditional understanding of what church meant, the woman's understanding of church was both startling and strangely refreshing. It compelled me to wrestle with what our local church might be overlooking and what it really means to be the church according to Jesus' calling.

Now, several years later, I find myself doing church in a similar way to her: on the street, or in a park, a home, a café or a restaurant. Looking back, I realise God planted a seed in me – a seed of rethinking and reimaging what it means to be the church in the world, through an unexpected encounter with an elderly missional leader.

My journey to Simple/Micro Church planting

My personal faith journey is deeply entwined with my journey into Simple/Micro church planting, shaped by God's providence.[1]

I am a single mother, an accredited Baptist pastor and a first-generation non-English background migrant. I raised my daughter on my own from when she was four years old, and last year she stepped into adulthood. My journey has been unique; yet this is the path God has placed before me.

As an evangelist,[2] missional leader and pioneer called to be a church planter, I have sought to respond faithfully to my calling through my study and ministry, and through my ordination and accreditation in 2019. In the years leading to that final step, the words of Acts 1:8 became a persistent voice of challenge: 'But you will receive power when the Holy Spirit comes on you; and you will be my witnesses in Jerusalem, and in all Judea and Samaria, and to the ends of the earth' (NIV). These words of Jesus confronted me with the question: Do I truly and deeply trust the power of the gospel and its ability to transform people's lives?

In discerning my call to church planting, I had to rely deeply on my strong faith in the gospel of Jesus. My personal circumstances were far from the typical image of a church planter with a good supportive partner or extended family network; I was a busy single parent with limited financial resources. Yet in that very weakness, I learned to rely on the Holy Spirit and the life-changing power of God. That conviction became my anchor and gave me the courage to prepare faithfully for church planting, even in the midst of the 2020 COVID lockdowns.

I did not set out with the intention to adopt the Simple/Micro Church model for my church planting. However, as I learned more about church planting through observation and experience, one question stayed with me: *Why are there so few new conversions and baptisms in many of the newly planted churches?* It was an important question to ask myself as I considered why I wanted to plant a church

I noticed a formula that characterised the more typical church-planting model: a group formed within the mother church or network, launched Sunday services and small group Bible studies, enjoyed fellowship as a church family and then started discussing and planning outreach programs or activities. Their starting point was usually a secure team structure and sufficient funding. But new members were often Christians who either relocated geographically or were invited by friends already in the church. In most cases, very few who joined were people without prior faith.

This made me ask: What then is the true purpose of church planting? Of course, compared to many established churches, new church plants can be healthier as they create a fresh culture, which is valuable. But I began to sense that this is not the ultimate purpose. That persistent question led me to reimagine the order of my own church planting. I came to believe that, however small the team might be, outreach (mission) should come first. I became convinced that discipleship and mission are not simply activities, but core factors for bringing a church into being in the first place. My reading of Scripture was that Jesus did not commission the disciples to plant a church or to start a church service, but to make disciples of all nations (Matthew 28:19-20).

A community of believers is a significant element of church. Non-believers may join a healthy community and discover the love of Christ and faith in Jesus within it. *Yet is building a healthy community of believers the starting point for church planting?* This is a question that has stayed with me.

These questions and observations led me to approach church planting from a different perspective. The model that resonated with me was the Simple/Micro Church model, as it allowed room for creativity and innovation. This model brings together two approaches to church. Simple Churches are an organic expression of church, built on relationships rather than an organisational structure. This kind of church can be described in the following way:

> [They] have no paid staff or property. They usually consist of a relatively small number of members, though often have a significantly larger number of non-members connected to their community. They are highly relational and flexible in their structures and approach. They can exist everywhere and anywhere being based around a variety of coalescing factors such as: a particular area, a workplace, a community group, a theme or purpose, a project or interest.[3]

A Micro Church, writes Brian Saunders, is 'a small community of believers, who love Jesus as Lord and Savior and engage in his mission'. Like the New Testament Church, it's a 'simple, small, fluid … and powerful' model of church 'where we see worship, community and mission overlap'.[4] I have combined these two models, as Micro Church adds a more explicitly missional framework to Simple Church. The COVID-19 pandemic provided providential timing and an opportunity that gave me the courage and determination to begin my Simple/Micro Church planting journey.

Kenotic posture and incarnational living

Grounded in the message of Acts 1:8, I started my church plant with the conviction that people's lives could be saved and transformed through the power of the gospel and my humble and faithful work. This posture of church planting was not based on the usual understanding of power or success; instead, it attempted to mirror Jesus' kenotic power. Hak Joon Lee writes:

> Kenosis is the paradoxical form of power that God uses in saving and bringing *shalom* (*koinonia* of all life) to the world. Kenosis tells that God is powerful enough to give up his own privilege in order to empower others. God's kenotic love is therefore powerful, not powerless or sentimental. Paul preached that this kenotic power of God revealed on the cross is the true wisdom and salvific knowledge for the world (1 Cor 1:20).[5]

This kenotic power was expressed and embodied in Jesus' *kenosis* – His self-emptying or self-giving that empowered the weak. In contrast to *dunamis*, which conveys a sense of explosive power (as in dynamite), the gospel of Jesus is most profoundly manifested as *kenosis*, or self-giving power, as in Paul's invitation to have the mind of Christ in Philippians 2:6-7. Through this self-emptying power, Christ became incarnate among us – He was born as a human and lived among us, experiencing life as we experience it. This kenotic embodiment by Jesus has continually challenged my faith and shaped my approach to church planting and ministry practice.

On a personal level, I had to learn to relinquish comfort. Instead of choosing a traditional and more stable model of church planting, I stepped into an adventurous one. Instead of a form of church that many could easily recognise and understand, I accepted a less familiar and often misunderstood model. Instead of thinking in terms of financial security or comfort, my motivation had to be rooted in Jesus' kenotic posture, and it was through this lens that I sought assurance of being on the right track. If the more difficult path was the way of Christ, I was determined to take it. Raised in a culture of success, I found that the kenotic way of Jesus required me to unlearn much of what I had once pursued. In short, planting a new model of church was my own journey of discipleship and meant clinging to the values of Jesus and walking faithfully in His way.

In practical terms, this has meant reducing my living expenses, adjusting my lifestyle, learning to be grateful for what I have and depending on God's daily provision – as the Israelites did when God sent them heavenly manna in the wilderness. Of course, my Abba Father has always provided sufficiently for me and my daughter!

Kenotic motivation and practice has significantly shaped me internally; I will now reflect on how it has shaped the way I express my Simple/Micro Church ministry practice.

Kenotic posture and incarnational practice: Simple/Micro Church

At the heart of my Simple/Micro Church practice is an incarnational approach – one that emulates Jesus' act of entering into our world, coming alongside us and immersing Himself in our experience. The BethanyHope group began its ministry on the streets five years ago. Just as Jesus reached out to the man at the Pool of Bethesda who had spent decades lying on the cold ground with no hope, waiting for healing (John 5), we sought to reach those who were living exposed at night. They were in as safe a place as they could find, but were still often vulnerable to violent attacks and neglect. BethanyHope started with no prior ministry experience, relying on kenotic hearts and the desire to follow Jesus the incarnational God. Our engagement with those experiencing homelessness was not a charitable activity or an act of good works; it was a practice rooted in discipleship and incarnational mission, following the example of Jesus who humbled Himself to dwell among us.

What our friends who were experiencing homelessness appreciated most was that we remembered their names, sat on the street beside them, listened to their stories with respect and empathy and showed sincere love and warmth, treating each one as a dignified and valued person. Once we established a bond of trust after a year of visits, they gladly accepted our invitation to share a meal with us at a restaurant. I still vividly recall their heartfelt reactions as they paused to read with appreciation the invitation cards bearing their names.

The BethanyHope Simple/Micro Church first met around a meal table at a Vietnamese restaurant in 2021. It was a small gathering of just three friends who were experiencing homelessness and our team of about eight. The location of our gathering – a local restaurant rather than a church – was a significant element of our incarnational practice. We shared lunch, prayed together, retold stories from the gospels and took turns reflecting on and discussing personal applications. I still remember our friends, who had been homeless for five, ten and more than twenty years respectively, all saying the same thing that day: while generous people had given them money or food, this was the first time they had ever been invited to a meal together. Their eyes filled with tears as they spoke. I will never forget that moment.

Every time we visited those who were living in the greatest poverty, as I listened to their stories and prayed with them, we felt Jesus' presence profoundly. This sense of giving pleasure to Jesus through our actions brought immense joy to all of us on the team and overflowed as hope towards those we came alongside and served.

Over the last five years, BethanyHope Simple/Micro Church has continued in this way, and we have witnessed five of our friends leave homelessness behind. As we built relationships, shared Jesus' story and prayed consistently with them, these men and women experienced life changes such as reconciling with family, starting work or obtaining housing through the public housing system.

Yet our church remains small, fragile and uncertain – more like a pop-up church, with no guarantees for tomorrow. There is no offering, no pulpit for preaching; instead, our gathering takes the form of conversational storytelling, practical help, emotional support, empowering encouragement and fervent prayers. BethanyHope might be unlike a mainstream church, yet the poorest and most marginalised who may not fit well in mainstream church settings have experienced transformative life changes through our relationships and regular practices. These are the treasured experiences I value deeply from my time in Simple/Micro Church work.

Another kenotic practice and incarnational posture is expressed through the BethanyHope Scholarship Program. This annual fundraising initiative selects children from low-income single-parent households entering high school and provides them with a one-off $500 scholarship. The gift may seem modest, yet for these families it often means being able to purchase a new school uniform.

The Scholarship Program was birthed out of my own lived struggles as a single parent when I first sent my daughter to high school. The costs felt crushing: laptops, uniforms, shoes, sports gear, bags and close to a thousand dollars in school fees during the first term, even in a public school. Centrelink payments such as the Family Tax Benefit barely scratched the surface. This hardship has been sharpened in recent years by rising house prices and the increasing cost of living.

Over the last five years, thirteen students have been supported through this scholarship. Each year, God has faithfully provided the exact amount needed. Most recipients are from migrant, non-English-speaking families, often with three or more children. The gratitude and tears I have witnessed testify to God's provision.

The story of one mother in particular still lingers in my memory. She and her son had fled domestic violence and were both deeply wounded emotionally. They faced the start of high school with nothing. The mother couldn't access government resources at that time due to the complexity of her situation. She came to see me, grasped my hands and wept uncontrollably. I wept with her and prayed for her.

I hear many other stories from mothers in serious financial difficulties. Time and again, these mothers have voiced the same aspiration: 'I want to live faithfully, and raise my children well, so that someday I can help another struggling single-parent family, just as I have been helped.'

The scholarship program has become not merely a means of financial aid, but a seed of discipleship and community. Each year we invite these mothers to our Mothers' Day gathering, sharing a meal and creating space for a gospel encounter. Some are Christians; others are not. One Buddhist mother heard about Jesus through this gathering; another who had left the church long ago joined our 'All-Life Family' Sunday group. Others receive the daily Bible reflections and questions I send out. One mother who received the scholarship in its first year later improved her financial situation and gave back generously to the fund, continuing the cycle of grace.

Through these practices, the theology of the incarnation becomes more than an abstraction. The Spirit moves in practical blessings like tears shared, meals eaten and scholarships given. God's kenotic love, poured out into vulnerable families, generates a ripple effect of discipleship and generosity. Though our community has not yet grown into a fully developed Simple/Micro Church with regular gatherings and worship, it nevertheless embodies the heart of a micro-sized church. Small and hidden acts arising from a faithful kenotic posture and incarnational practice spread Christ's tangible love and practical care, revealing the Kingdom or reign of God.

The BethanyHope Homeless Group and the BethanyHope Scholarship Program are expressions of a church that goes out among the marginalised, entering into their struggles with empathy, offering comfort and leading them towards Kingdom hope. Our goal is to empower them so that, in their daily lives or by joining our team, they in turn may become the hands and feet of the kenotic Christ with us.[6]

Our principle has always been to remain at a scale we can manage. Whether it is for one family, or even just one person, we simply do the little things we can. We do these things faithfully, seeking the help of the Holy Spirit. We are like the little boy who offered his five loaves and two fish to Jesus. It is Jesus who performs the miracle of feeding the five thousand. In practicing Simple/Micro Church, I only take up the small tasks I can faithfully handle. And then I see the great works of God.

The place of Simple/Micro Church within the Kingdom ecosystem

One of the challenges of Simple/Micro Church is understanding how it relates to other expressions of the church. The notion of a Blended Ecology or Mixed Ecology has been used to describe how various expressions of the church – such as Simple/Micro Church, and the more traditional forms such as Neighbourhood Church, Regional Church and Resource Church – can work together.[7] A Blended Ecology is characterised by diverse leaders and models of church, all held together by one vision of multiplying communities of faith. This diversity is like a beautiful orchestral performance, each instrument with its own unique voice, not competing or comparing, but working together to create harmony, embodying unity through the rich diversity of God's people and expressions of church.

Simple/Micro Church is an essential element of this Blended Ecology. Through creative approaches such as the BethanyHope group and scholarship program, it is possible to fill the gap that other models of church are often unable to fill. We can think of a Blended Ecology as an ecosystem. In a forest, there are large trees, medium size trees and wildflowers beneath them. All these plants together contribute to the health of the ecosystem. BethanyHope is like the dandelion – a delicate wildflower. The vitality of wildflowers is beyond imagination. And most importantly, the life force of the wildflower is sustained by the Creator God.

Dandelions are fragile, swaying in the wind. Their life cycle is certainly different from the large, towering trees, yet they scatter countless seeds that are carried by the wind. The quiet influence of dandelions is a picture of the life-giving impact of Simple/Micro Churches. In an ecosystem, what matters is not the size but the diversity of all living things, whether large or small, that contribute to the multiplication of the whole ecosystem and to its flourishing.

This vision of a Blended Ecology captivated my heart when I first joined the Baptist denomination five years ago. I was looking for a space where women in leadership could plant churches, and found that my desire to plant a Simple/ Micro Church was aligned with the denomination's vision for a Blended Ecology. Remarkably, I was also able to join the denomination's Church Multiplication Team as a part-time mission catalyst. The convergence of vision and opportunity was nothing short of providential.

Challenges

The first major challenge facing the Simple/Micro Church model is measurability. Over the last five years, I have continually asked myself: *Am I doing this right? What exactly is my metric of success?*

A popular innovation model is the Build, Measure, Learn cycle.[8] This model is designed to help you consider where your organisation or church is at, discern how you want to measure outcomes, learn from that data and come up with new ideas for implementation. The model has helped me to formulate my metrics for evaluating our ministry. Our metrics include: *How many people experiencing homelessness are we intentionally building relationships with and regularly engaging in meaningful communication? Are BethanyHope members growing in understanding and insight toward people experiencing homelessness, increasingly reflecting the heart of Jesus? How many of our homeless friends are walking alongside BethanyHope and gaining renewed hope in life – whether in practical ways, spiritual ways or both? How many homeless friends are participating in BethanyHope worship, coming to know Jesus and growing in discipleship including through baptism? How many homeless friends are developing the hope and potential to serve other homeless people or to participate in leadership within BethanyHope?*[9]

These are different metrics to those commonly used in traditional church-planting models: how many people gather each week, how much the numbers increase or how much is collected in the offering. By defining success in this way, I have found a sense of freedom as well as clarity about where to focus my attention and where to invest more deeply.

The second major challenge is sustainability. The model of bi-/co-vocational ministry – whereby a ministry leader also works in a full-time or part-time non-ministry paid job – is appropriate for Simple/Micro Churches due to their size and scale. However, the highly relational nature of this model, and the reliance on volunteers, creates a challenge to its long-term viability. This gives rise to the criticism that the Simple/

Micro Church life cycle is limited. If there is a shortage of volunteers or the balance between a full-time job and ministry responsibilities is disrupted, practitioners are often forced to step away from their ministry.

I work on a scale I can manage with my current team while simultaneously raising leaders to pursue a strategy of multiplication. However, as the demands of ministry grow, it will be essential to establish a system that can be supported by at least a part-time paid role. Embracing the Kingdom ecosystem and establishing partnerships with Neighbourhood or Resource churches is vital.

Future hope

The Blended Ecology approach offers hope for the flourishing of the church. By encouraging a greater acceptance of different models and expressions of God's kingdom, a Blended Ecology approach ensures both the sustainability of the Simple/Micro Church and the health of the wider ecosystem.[10] A partnership between diverse expressions of church can enable more effective evangelism as it can empower Simple/Micro Churches to connect with spaces that traditional churches may not be able to reach as easily. At the same time, it can provide mature leaders within the traditional churches an opportunity to live out their missional calling in the midst of their daily lives: they can lead Simple/Micro Churches during the week. Rather than remaining inwardly focused, the church must look outward. The missional calling of believers is not limited to serving in Sunday church activities or church programs, but is also about asking: *How do I embody my personal missional calling as salt and light outside the church on Sunday? How do I, in that space, lead people to Jesus and make disciples?*

Through BethanyHope and in my work at the Baptist Association, I have witnessed the rise of lay missional leadership. This has been an outworking of the Blended Ecology, with all forms of church working together.

Most of the BethanyHope team members belonged to their home churches and were already involved in other ministries; however, they carried a specific calling and deep conviction to come alongside those experiencing homelessness. They felt hesitant about doing this alone, even finding it hard to approach and talk with people experiencing homelessness on the streets. They struggled to imagine how they could introduce them to Jesus and share the gospel message. They saw Simple/Micro Church as a way to come alongside these people. Through BethanyHope, they have seen how it is possible to effectively empower and lead even one person to Jesus through alternative forms of ministry and to see their life transformed. They have been able to serve together, share their challenges, discuss how to do better and pray together. This calling to come alongside those experiencing homelessness has brought people great joy and fulfillment, and I have seen this lead to spiritual growth among the team and within myself.

This kind of missional leadership is not just for a select few. Every believer is called to embody the Spirit of God the Father who defends the widow and the orphan by practicing holiness in tangible ways (James 1:27). This will look different for everyone, but in every case it means living out Christ's kenotic love in daily life. In doing so, believers can explore and live out their own missional calling, becoming a scattered, weekday Simple/Micro Church, while still being part of or connected to a traditional church. My hope is that mainstream churches will cultivate concrete strategies of discipleship and mission, releasing missional leaders who can engage in these creative Simple/Micro Church ministries. For this to happen, church leaders could identify these people and release them to serve in their daily lives, encouraging and equipping them to be local missionaries. In this way, the vitality and health of the whole ecosystem will be strengthened and together we can participate in the nurturing and growth of God's Kingdom.

Trunks of trees and elephants

Growing up as a second generation South African Australian meant that church was a massive part of my family's life. Every week you would find my mum and dad marching their little herd of children into the Sunday morning service – usually late, of course. There was seldom a week when the whole family was not sitting in the pews. Plus, with my dad as our Sunday school teacher and my mum coming from a long line of church planters, ministers and missionaries, exploring faith and spiritual curiosity weren't seen as topics solely for church life. We had these faith conversations everywhere and anywhere.

Perhaps it's because of this upbringing that conversations about faith seem to follow me, often popping up in the most unexpected places. Whatever the cause, I have come to realise that I love curating spaces that promote opportunities for spiritual curiosity and a sense of belonging. This chapter highlights those sacred connections and conversations within the digital world.

Before jumping into the sacred, I need to address the elephants in the room. Many are still unconvinced that real, authentic relationships can exist within the digital realm. Even more people are worried about the long-term implications of digital connectivity on an individual's wellbeing. When we then factor in concerns about the ecological impact of digital technologies, the need for greater ethical standards and the ever-growing list of safety requirements, it becomes hard to see through the dense forest, filled with what appears to be wild and unruly trees. Though not the purpose of this chapter, it might be helpful to explain my personal view of these elephants. They're best summed up in the words of scientist and religious scholar Ian Barbour. Barbour suggests that for digital connectivity and technology to be appropriate for all humanity, it needs to be 'economically productive, ecologically sound, socially just, and personally fulfilling'.[1] A profound statement.

However, I want to say more about the trees, as they have helped me to understand my own theologies and practices.

The imagery of wild and unruly trees is not usually connected to goodness (with the exception of the current 'rewilding' metaphors used in community engagement). Mainstream Christian theology, as well as an abundance of biblical narratives, usually speak of trees in a tamer manner – as individual, isolated, trees or by breaking them down into pieces. Particularly when it comes to new, fresh and emerging expressions of community, the language and imagery drawn from trees is exhaustive. Planting. Fruiting. Fruit. Good fruit. Seeds. Seedlings. Saplings. Then we get into the supportive roles that communities could offer these new expressions. Transplanting. Seeding. Budding. Sheltering. Supporting canopy. Mixed ecology. Not all the language around emerging communities is inherently problematic, but many of these metaphors have shifted from being descriptive methods to becoming prescriptive models of community formation. This mightn't be so terrible if they didn't reflect a deeply Eurocentric approach to mission, where movement occurs from the centre toward the margins.

More importantly, it becomes difficult to practice when paired with a theology that calls us beyond colonial forms of mission. We need to find new ways of speaking about and practicing emerging expressions of Christian community to resist replicating the very power dynamics we claim to dismantle.[2]

So, what if we saw the forest as more than just a metaphor for disarray or complexity?

What if instead of seeing the digital forest as a chaotic or tangled place, we allowed ourselves to notice what is quietly emerging here? Because this wild and unruly woodland – dense and unpredictable as it may seem – is not barren. It is a living, breathing world I've been watching grow, not from a distance, but from within.

The digital forest

The digital forest is not a foreign ecosystem I wandered into by accident.[3]

I can barely remember a time before screens – before computers, phones and televisions. I've grown up entangled in the gnarled vines of this digital world. My social, physical and spiritual development has unfolded alongside digital media. My very being has been formed by the forest floor of a hyperconnected, digitised, ever-evolving world. To borrow academic language, growing up in the digital age means that digital technologies are 'indispensable not only to how one conducts everyday life but also to how one's ontological existence is constituted'.[5]

No longer are digital technologies seen as just a tool to use or to glean information from. Instead, we inhabit a digitally integrated world where connectivity shapes how we live, how we relate and who we are.

From a sociological perspective, the contemporary world has little need to distinguish between digital and non-digital activity, as both continually shape and influence the public square. This becomes especially important when it comes to meaning-making and identity formation, particularly in spiritual life. The distinction between what is 'digital' and what is 'real' holds limited relevance in this context. As author and artist Margaret Wertheim writes, 'Just because something is not material does not mean it is unreal, as the oft-cited distinction between "cyberspace" and "real space" implies. Despite its lack of physicality, cyberspace is a real place. I am there.'[4]

Likewise, others argue that the products of spiritual culture – practices, beliefs, symbols – remain valuable even when they exist only in imagination or shared digital experience. They don't need to be physically manifested to be real or meaningful.[5] The digital is not merely transactional – it is not a stagnant realm of data; rather, it is made up of active habitats of spiritual formation. Real places where belief, belonging and becoming take root.

When we take the time to notice this living, breathing world, we begin to see sacred life emerging – in late-night DMs, within posts where grief, joy or sorrow is shared by strangers. Life grows in the imperfections: in awkward livestream silences, in lagging connections, in the rawness of unfiltered prayer. There's a kind of beauty here, in these unpolished gatherings where community has formed not by strategy, but out of a shared need and unexpected grace. Life is being lived here. Communities are forming. Gatherings are taking place. Friendships are sustained, families nurtured and memories made within the digital world. And if we can manage to hold these all together through faithing conversations and spiritual exploration, we then have something that starts to look awfully like church.[6] It might not resemble the kind of church we know, at least not through traditional lenses. But if you linger long enough, if you listen with the same reverence we give to ancient liturgies, you begin to see it: this wild and unruly forest is alive with sacred patterns and sacred people. All we need to do is join in the holy chaos.

For someone like me – someone who loves curating spaces of spiritual curiosity and shared belonging – the question began to shift when I stopped holding my experiences of faith communities and digital communities apart. Rather than asking how we might bring inherited missional models into this digital ecosystem, I began wondering: How do we tend, cultivate and nourish the sacred practices and rhythms already unfolding here?

And the digital forest did what it does best – it connected.

A newspaper article about a youth community running into a burning building began to make its rounds, and somehow it landed me on OddRev's social feed.[7] The algorithm, in its quiet ways, noted our mutual love of board games and our shared roots in the Uniting Church of Australia. Though we lived nearly 100 kilometres apart, the forest wove our paths together – two practitioners drawn into conversation about ministering through board games.

We started to share about our love of chaplaincy, the traditional church communities we belong to and the new ones we've helped form and shape. We swapped stories as dreamers, ministry agents and then as gamers. Coming face-to-face with another forest-born practitioner left little room for awkward silences. Soon we were sharing stories about the discipling conversations we had held in Zoom rooms and the deep connections nurtured with family and friends across time zones and continents.[8] Naturally these stories eventually gave rise to a question: What kind of faith community would emerge if grown solely by, from and within the digital world?

This germ of an idea initially led to a regional offshoot of a larger ministry network.[9] Then, over the years, through shifting ministry teams, changing church appointments, evolving pastoral needs and one big, ugly, global pandemic, it became clear that something more was needed: a community dedicated to tending, cultivating and nourishing the sacred practices and rhythms of this digital forest.

And so, together, we welcomed Sonderverse.[10]

Sonderverse

It's not the kind of church most people would recognise. There are no pews, no stained-glass windows, no organ – not even a guitar. This kind of church doesn't offer the smell of old hymnbooks or the wooden ceilings where each beam feels steeped in the faith of those who came before. Rather, the digital world offers its own realness and has its own subcultures, each with their own language, rituals, aesthetics and norms. One of the first signs you've entered such a space is the presence of handles, and in this world, I go by PastoralHare.[11]

What's taking shape in Sonderverse doesn't follow traditional liturgical structures, yet it is unmistakably church. For many of us, this space has become our sanctuary, where we are able to ask questions we don't yet have language for and listen to the wondering of others.

Sonderverse is a digital ecosystem built for community, faith and exploration. It's a place where belonging doesn't come with conditions, where belief isn't a prerequisite and where curiosity is not only welcomed but encouraged. In gamer language, Sonderverse is a community where nobody is an NPC.[12] Everyone matters. Everyone has agency. And fittingly, Sonderverse lives up to its name. *Sonder*: the profound realisation that every person you encounter is living a vivid, complex life, full of their own connections, struggles and story arcs.

To be in a state of sonder is to see differently. It's to remember that '... each of us is at once a hero, a supporting cast member, and an extra in overlapping stories'.[13] In the average week, you will find us gaming together, streaming together, praying together, laughing, creating and learning what it means to live whole, meaningful lives. Alongside this we offer a gathering time every Monday night at 8 pm AEST.[14] Here, we wrestle with the big questions through progressive theology, celebrate and affirm the diverse spectrum of identities, abilities and sexualities, and hold space for the messy work of deconstruction. As we're a digital community, we take the need for authenticity both on and off the screen seriously.

Because of this, we have managed to linger within the digital forest as a faith community, dedicated to tending and nurturing the sacred stories within it. Of course, to capture the fullness of a community with just a handful of moments seems like an impossible task. So what follows are just some sacred moments that give a glimpse into our daily lives as Sonderers. These stories offer a window into the kind of church that is quietly growing within the digital world. And perhaps, in sharing them, they might also invite our more traditional church structures to reflect on their own rhythms and ways of being – and maybe to hear God whispering something new.

Sacred stories

One could argue that there's nothing more frustrating than a buffering video or a lagging internet connection. These moments aren't just annoying – they're disruptive, especially when you're trying to connect with others. Regardless of whether you're a digital native or just finding your way through the online wilderness, lag and buffering are universal experiences.

I remember one gathering where we were only managing to transmit about seven seconds of connection for every thirty seconds of streaming. Take a moment to imagine yourself talking to someone on the phone and for every thirty seconds you only received seven seconds of conversation. Despite the audio and video being in a constant state of buffering and catch-up, the community didn't log off. They waited. What could've felt like failure instead turned into something surprisingly holy, because at this moment we remembered that the digital world isn't just a continuous feed of content or entertainment. This was a community of people, undisturbed by the chaos; each of us had sat in this liminal space before.

This story reminds me that the digital forest grows a different kind of grace and patience.

No matter how much upskilling you do or how much you prepare, the digital world demands a different kind of leadership. One that's rooted in vulnerability, flexibility and tenacity to roll with Plan B ... or C ... or even Q.

I think one of the reasons we've learnt to lead out of this vulnerability is because we're gamers. We're familiar with an ever-changing landscape that requires us to constantly adapt, with its glitchy mechanics, sticky keys, plot twists and side quests. In gaming you learn by trying. You pay attention to patterns. You listen for the story under the surface. You constantly fail, and that's the point.

Gaming trains us in a particular kind of spiritual agility – one that is curious, attentive and reflective. Much like music, art and books, gaming helps humanity make sense of its inner world, creating scenarios where you can try on identities, test choices and wrestle with big questions about justice, power, redemption, grief and hope. Of course, people often assume that because we're a gaming community, Sonderverse must be only for young people. But that couldn't be further from the truth. Our community spans from eleven to seventy-three years old. These people tune in, game, create, pray and do life together.

Gaming across generations adds a depth and richness to the stories we tell and the questions we ask. We're given the opportunity to reflect on how these shared moments shape our everyday lives and reveal something of our relationship with God, with creation and with one another. In other words, our discipleship model is gaming together.

I don't mean we play specifically Christian games or try to wedge Christian stories and practices into them – we don't need to force faith into these conversations. Games are designed for meaning-making, and God always manages to show up. Like the time two bears wandered into a post-apocalyptic world overrun by zombies.[15] It was a moment of gameplay we didn't see coming. One minute we were gathering supplies to build our makeshift fortress and the next we were deep into the book of 2 Kings, talking about Elisha, divine justice and prophetic rage. An unexpected side feature suddenly became the main point of conversation – and, if I'm honest, it led to deeper reflections on who God is and what God might be saying than many of us have experienced in traditional church settings.

Of course, zombies aren't everyone's cup of tea. And not every moment in Sonderverse is filled with dramatic plot twists or unexpected bears. The digital forest holds all kinds of people, all seeking a community where they can belong. There are many reasons why people might feel unseen, unheard or on the margins of more traditional communities. This is especially true for those with diverse sexualities and abilities. Unfortunately, the institutional church has not always been able to offer the kind of safety people have needed, and at times has contributed to deep emotional and spiritual pain. These experiences don't mean everyone wants to throw away God, but for many even the physical church building has become too foreign, or too tangled with pain, to feel like a safe place to return to. Sonderverse offers a space to connect from the safety and comfort of one's own home. What a privilege it is to be welcomed into each other's sanctuaries.

Being able to transcend time and space is one of the quiet miracles of Sonderverse. We've met people in their homes, on trains, even gathered around the dinner table with family. We've had people connect from across the globe in search of someone to help them navigate discernment, to pray with them or to help unpack Scripture. One of the most surprising parts? These conversations are happening on Twitch – a platform made for gaming. Who would have imagined that someone would go specifically to Twitch to search for 'Christian community'? But they are. And this is exactly why showing up in these spaces matters.

These stories are just fragments. They don't capture everything, but they give us the opportunity to see that church in the digital world looks different – and somehow still the same.

The sacred belongs here, too

So, what has being part of a community dedicated to tending, cultivating and nourishing the sacred practices and rhythms of this digital forest taught me?

Firstly, I have learnt that digital spaces do not lack spiritual encounters, but people of faith often struggle to recognise them as such. Too often, the wild and unruly trees are overlooked rather than seen as a place where the sacred not only exists but also belongs and grows.

My second learning is that what it means to exist as human beings has profoundly changed. The church, as a liturgical tradition that has transcended millennia, does not *need* to enter this digital forest at all. This is precisely why even a global pandemic wasn't enough to truly launch the church into the digital age. During COVID, the church took a momentary detour through the digital forest. For many, it was seen simply as a necessity during uncertainty – a placeholder rather than a place where the sacred was already alive and flourishing. The church, by and large, failed to see that the digital space wasn't just a substitute; it was already a sanctuary.

And yet, the digital era has well and truly begun. Whether we're ready or not, it is changing how people experience life, connection and spirituality. This is not a threat to the church – it's an invitation. This is, in many ways, the most exciting part of theology: making meaning of our lived experience in relationship with God.

But please, do not hear this invitation incorrectly.

Do not come into the forest ready to clear the land, build steeples and replicate what has always been. This forest does not need saving. It needs noticing. And if the church is willing to pay attention, it might just discover that the canopy of trees is, in fact, God's own tent.

So come ready to listen and game with us. To tend and cultivate the sacred stories already alive. Come not to control the narrative, but to co-create it. Because here in the digital forest, God is calling.

And if you hear that call – if you begin to sense God in the unexpected – then there are two postures that may serve you well on the journey. The first is to take of your shoes, and the second is to be willing and ready to start baptising some extraterrestrials.

Take off your shoes

In the book of Exodus, we're told of when Moses was tending the flock of his father-in-law, Jethro. Near the base of Mount Horeb, Moses stumbled across a bush that was on fire, yet the branches were not burning. Moses edged a little closer to this curious sight and heard the Lord calling to him from within, 'Take off your shoes, for where you stand is holy ground' (Exodus 3:5, my paraphrase).

There are many reflections that can be drawn from this

story. I would like to add a little poetry alongside it to establish a spiritual posture for the digital world.

> Earth's crammed with heaven,
> And every common bush afire with God:
> But only he who sees, takes off his shoes,
> The rest sit round it, and pluck blackberries,
> And daub their natural faces unaware
> More and more, from the first similitude.[16]

Elizabeth Barrett Browning invites us to reimagine the everyday as sacred. There isn't a moment that exists beyond God's presence, no matter how ordinary it may be, or whether it is acknowledged or missed.

It was in a place of the holy ordinary that Moses met God – at a bush at the base of the sacred mountain, not a mighty tree perched at Mount Horeb's peak. And when Moses heard God calling from the unexpected, he slowed down, took of his shoes and listened.

So, if you find yourself aware of God calling from deep within the digital forest, then perhaps it is time to take off your shoes.

Baptising extraterrestrials

OddRev once told me about a book called *Would You Baptize an Extraterrestrial?* by Guy Consolmagno and Paul Mueller.[17] And while I speak openly about encountering God in unexpected places, I'm aware that not everyone will recognise or understand what I am going on about here. For many, I may as well be talking about the time I stumbled into Endor and ran into a tribe of Ewoks.

Often when we're faced with something vastly different from our normalities, we struggle to recognise what God is saying. Even if you've heard God calling from deep within the digital forest, it can be hard to name the holy if what you're encountering feels unfamiliar and strange.

So, along with taking off your shoes, are you ready to talk about aliens?

All jokes aside, the title of Consolmagno and Mueller's book is intentionally provocative and is supposed to be a little bit uncomfortable. Issued by the Vatican in 2018, the book was written to challenge our own theological assumptions when thinking about the boundaries and limitations of God's grace and presence. Because Consolmagno and Mueller are not really writing about aliens at all. The question of baptising extraterrestrials is to help stretch the assumptions we carry. It offers us a playful point of entry to some deep ontological questions, and at its heart it explores the practical implications of a truly cosmic God.

Perhaps the discomfort we feel at the thought of baptising an alien reveals less about the limits of God's grace, and more about the limits of our imagination. Because maybe it's not such a far fetched idea that God is flickering within the digital spaces that are often overlooked or dismissed. And as in Barrett Browning's poem, we have been invited to reimagine the everyday as sacred and perhaps ask whether it is not actually God's presence that is limited, but our own willingness to see it.

The invitation

If you take this invitation seriously, if you slow down enough to notice the sacred flickering in unexpected places, if you have heard God whispering from the holy ordinary spaces, you are ready to walk on holy ground, ready to challenge your own assumptions and beliefs. Perhaps you have already found yourself tangled among the trees.

Here, we are all invited to reimagine what it means to be the church, the body of Christ, in an era that is hyperconnected, digitised and ever-evolving.

If you feel the call to step into this unfolding story, to listen and to learn, to question and to grow, then know this: you are not alone.

Welcome to the forest of wild and unruly trees.

Liminal

Cyrus Kung

Throughout my life, edge spaces have shaped how I think about faith, and they have informed my ministry, both consciously and subconsciously. They have also influenced both how I view the challenges before me and how I posture myself to see hope present in the world.

In this chapter, I will highlight the edge spaces or communities I have ministered in that have been pushed to the edge from/by the centre: an ageing Anglo-Australian congregation, and Chinese first-generation and second-generation congregations. I will then explore how these edge spaces can be extraordinarily creative because of their liminality. I will also show the ways in which edge spaces can breed fear and marginalisation, and what it looks like for these communities to address this. I will conclude by offering a hope-filled way forward for the Australian church.

Transitions: A context not my own
Coming out of the COVID-19 pandemic, like many people

around the world I found myself tossed into a life of transition. Part of this transition was entering into a role of ministering in a congregation where most of the members were over the age of eighty. Having ministered primarily in congregations of under-forties, something about this radically different context both challenged me and sparked my curiosity about what it means to live in a place different to my own.

As I worked alongside these older Anglo-Australian congregants – most of whom were women, and many of whom had been leading the church for more years than I had been alive – I found myself reflecting on what I had to offer as a minister in this context. I became curious about what it was that made these women still willing to be a part of the church council, serve so diligently, drive to meetings and be so active in the life of this congregation.

In many ways this ageing congregation represents the *centre* of our inherited church, but in other ways it represents the *edges* of our society and the marginalised amongst us. This congregation has remained tremendously faithful to what they were given but continues to come face-to-face with what it means to be limited by their age and capacity on a daily basis. There are many congregations across the country that share this struggle, continually hitting the wall of their own capacity as they face ageing, reduced mobility, irrelevance and disconnection from their surrounding community. I am always eager to see change in spaces like this, yet I am continually humbled by how much life congregations like this have lived.

One of these humbling experiences was learning that one of the relatively newer members, aged ninety-six, had started serving in the church council since her husband had passed away almost twenty-five years earlier. It was actually the first time she had taken on formal leadership in the church. This woman had been doing this 'new' thing for almost longer than I had been alive. This realisation had me reliving a phrase I held closely during my time as a youth pastor in a Chinese Church: 'I have eaten more salt than you have rice.' I felt humbled and out of my depth dealing with issues facing a community I did not personally relate to. I found myself asking the question Moses asked as he found himself in a liminal space in the desert: Who am I? And who am I *in this context*? How can I possibly recognise God in a place that seems so foreign?

It is in these questions that I found myself contemplating Jesus' ability to transcend boundaries. He entered into the liminality of others by walking at the edges with them. Liminality refers to the space or time of transition in between two physical places or life stages. In liminal spaces, a person or community may experience disorientation or uncertainty, yet 'The very vulnerability and openness of liminal space allows room for something genuinely new to happen.'[1] However, liminal or edge spaces can also be places of fear and marginalisation; they can be places people find themselves pushed to, sometimes causing them to become trapped and disfigured.

A context I know best

I grew up in the Chinese church community. It was a flourishing church, full of spiritual growth, food and of course people. Yet we all know that where there are people there is also conflict, politics and brokenness. I am proud of the Chinese church I was formed in, but I am also aware of the challenges of growing up in it.

The Chinese church was a reasonably safe space for me growing up. In many ways it was the place where I was most at home, where I felt culturally safe and where I felt like I belonged. It was a place where everyone looked like me – dark hair, dark eyes and not too tall. However, in other ways the space had its challenges. Respect for elders was seen as a biblical, theological and cultural expectation. Elders made all the decisions and kept us on track, and obedience to them was essential for cultural cohesion.

I grew up amongst the oldest of the second generation in the church. It was a place of privilege in some ways – we were the first-born of the newly emerging first-generation Chinese congregation – but in other ways we also knew that with this respect and honour came expectation and responsibility. As children, we walked down the hallway and slipped into the rooms adjacent to the 'main service' for worship. Our programs were run in English and changed form with each stage of life: Sunday school would become youth group, youth group would become young adults' groups and young adults' groups would eventually become the English service. We were motivated by and obedient to what the first-generation leadership wanted. We ran the services, looked after the children and even helped with the music and audiovisual equipment for the main service. I stacked a lot of chairs and moved a lot of equipment in my young adult life, first for the main service and then for our English service. As we aged, the English service also aged and grew in numbers. Evangelism was not necessary for our service to grow; it grew from the evangelism of the first generation and their ability to keep having children.

The first generation loved the Chinese church space because it gave a voice to their community – a group of people that longed both for their motherland and to find their place in their new home. As the second generation, we participated in this community but often felt like it was not our own. And as we grew older, the divide between life in mainstream Australian society and the Chinese community grew wider. We were obedient, but we always had questions. One of those questions was: Why were things so different in church to the world out there? Conflict was always bubbling beneath the surface and only ever erupted when those leaving the church felt they were free to voice their frustrations. I was a youth leader in the church, which wasn't easy within this tense dynamic. Over the years, I occasionally put my effort into confronting the leadership and rallying for rebellion and disobedience, which led to disharmony. At other times I engaged in and facilitated meaningful dialogue and heart-warming acts of reconciliation between cultural factions.

In my own personal story of the Chinese church, I have seen two clear types of edge communities. The first edge community was the immigrant generation, pushed to the edges by the dominant Anglo-Australian culture and the Anglo-Australian church. The second edge community was the second and subsequent generations who were pushed to the edges of the immigrant church by their elders because of their youthfulness and Western cultural influence.

A faith that doesn't fear the grief of transitions

> Let us, therefore, learn to pass from one imperfect
> activity to another without worrying too much
> about what we are missing.[2]

As communities experience change and come to terms with the liminal or edge nature of their transition, they grieve.

The ageing Anglo-Australian congregation, moving from the centre of society to its edge, experience grief as they are slowly excluded or displaced by the emerging generations due to their diminishing capacity. For the first generation in the Chinese church, grief is felt most deeply in the transition from one country to another, in the experience of trying to hold onto tradition whilst embracing the present reality of living in a foreign land. For the second generation in the Chinese church, the grief is internal as we navigate our turbulent identity and try to find our voice within two conflicting cultures. Living in edge communities means living in liminal spaces, and this means being comfortable with transitions; not fearing what is lost, but embracing both the life and death of things that come and go, knowing that God is with us in all of this.

Spending enough time grieving, and fully engaging in the loss of what was, is essential for communities thrust to the edges. Being heard, having the time to slow down and having opportunities to speak this loss out loud are important.[3] However, these spaces can be difficult to navigate when we focus on the fear of loss rather than on liminality as a doorway to unwavering deep hope. Old Testament theologian Walter Brueggemann writes about how this fear can manifest as a denial of the grief that is clearly present. He uses Jeremiah's contemporaries as an example of those who remain in denial about the possibility of a Babylonian exile. Jeremiah, on the other hand, leans into this great loss and enters fully into this season of grief with Judah.[4] Brueggemann writes: 'In God's attentive pain, healing happens. Newness comes. Possibilities are presented. But it all depends on being present with God in hurt, which is incurable until God's hint of healing is offered. We wait along with the poet, to see what the tone of the next "therefore" will be'.[5]

In the ageing congregation I was in, there were clearly those who embraced the grief of ageing, and those who adamantly denied the reality of their ageing and waning capacity. Amongst the first generation in the Chinese church, some remained entrenched in the values and behaviours of their home country. Yet in their home country these values and behaviours had changed, so the first-generation migrants had created a time capsule of a culture that was disconnected from the motherland. Change and imperfection are a given in edge spaces, yet as one thing fades away and ideals are challenged, grief comes in and may not leave us until a new thing arrives. The challenge with liminal spaces is that the new thing often has not yet made itself fully known, and this creates a holding place, a place of in-between imperfection. As the Trappist monk Thomas Merton writes:

> The secret of the imperfection of all things, of their inconstancy, their fragility, their failing into nothingness, is that they are only a shadowy expression of the one Being from whom they receive their being. If they were absolutely perfect and changeless in themselves, they would fail in their vocation, which is to give glory to God by their contingency.[6]

It was Adam and Eve's desire to be as gods, changelessly perfect in their own being, that led them to taste the fruit of the forbidden tree.[7] Yet it is in this liminal space, where grief comes and goes, that we find both brokenness and hope, both death and life – a picture of Christmas and Easter, the-now-and-the-not-yet of God.

Asian American theologian Jung Young Lee articulates

an identity of liminality – or what he calls the 'in-between' – that is shaped by being at the edge of two centres, Asian and American.[8] He describes this space as one of marginality (in-betweenness) that places you simultaneously in both and neither of these contexts (liminality). Drawing on his bicultural identity, Lee articulates that this place of the in-between can resemble the in-between nature of Jesus being fully divine and fully human, the place between the incarnation and the cross.[9]

Finding space to invite people into the grief of the liminal or in-between is an artform. One way I learnt to do this was by creating spaces for story-sharing in the second-generation Chinese context. I set up a sharing community that would rotate speakers every week to allow for one person to share their life story for an hour. I would start the session by telling the person they had one hour to speak and that no one should interrupt them until they had five minutes left. The person sharing would often be apprehensive, unsure if they could talk for an hour. However, once they had started they would continue to talk, and when the time came for me to tell them they had five minutes to go, they would realise they had only covered their early childhood. They would then rush through the next twenty or more years of their life in those last five minutes.

From this form of deep listening, I learnt that most people have never been asked to tell their stories, to share the good and the bad parts of their life with others who were just present to listen. One hour is not enough to share all of who we are; a hundred hours would not be enough! Participants in this story-sharing space would often tell me, 'I don't think anyone will ever know who I am fully, but that's ok.' There was grief in this statement but also joy, hope and a peace that came from being ok with sitting in this in-betweenness.

There are many ways we can learn to share in the grief of those at the edges. I wonder what these might be for you and your communities.

A faith that seeks for justice: acknowledging and naming marginalisation

Having discussed the fear of the grief that arises in times and places of transition and how the hope and peace of God can be present in this, I would like to explore what engaging with this grief does *not* look like. Asian American Theologian Sang Hyun Lee distinguishes liminality from marginalisation:

> By making a distinction between liminality and marginalization, we avoid the danger of romanticizing marginality. Marginalization is dehumanizing and oppressive. ... The liminal space that also results from marginalization, however, has the potential of being used as a creative space of resistance and solidarity. Marginalizing space and liminal space overlap. bell hooks, an African American womanist theorist, explains, "I make a definite distinction between that marginality which is imposed by oppressive structures and that marginality one chooses as the site of resistance – as location of radical openness and possibility". I choose to call hook's second marginality "liminality".[10]

Whether it's an ageing congregation coming to terms with their limited capacity, first-generation migrants transitioning to a new land or a second-generation migrant like me trying to find their own voice, living in edge spaces calls us to distinguish between liminality and marginalisation. It is important to address the grief that is a normal part of transitions, but it is equally important to seek justice by acknowledging and naming the marginalisation that may be present.

Naming marginalisation

Differentiating liminality from the marginalisation that comes from oppression can be difficult. While liminality describes transitions in time and place that are the result of circumstances beyond our control, marginalisation is the result of the actions of one group towards another. Naming marginalisation can expose those who wield this power, and this can be unsettling for all involved. However, it is important to address this marginalisation at both an institutional and personal level. At the institutional level, we may need to confront and engage with the power dynamics within our systems. At the personal level, we may need to engage with our internal biases, internalised racism or inherited toxic theology and values.

In the Chinese church I grew up in, marginalisation came firstly in the form of racism and exclusion as we navigated the dominant Anglo-Australian context and the inherited Western church structures in Australia. Our church met in a building that was not our own, relegated to midday services and the setting up and packing down of equipment multiple times a week for our various activities. I have distinct memories of making sure that all our equipment, food trays and rice cookers were left meticulously clean and tidy so that we would not be considered bad guests in the building. We paid rent to the hosting congregation and I made sure I gave an extra big smile to their members as they left the building so as not to look like I was frustrated with them for finishing late. As their small congregation would leave, I would set up the church for the 'adults' before rushing upstairs to plan for the arrival of our volunteer kids' ministry leaders (who would often outnumber the parishioners in the morning service before us). Even as a teen, I was aware of the unspoken rule to revere those in the Anglo-Australian church even though they seemed old, small in number and a little irrelevant. I was never sure if this was an expression of my Chinese heritage, which taught me to respect my elders, or a subtle form of internalised racism as a result of being part of a Chinese church in a foreign land.

When we had set up and were preparing to lead the kids and youth ministry upstairs, those of us who were second-generation faced another form of marginalisation – the need to navigate multiple cultural contexts while being obedient to the leaders and church elders at all costs. How we ran our service or prepared for the kids' ministry was always discussed with and approved by an elder 'adult' present. If there was a large event we were obligated to be involved and to contribute, since we were 'blessed to have so many gifts and talents, having grown up in Australia'.

These tensions came into conflict with Western ideals of individualism and independent thinking. Unable to articulate and identify the differences between their two cultures, Chinese and Australian, the second generation subconsciously accepted and often reproduced the attitudes of their elders – attitudes such as patriarchy, authoritarianism and internalised racism.[11] These were the same attitudes that contributed to the marginalisation of the second generation, yet it was difficult to name these subtle forces as those of the first generation were often well-meaning, making the second generation hesitant to offend them. Further, these forms of marginalisation were often articulated as 'cultural norms', masking their oppressive nature. Asian Australian Pastor Grace Lung writes:

> Asian Australians struggle to articulate their ethnoracial identities, often labelling themselves in exclusively "cultural" terms for adopting color-blind language. This is likely because Anglo-Australian society and faith does the same while functionally denying that systematic racism exists. Racism is largely spoken of as overt acts, mostly occurring in the past.[12]

The ageing Anglo-Australian congregation has also experienced marginalisation, resulting from a decline in mobility. Some of this is the result of the normal process of ageing. They find it increasingly difficult to get to Sunday services and other gatherings. Those who love to bake for morning tea now find themselves spending all of Saturday to accomplish tasks that would previously have taken them an hour. The pressure placed on them to do all these things comes both from their own internal understanding of what it means to be a good Christian and the church structures that have shaped what is considered necessary for them to continue to be a church. This generation also faces marginalisation as a result of existing social structures that limit their access to essential services. For example, to access resource materials for services, to pay bills and to withdraw funds, they now need to embrace online and digital services.

Naming marginalisation is the first step to addressing its consequences and to distinguishing it from the normal grief of transition I discussed earlier. If we are too afraid to name the things we face, they will only accumulate and require more urgent attention later. Naming the marginalisation before us – those things that seem out of our control, that oppress us and disfigure our potential – can be the first step towards creating spaces in which we can begin to seek real justice.

Seeking justice in edge spaces is difficult and messy. I wonder what this has looked like in the spaces you have been a part of.

Confronting liminality and addressing the grief of marginalisation

Finding space at the edges where you can sit and sabbath, listen to, reflect on and grieve the hurt that comes from marginalisation is just as important as being attentive to the grief of being in a liminal or transitional space. In this section, I will share two stories of hope, one relating to marginalisation and the other to liminality.

I experienced the process of listening when I was in the Chinese church. Marginalisation amongst the second generation often presented itself as the pressure of performing and not being able to vocalise our opinion. Despite being adults ourselves and often holding university degrees and being in professional roles, we found ourselves continually deferring to the thoughts and opinions of the elders. Finding ways in which the second generation could connect to the first generation in a way that didn't feel threatening was key to addressing this marginalisation. To this end, we created opportunities for conversation and for hearing one another's stories. This was about intentionally making space for an imaginative stance that allowed us to hear the other in a fresh way.

A number of elements were needed to ensure the success

of this initiative: having an outside facilitator, using a neutral space, allowing the work to be slow and intentional, and planning events together that sat within a two- to five-year timeline. At the end of each session, it was always a gift to hear a young person who had known an uncle or auntie for their whole life say, 'I have never heard that story before.' These types of imaginative engagements broke barriers and created space for the second generation to feel connected. As Cindy Lee writes, 'We need to share our dreams with one another and discover the areas where our dreams overlap.'[13] There is no easy solution to the intergenerational tension that is experienced around the world by diasporan communities of many backgrounds, but I have learnt that slowing down, listening and creating space for genuine community and relationships is a good place to start.

I was able to apply some of what I had learned in my time at the Chinese church to the ageing congregation I found myself in during COVID-19. I spent most of my first year hearing the stories of the older people as they confronted the reality of ageing. I visited their homes and asked about their struggles, not just in the church but also in their own lives. I heard stories of losing their breath at night and struggling to get to the phone to call an ambulance. I heard stories of needing to spend a whole day and a half to bake the carrot cake for morning tea. I heard stories of them being given phones and iPads that simultaneously confused them and made them feel guilty for not using them. I listened to their stories and let them speak freely.

Hearing the congregation's stories and being attentive to their grief gave me a deeper insight into their liminality and the tensions they were holding in their transition. After many robust conversations about the future of their church and their missional objectives, they decided to host a choral concert for other seniors in their neighbourhood. Their original intention was for this to be a way of bringing young people into their church. However, as we discussed this idea, they were able to let go of the perceived need to have young people in the church and decided instead to aim for their own peers.

The choral concert did not save their church and it did not bring in more young people to run their programs, but what it did do was give those who were present a glimpse of hope and a sense of normality in the midst of their ageing. I visited the congregation recently and saw a photo from that day still on their noticeboard. One of the ladies remarked that the event reminded them that they had a place amongst the ageing community in their suburb. I encouraged her that God is present in all sorts of ways in their community and that this might look different to the way it used to.

They are continuing to work out what it means to live in the liminal space that comes with ageing, learning to let go of things that have always been and reaching out to discover what can be. And I am continuing to learn that grief is a normal part of transition and that, at the same time, listening deeply to communities coming to terms with this transition can be an incredible act of love.

In conclusion

Living at the edges has taught me that liminal spaces can mirror the Gospel itself – specifically the cross, where death and life, and brokenness and hope, intersect. Yet the edges are not always romantic spaces. They can be marked by genuine loss and the sting of marginalisation. However, it is here that

God's transformative work becomes the most visible. For faith to flourish at the edges, two movements must happen together. First, we must sit with the grief that transitions bring, whether it be caused by ageing bodies, displaced identities or fractured belonging. This grief must be given voice. As Brueggemann reminds us, it is in God's attentive presence with our pain that healing happens. Second, we must seek justice by naming and addressing that which pushes people to the margins. The racism, patriarchy and other forms of exclusion that push people to the margins are not unfortunate circumstances but injustices requiring confrontation. When we hold these two movements together – grieving well and seeking justice boldly – creative potential emerges. Seniors fill their church with hope. Second generation voices find peace in incomplete identities. Immigrant churches imagine new forms of mission. As the Australian church as a whole finds itself in a liminal space, moving from the centre to the edge, the question is not whether we will face transitions and marginalisation, but whether we will face transitions and marginalisation with fear or with faith. The edges are not where the church dies, but where it learns again what it means to truly live.

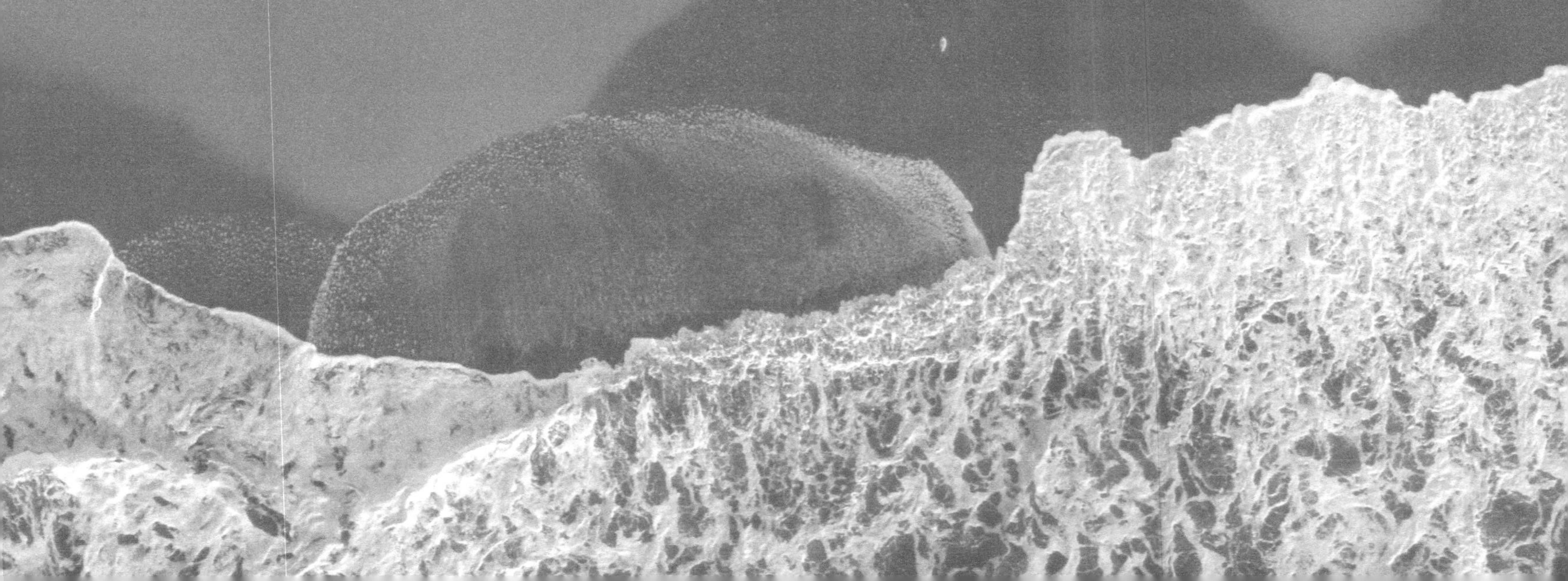
THEOLOGY

A Prayer for Walking the Edge / Jono Ingram

God of the wild places,
of narrow paths, rocky ridges,
and deep forest valleys –

Here I am
standing on top of a mountain looking out,
no longer in the centre fenced in by certainty,
but balanced on the edge,
where faith feels thin.

Standing on the margins of belief and belonging,
I discover that You are already here
not calling me back to safety,
but beckoning me forward,
an invitation to traverse with You further along the
spur.

Teach me, O Creator, to listen
to the ground beneath my feet,
to the rhythm of breath and heartbeat,
to Your quiet voice
that does not shout directions
but invites attention.

Shape me into one who trusts the edge itself
not because it is safe,
but because You meet me here.

Amen.

Decolonisation

/ Naomi Wolfe

... the aborigines capable of only a limited improvement. Have no knowledge of a Supreme Being. Death attributed in all cases to human agency. Numbers in the Murray and Darling tribes. Infanticide prevalent. Their diseases and physical sufferings. Cannibalism. Marriages. Probable future of the aborigines. ... Bennilong and the Native Police, instances of failure to permanently improve the aborigines. The aborigines doomed to become extinct.[1]

Note: This chapter uses storying, an Aboriginal methodology, for both theological act and as literary method, grounded in relationship, responsibility and memory as a practice of truth-telling. I invite you to consider this methodology and theological reflection of storying as a prophetic witness to the Church as you navigate this chapter.[2]

Let me tell you a story:
There was a Sunday school room of children from the

neighbourhood, various shapes and sizes, colours, but all the one creed – of the parish Anglican variety. Miss Smith (not her real name, but if you know, you know) had arrived early to St Stephen's after driving the local streets at such a speed that made even the local copper pray. She was ready for another week of faithfully teaching the generations of local children as she had done for the previous fifty years. And for those children who did not respond appropriately, she did not spare the rod.

She settled the class with a stern glance that would have made even St Peter straighten up, ready for Bible learning. She read aloud, saying, 'Let the children come to me, for the kingdom of God belongs to such as these.' She spoke further to the children: 'God so loved the world that he gave his only Son. God loves all people.'

The children heard. They wrote it on individually designed bookmarks and promised to commit it to their hearts.

Miss Smith continued with her lessons, not all from the Good Book, but spoken as truth all the same. The teacher spoke of the local people who did not know God – the Tommeginer.[3] She spoke of how they lived in darkness and sin, and how their ways were the wrong ways and must be left behind. She spoke of the local people who had died out because of their sin, and their shame, and not knowing God. She looked around the class and murmured about the 'remaining touch of the tar brush'.[4] Her words were heavy, capturing shame in her pedagogy.

One girl asked, 'But Miss Smith, if God created the whole world, and all the people, and God is love, then why are the other people bad? And doesn't God love them too?'

Miss Smith's stern eyes had a mercurial flash, and she replied, 'God does love everyone, but some first must be changed. Some people's creation and their ways were not pleasing to God!'

The girl tried again. 'If God created them that way, why would he be upset?'

Miss Smith got up slowly and determinedly and walked to the door. She opened it, smoothed her hands down her dress and quietly told the girl, 'Get out of my Sunday school. Get out now!'

The girl's legs trembled but she carefully got her Bible, her pencils and her bookmark and made for the door. She didn't say a word. As she made her way through the doorway, she felt the strong sting of Miss Smith's hand slap the back of her legs, with a quiet and angry, 'Get out, you touch of a tar brush hellion.'

The girl left, upset both in body and in mind. She had so many questions. She had heard the stories of the Old People who were part of the land, had cared for it, how they had lived off and with the lands and waterways and how life was as sacred as any story heard in church and Sunday school. She wondered how, if the people and their place were created in God's image, they could be evil.

The girl resolved to find a way to understand, and as her legs and her pride smarted, she would find a way to help Miss Smith understand the true nature of God who did love everyone, that no one was created evil, and importantly, the meaning of the word 'hellion'!

It's January 2026 now and that girl is all grown up, but the incident with Miss Smith remains firmly in my memories long after the pain of that leg slap has disappeared. I never felt welcome in Sunday school ever again. From that day on, I always felt on the edges of relationship with church and theology. But that memory has become part of the foundation for my commitment to decolonising Christian theology in Australia. It is an incident I now use to remind myself that there can be a way of reconciling traditions, wisdom, faith and practice.

For many years, I would pray for myself, my family and my ancestral lineage to be healed and accepted by God. As I read more, grew older and had the good fortune to encounter a variety of theologians, parish priests and religious sisters, I began to realise that those types of prayers were unnecessary. But I didn't know how to replace those unnecessary and deficit-based prayers. Both my parents were avid readers and suggested that perhaps I might like to explore what our local library had by way of theological books, believing that I might find hidden gems that could be strung together. The local librarian took pity on me, suggesting I might like to see what the local minister's fraternity might offer from their collections.[5] It was a wonderful suggestion. The local Baptist minister introduced me to John Bunyan and Charles Spurgeon with the expressed hope that I might be baptised by full immersion; and the local Catholic priest gave me the writings of Karl Rahner, Gustavo Gutierrez, Rosemary Radford Ruethur and Karol Wojtyła (the future Pope John Paul II). The latter two's work would intersect with my academic theological work. The Anglican vicar introduced me to the writings of John A.T. Robinson and C.S. Lewis. I can remember speaking with one of the ministers of a non-denominational church who cautioned me about 'asking too many questions, lest I open the door further for the devil to come in permanently'. That caution, and my less than enthusiastic response to it, he had no recommendations for reading other than 'the Bible, the only book you'll ever need'. I left his study with assurance of prayers and a new copy of the Good News version of the Bible.

My theological appetite in those days was raw and unbridled. I would devour any theological, spiritual or philosophical text available to me, searching for answers, for ideas, for peace of mind and, importantly, for connection. I would review microfiche, looking for reports of gatherings and sermons that might help to understand the ideas of the past. I was looking for specific reasons why Aboriginal peoples and others were seen as less than, as deficit, as objects needing salvation and requiring greater attention than non-Indigenous peoples. It was an often frustrating process. As fellow trawlwoolway priest Garry Deverell notes:

> ... from the 1820s right up until the 1990s, the public imagination of this country was dominated by a great silence about the stealing of Aboriginal lands and seas, the long war between invaders and native warriors, the systematic attempts to destroy whole cultures and nations, and the forced separation of Aboriginal and Torres Strait Islander children from their families. School children were taught that the land was largely "empty" when white "settlers" arrived and that the few natives who already lived here soon died out because of their stupidity and their failure to cultivate the land.[6]

As a historian and a theologian, I enjoy diving into primary sources from colonial times and uncovering evidence that the church and wider society have forgotten, have ignored or may well want to forget. A while ago, I was tracking down a rogue quote from a colonial source and stumbled across the words of Hugh Jamieson to Bishop Perry cited at the start of this chapter. And there they were – the lurking yet forceful echoes of eurocentrism and racial superiority that have contributed to institutions of Australian Christian institutions in Australia. Jamieson's letter gives us an insight into colonial theology and how Indigenous peoples were seen by those outside their communities. These echoes still need to be acknowledged, uncovered and repented of.

Australian Christianity frequently imposed a missionary religion and an image of Jesus Christ that was shaped by European power, by empire and through racial hierarchy. It imposed a faith of a Caucasian imperial Christ who, along with the rest of the Trinity, arrived alongside colonisation. These representations often rendered Aboriginal peoples as objects of mission rather than as interlocutors of existing relationships with God. Fellow countrywoman from lutruwita, Aunty Lee Miena Skye, notes that 'if initially the colonialists had taken the time to thoroughly understand the Aboriginal ways, then a considerable amount of violence could have been avoided'.[7] This was not just violence towards Indigenous lands, waterways, native flora and fauna, families and their children; it was also theological and epistemological violence. Wiradjuri Elder Pastor Neville Naden puts it, frankly, describing colonisation as 'any illegal or legal action that breaks the spiritual ties of people with the land'.[8]

Australian iterations of colonial Christianity carried out epistemological and theological violence by rejecting the validity of Aboriginal ontologies and reframing them as heinous, superstitious, erroneous or absent. It was unwilling to see them as complex and articulate systems of law and lore, knowledge and relationship. Christian theology in Australia was formed by empire and the assumptions of the Enlightenment, incorporating universalised European categories of land, truth and personhood, thus separating faith from Country. It also cast Aboriginal worldviews (spiritualities) as incompatible with revelation. In doing so, the Church directly contributed to dispossession, cultural erasure and silencing of Aboriginal knowledges, disrupting the transmission of law and lore, and transitions, rituals and responsibilities across generations. Yet non-Indigenous ally and theologian Rev. Chris Budden reminds us that:

> All theologies are always contextual. Theologies arise within communities bound by time and geography, by language, discourse, and knowledge shaped by traditions and times. Some theologies claim to be universal and imply that self-consciously contextual theologies are limited and interest bound. In reality those who claim to speak a universal theology are actually asking that their own limited interests and perspectives should be accepted by everyone.[9]

A decolonising shift away from such a narrow form of theology invites the whole Christian community to reimagine Jesus through the lens of Aboriginal relatedness, through an *Imago Dei* that includes an Aboriginal creation through and the suffering, resilience and survival of Aboriginal peoples. Such imagination affirms that Jesus is encountered through the colonised, the displaced and those seeking healing and belonging. This approach recovers an embodied and contextual Christology – God with us on Country – recognising that Jesus is not alien to these lands but present within its histories, wounds and, importantly, hopes.

I kept aside my ruminations of Bishop Perry's and wondered what his response to Jamieson's remarks about the so-called 'the aborigines' might have been. I wondered how his response translated into his pastoral care of the 'aborigines' and settlers under his care. I wrote myself a note to do some more research on Bishop Perry and perhaps include him as a case study one day, or even write an article! Meanwhile, my musings about decolonising theology and my brief interaction with pioneer letters brought forth a memory from several years back of an interaction with a non-Indigenous theologian whose expertise was not Indigenous theologies or spiritualities.

Let me tell you a story:
He leans back, generous with unsolicited advice.

'If you want my advice,' he says, 'you should write more. Get that Aboriginal and Torres Strait Islander spirituality into some serious publications. Conferences and community actions are all very well, but if you want to be taken seriously, you need to get published.'

I nod, wanting to be respectful but also to be understood. I explain – briefly, politely – that I am working on an article. That it's a heavy season. Teaching. Kinship care. Managing my health. Trying to be there for both community and institutions.

He frowns, kindly. 'Well, some time management is in order. You really should carve out some time and knuckle down.'

I thank him. I explain I'm balancing several expectations. I mention the joy and support of co-writing with others, the way collective work sustains me and the way I think I can give back to Elders, community members and fellow academics.

He brightens.

'I've actually got a bit of an interest in this area. Send me some things to read – maybe some ideas you've had.'

I say yes. I send readings. I send a draft. I send labour shaped by community, obligation and care.

He responds with nothing. Silence. Not even generic politeness by acknowledging receipt of email.

The following year, he celebrates his new publication on First Peoples theologies loudly on social media.

No mention of the people.

No mention of the labour that fed the work. No visible work of decolonising himself, his methods, his institution or his faith.

Just the shimmer of the 'Indigenous' as concept – portable, publishable, safely exotic.

Unchallenging and unchallenged.

I scroll past.

Time for more coffee.

There is a bitter irony – and an unspoken privilege – in the ease with which a non-Indigenous theologian can write about Aboriginal and Torres Strait Islander theologies while Indigenous academics themselves remain excluded structurally from the institutional support, the time and the space required to publish. Decolonisation can never be achieved by merely acquiring knowledge or by circulating fragments prioritised by a European academic lens. What is required is the relational, slow and unsettling work of interrogating one's authority, methods and relationships to text, to history and faith. In contrast, the response of this theologian was not to decolonise theology – it was to reproduce it while at the same time reinscribing familiar non-Indigenous hierarchies of productivity, expertise and ownership. This matters to me because of the many Aboriginal people who live at the edges and margins of the church, striving to be both Christian and Aboriginal, still waiting for institutions to offer more than scraps of inclusion, welcome and understanding. As Goenpul woman and professor Aunty Aileen Moreton-Robinson argues, decolonisation encompasses exposing and upending dominant assumptions entrenched in Western epistemologies that have controlled knowledge production and marginalised Indigenous knowledges across Australia.[10]

This places a profound responsibility on educators and theologians to do more than include Aboriginal and Torres Strait Islander content in curricula. Existing theological curricula, interpretations and structures will be reproduced if they are not prepared to recognise and understand how theology has been used to dispossess, silence and spiritualise injustices to Indigenous Country now known as Australia. Therefore, there must be a focus on actively decolonising the formation and training theological students receive. These students go on to shepherd congregations and shape ministry practice, and their training needs to equip them to speak with moral authority and to critique the church's role and place in the continuing colonial project. This is important for Indigenous theological students, as well as multigenerational settler students and those more recently arrived. A decolonised theological education must shape ministers from all communities so that they are capable of critically engaging with their own traditions and beliefs, re-examining their faith practices and developing ethical relationality that has a place alongside Indigenous communities in the urgent and substantive work towards biblical justice – truth-telling, reconciliation and engagement with treaties – not as abstract ideas but as lived and living ecclesial responsibilities.

Let me tell you a story:
It was only a few weeks after the 2023 Voice Referendum, long enough for the headlines to thin but not long enough for the bruising across community to fade.

I clicked on the Zoom link. Ah, Zoom, that love-hate function of modern theological education. I waited for my colleague to arrive. We were meant to be talking about programs – budgets, timelines, deliverables, compliance stuff. The peel of an email arriving, and my laptop alerted me to less than fifty percent battery. Ordinary workday things.

And then there were two of us on the Zoom, as planned. He shifted in his chair before we began. 'I know we're meeting to talk about programs,' he said, 'but I just wanted to touch base about the referendum results and ask how the Aboriginal community was feeling, you know.'

I exhaled slowly, and took a mouthful of coffee, wishing I'd made two cups.

'You and everyone else have been asking that question,' I said. 'There isn't a single answer. But I can tell you that many Indigenous people are worried about racism increasing – even in church communities.'

He looked genuinely surprised.

'Oh. Is there still racism towards Aborigines? I didn't know. I haven't heard of any racism.'

'Yes,' I said, calmly and I hoped evenly. 'There's a lot of it. And some racists feel more emboldened since the result.'

He frowned, processing, then tilted his head. 'Will the Aborigines have to pay that money back?'

'Money?' I said, my mouth already slightly open.

'You know,' he continued, 'for the cost of the referendum and all that.'

There it was. Money as the issue, again. My jaw dropped just enough that I felt it, then caught it.

'The referendum was a federal government initiative,' I said carefully. 'It met parliamentary and legal requirements. It wasn't something many Indigenous communities were even asking for.'

He waved a hand lightly. 'Yes, well, it just seemed like a waste of money. As a recent migrant to Australia, I'm not sure why I should be held accountable for things done in colonial times.'

I picked up my coffee cup, still wishing I had made two coffees. 'There's a lot to unpack there,' I said. 'But we have other priorities for this meeting. Could we schedule another time to talk through what you've just said?'

'Yeah, sure,' he replied. 'We should get on with the proper work. I just think it was a lot of money. It doesn't concern me or my family – we've come recently. We've worked hard for what we have, and so could Aborigines – oh, not you,' he added quickly, 'the other ones.'

Inside my head, something shatters noiselessly. 'Let's meet another time,' I said again. 'You can email me when you're free.'

'Yeah, yeah.' He paused. 'I didn't vote anyway. There wasn't enough information.'

Silence stretched between us. It has a weight to it, like humidity before a storm. I wonder if I should leave the Zoom, blaming technology or internet connectivity. The silence stretching on and on.

I nodded once, slowly. 'So,' I said, my voice returning to its professional register, 'shall we talk about the programs?'

And just like that, we did – while everything else unsaid sat heavily in the Zoom and in my lounge room, unacknowledged, waiting.

I scan my email regularly for his name and for an invitation to make that time to meet to talk about the referendum of 2023. It never arrives. A missed opportunity to uncover and tease out the theological and societal racism lurking? Sure. A missed opportunity to think about theology and faith with a strong coffee? Never.

That conversation has stuck with me. It set my ADHD brain off on tangents around a range of topics – assimilation, migrant theology, diaspora theology and that go-to topic of academics, postcolonial theology. It got me thinking about theology – the study of God that is woven into every aspect of my life. It got me thinking that decolonisation cannot be a one-size-fits-all for all Christians, all traditions, all communities, in all places. Thankfully there have been hard-working, tenacious Aboriginal, Torres Strait Islander and Allied scholars who have continued to 'fight the good fight'. Aunty Phyllis Pitchford brings home for me and others how important this fight is:

> ... they were stripped of their culture, they were stripped of their language, they were stripped of everything. They tried to teach them Christianity, trying to really push them into the white man's way of life and of course it wasn't going to work. They had their own beliefs, their own cultures, their own heritage and they wanted to remain that way. It was really traumatic, very traumatic for our people.[11]

I wonder how many Christians across Australia are truly aware of this reality. Professor Mark G. Brett, who has worked consistently and tirelessly on decolonising biblical studies, notes that 'the lived experience of Aboriginal Christianity in Australia remains largely hidden from wider churches'.[12]

Decolonisation is just as important for more recently arrived Australians as it is for the rest of us. It helps migrants to understand how Christianity in Australia is shaped by settler colonial history, and that therefore all of us require an ethical re-grounding on these Aboriginal lands if we are to avoid simply continuing the inherited European traditions. It provides an opportunity for migrant communities to avoid any unintentional alignment with colonial power structures, especially when they themselves have experienced displacement, racialisation and marginalisation elsewhere. Adnyamathanha Elder and theologian Aunty Denise Champion reminds all of us that:

> There's a much older story that has stood the test of time in this land of the universal Christ and the birth of the universal church that is not being acknowledged. As Aboriginal peoples we hold knowledge, understanding, and wisdom that not only our own, but all peoples, need to learn from – language for God, wisdom for God's people, and challenge for the way ahead. For the church to be complete, our voices must be heard.[13]

Theological decolonisation is therefore an invitation into this old, old story, and it is a clarification. It is an invitation into right relatedness with Aboriginal and Torres Strait Islander peoples, flora and fauna, lands, skies and waterways rather than connectedness by default or choice with settler norms and ideas of whiteness. It is a clarification that belonging in Australian Christianity cannot be divorced from responsibility to Country and an acknowledgement of Aboriginal and Torres Strait Islander sovereignties, not just their own personal culture or denominational membership. Quandamooka Elder and theologian Aunty Evelyn Parker invites all Australians to recognise that an essential component of Australian theology is to recognise that:

> ... the sacredness of God is all around us. We feel, hear and see him in people, churches, cathedrals, the land, sea and sky. He speaks to us in the language we understand, and we continue the special relationship with him that our Ancestors once had. It is this great gift that has been given to Aboriginal Christians – they are well equipped to share with non-indigenous Australians the knowledge of finding the Lord in the soil of the wonderful land where the Ancestors once walked.[14]

Decolonisation opens space for the inclusion of non-Western theological traditions and expressions of faith that can contribute to and dialogue with existing Indigenous and non-Indigenous expressions. In doing so, it challenges the emphasis on assimilation into a very narrow western and dated European expression of Christianity. Christian practice and witness can be strengthened by grounding faith, biblical interpretation and ministry in truth-telling, humility and justice – the antidotes to the silencing of stories and experiences of historical and contemporary harm. Decolonisation of theology can equip Christian leaders to engage ethically with theology in the public square, and to hold conversations of integrity about truth-telling, reconciliation and treaties rather than drawing on inherited assumptions and misunderstandings. Importantly, decolonisation prevents further silencing, marginalisation and erasure of Indigenous peoples by Australian Christians, providing an opportunity for them to contribute to a church and a living faith that is honest about history, relational to people and place, and faithful in these lands, this embodiment of Creation.

Let me tell you a story:
The gathering did not begin with an agenda. It began with people arriving – Aboriginal and Torres Strait Islander Elders, community leaders, theologians, historians, church workers, students and whitefellas – some known to one another, others meeting for the first time. Some were Northern Hemisphere ring-ins from the NAIITS: An Indigenous Learning Community. They came by different means: planes, trains and one professor arrived on his bicycle. Some were collected from airports by allies who rearranged workdays and family commitments; others arrived holding food, stories and long memories. What brought them was not an institution's invitation or a funded project, but a shared conviction that theology and history in Australia could no longer be taught, researched or practised as if colonisation were peripheral to their foundations.

Elders spoke first – not to open the meeting formally, but to locate us: in Country, in relationship, in responsibility. The questions that followed were not framed as curriculum design problems or issues, but as ethical ones. What does it mean to teach theology on stolen lands? Who controls our knowledges and who bears the cost of its extraction? What would postgraduate programs look like if they were shaped not by disciplinary inheritance alone, but by accountability to Indigenous sovereignty, Law and lived experience?

Decolonisation, in this gathering, was not spoken of as a metaphor. It was called a relinquishing: of ownership of ideas, of control of methods and of certainty about outcomes. Non-Indigenous scholars listened as much as they spoke. Elders reminded them to hush when they forgot themselves. They did the same to the mob who did likewise. Indigenous participants refused to take on the role of consultants brought in to 'add content' – the black cladding approach. Instead, they asserted the reshaping of the very questions being asked. Learning was imagined not as transmission, but as andragogical formation – slow, dialogical, relational and demanding of humility from those accustomed to authority, and perhaps those seeking it!

It was not a flash event. There was no budget, no glossy prospectus or commissioned feasibility study. What sustained it was big-heartedness: church communities giving donations for the purchase of textbooks and internet dongles; people cooking casseroles and soup late into the night; donated time, shared vehicles, spare beds and patient children. Resources appeared because commitment preceded funding, not the other way around. As Aunty Janet remarked several times, 'If we waited for funding, we'd get nothing started, and nothing done!'[15]

By the end, what had taken shape was a shared resolve: to develop theological postgraduate programs that would make space for Indigenous and non-Indigenous students and staff to learn differently; to provide an opportunity to form ministries accountable to Country and community; and to track right relationship rather than institutional kudos and prestige. The hope was modest and profound at once – we didn't want to perfect the disciplines, but to begin again, together, in truth, with courage and with care. The hope was strong, and the mandate was the decolonisation of theology. This Indigenous-designed, Indigenous-developed and Indigenous-led consultation, auspiced by the University of Divinity, led to several outcomes: an Indigenous theologies program through a partnership between NAIITS and Whitley College;[16] the development and launch of the University of Divinity School of Indigenous Studies;[17] and the graduation of fourteen students (including nine Aboriginal and Torres Strait Islander and world Indigenous graduates).

As I reflect on the acts of decolonisation already completed, I am both proud and sad. Sadly, some of these decolonisation initiatives have either paused or ended. As I contemplate yet another cup of coffee, I am reminded that the decolonisation of theology in all its forms has only just begun. It's not a task that leaves you unchanged; it demands time, patience and a willingness to be unsettled. It calls you, me and churches of all denominations and agencies into a sustained self-interrogation – exploring inherited theologies, historical silencing and structures of power that continue to privilege some while excluding others. This work requires humility and attending to the discipline of hearing the painful truths without defensiveness. It involves knowing when to stay silent or wait to be invited to speak in spaces that are not your own. It requires a refusal to commodify or extract Indigenous knowledge for personal or institutional progress. Decolonisation of theology is about being faithful, not the master. It's an ongoing commitment to do the work, to dismantle that which harms and to be accountable to relationships even if those are slow, uncomfortable or costly.

We might wish that such stories are merely a literary device.

We might argue that they reduce the individuals involved to little more than caricatures – that they lack nuance, that they fail to account for the fullness of the other person's life, intentions or complexity. Yet these stories are not fictional. They are drawn from actual events. Names, locations and genders have been altered to protect those involved, but the encounters themselves are real and painfully recognisable to Aboriginal people. They are representative not because they are exaggerated, but because they are repeated.

This is how humiliation operates. This is how structural bias and everyday racism are experienced. This is how trauma works. In moments shaped by power imbalance, prejudice, and microaggression, the encounter is not experienced as layered or contextualised; it is experienced as totalising. Everything else falls away. The body remembers the moment as shock: stripped of background, stripped of intention, stripped of narrative safety. If the story feels flattened or surreal, that is because it was lived that way. It did not feel real at the time either.

In the aftermath, as I carry the cultural and emotional labour of rebuilding my sense of self, these moments can feel almost fictional. Did they really say that? Did she understand what she was doing? Would anyone believe me if I told this story? If I speak, will I be asked to soften it, to reframe it, to make it more palatable or accessible? Will my pain be met with care, or with another request for translation, explanation or emotional regulation? In this way, the burden compounds: the original harm is followed by the labour of managing how it is received.

Ironically, questioning whether these stories are 'accurate' or 'fair' reinscribes the very dynamic they seek to interrogate. Aboriginal people are repeatedly reminded that dominant, non-Indigenous society has long positioned us as caricatures –

an act of cultural control that resists genuine decolonisation. Many non-Indigenous Australians have been socialised to understand Aboriginal peoples not as contemporaneous, complex human communities, but through simplified and contradictory images: the 'ancient traditional', the 'symbolic custodian', the 'traumatised subject' or the 'grateful beneficiary'. These caricatures flatten agency, erase diversity and deny the adaptive, living and intellectually rich nature of Aboriginal lives.

As a result, interactions are often shaped by expectation rather than relationship. Aboriginal people are encountered as representations to be managed, consulted, corrected, admired or cautiously avoided, rather than as people who carry authority, difference, expertise and accountability across their own communities. This caricatured lens enables the continuation of the settler-colonial gaze: one that allows non-Indigenous people to feel benevolent or well-intentioned without undertaking the deeper work required by decolonisation – the work of listening without defensiveness, of sitting with discomfort, of accepting accountability and of sharing responsibility.

Aboriginal people, within the Church and outside of it, will tell you of their own experiences that are like the ones you've read in this chapter. Decolonising our faith, our church structures and our understandings of ourselves and one another will be neither easy nor comfortable. It is, nevertheless, a journey that must be taken. Will you join me and others as we seek decolonisation?

Malagigiri

Cliff Bird

This is the story of something I experienced when I was nine years old.

In the mid-2000s I was at St Mark's National Theological Centre in Canberra, where I was living on campus. While doing my doctoral research on land as a 'household of life' in my native Solomon Islands, this pivotal experience in my life-story resurfaced. There were many experiences that shaped me as I was growing up, but this unexpected occurrence turned out to be one of the most profound and defining. It was, and still is, one of my reference points for trying to understand many things, including God's interactions with/in nature, and the unexpected ways in which healing and wholeness are interwoven and interconnected with nature. This experience raises questions about God, faith and the manifold relationships in God's and our world.

There are two Indigenous and religio-cultural concepts that best capture this experience: *mana* and *malagigiri*. According to the Indigenous knowledge and epistemology of my people, *mana and malagigiri* intertwine. These rich concepts defy any simplistic English transliterations and have various shades of meaning.[1] As a noun, *mana* can be understood as an otherly-endowed 'blessing' upon and 'function' of a human figure or human figures, or alternatively as culturally-inherited hierarchical status, power and authority. It is given to people in leadership, who are expected to exercise it for the common good of the community. As a stative verb, *mana* can be understood as being embodied in the natural processes: weather (sun, rain, winds, breeze etc.), local environment and fecundity of the soil. For example, a food garden that produces a good harvest is because of a combination of all of these – not because of an otherworldly power. From this perspective, *mana* is not an external subject or source, but an innate ecological pro-life-energy and potential.

Malagigiri can be described as effulgence of sacred charisma; outpouring of spiritual authority (akin to the Old Testament Hebrew original use of 'glory'); and vibrancy of sacred spirit. In a nutshell, *malagigiri* is a kind of power, authority and charisma that is embodied in a subject (human person or otherwise) and is emanating from and animating that person or subject. In my story, my healer embodied *mana* and *malagigiri* – he was a manifestation of both!

Perhaps some who read this piece will find the story hard to believe and will become very sceptical, even seeing my story as superstitious. I have no control over how each reader will react or respond. I am reminded of the words of Daniel L. Migliore:

> Questions arise at the edges of what we can know and
> what we can do as human beings. They thrust themselves

on us with special force in times and situations such as sickness, suffering, guilt, injustice, personal or social upheaval, and death. Believers are not immune to the questions that arise in these situations. Indeed they may be more perplexed than others because they want to relate their faith to what is happening in their lives and in the world.[2]

I invite the reader to read on with an open heart and mind, and to ask: Where is God in this story? What does this story tell us about God and how God works? Or what and whose kind of theology or theologies does this story invite us to explore and deeply contemplate? How does this story help us navigate complex questions around the Bible and theology?

Before I share my story, let me give some background.

Primacy of relationships

In my early years I was formed, nourished and sustained by multiple relationships, including but not limited to relationships with family and with nature. These relationships planted a seed and nurtured my theological meanderings and explorations, especially my worldview that the whole of life is interconnected.

Relationships with family

My early life story is in large part the story of my parents. The very fabric of who I was and who I have come to be was woven in loving, kind, generous, respectful and affirming relationships within both my nuclear and extended families, and my parents and grandparents were the most influential authority figures in my formative years. They were my teachers! They did not have the opportunity to enter the Western education system in their prime due to inaccessibility, isolation and the devastation brought about by the Second World War. Yet they raised my siblings and me with the breadth and depth of the knowledge and wisdom they had acquired in the everyday 'school of life' rooted in Indigenous-traditional knowledge, values, disciplines and practices.

My parents were subsistence farmers in the Solomon Islands. They were very knowledgeable about plants and their uses, the rhythms of nature and times for planting and harvesting, and the taboos, restrictions and rituals to observe, including especially the centrality of prayers before and after every activity. We would pray before we started work on our family food gardens and again when we were ready to return home. My mother would use plants and herbs that were known to have curative and healing elements to deal with illnesses and wounds. My father was an avid and highly knowledgeable fisherman; when I was about five years old, he started to teach me what a fisherman is and what s/he does. There was so much I learnt, including the centrality of prayerful engagement with the elements.

My parents were also very committed church people. They grew up under the influence of Methodist missionaries and teaching, and the Christian disciplines of family devotions, village/community worship and service to the community were important practices. My father was duly appointed as a lay pastor and my mother a leader in the Women's Fellowship. They were self-taught leaders. My family was commonly referred to as a *tatamana lotu* – a Christian family. All of this and much more contributed to the forming and broadening of my knowledge and experience.

Relationship with nature: land, sea and skies

Growing up in the village meant being attached to the land and seas and skies every day. I joined my parents in their daily work and was infused with knowledge of subsistence methods and shifting cultivation. I walked to school either on forest footpaths or along beachfront tracks and marvelled at the beauty and wonders all around. Along the bush tracks there were flowers, butterflies, spiders and spider webs, frogs and toads, lizards, centipedes and millipedes, creepers and climbers, vines and palms, possums, snakes and so much more! In the water along the shoreline footpaths there were fish of all sorts, seagrass, seashells, sea snakes, crabs, reef sharks, eels, crocodiles and so much more.

I joined my uncle as he traversed mountains, valleys and rivers and took in the stories and knowledge embedded in all of this. I learnt about sacred sites and taboo places, plant names and uses, tree species for building houses and canoes and tools, medicinal plants and herbs, totems and their religio-cultural significance, sounds and silences and what they mean, how to trace feral pigs, spirit abodes and journeys and stories, and so much more.

From my father I received worthy traditional maritime knowledge and skills: fish names, spawning times and seasons, habitats of different fish species, tidal and current movements, different fishing methods, how to trace octopus on reef flats, the connection between tidal and current movements and the moon and its phases and how all of this connects with fish species and spawning times, the importance of sea cucumbers (beech-de-mer), corals and giant clams, and much more.

All of this was critical in my upbringing. From a relatively young age, my Christian life was shaped by familial and communal relationships as well as my connectedness to/with the land and seas and skies. I experienced the divine in my family, in my community and in my continuous interactions with everything in, around and above me. For instance, before every fishing trip, my parents would remind me that God is always present. I would pray to God and then read the skies (types of clouds, time of day, moon phases), study the sea (tidal and current movements, fish movements) and look to the land (mountains, hills, islands, islets) as the markers for my fishing spots. My knowledge of God during my young days was not an abstract and philosophical one! It was experiential and tangible – from experiences in/with the family to experiences in/with the land and sea and skies.

All of this became the cradle of my theological journeys and meanderings, which would eventually form me into 'a fisherman who romances theology'. The interconnectedness of all life was a deep insight that helped shape the substance of my theological orientation and work later in life.

Innocence of faith ruptured

A major shift happened as I was transitioning into high school. As self-taught and self-motivated church leaders, my parents started to read Christian literature (noting that there was not much that was available to read at the time!). My father began to read about the work of the World Healing Crusade (now called the World Healing Centre), a Blackpool-based religious organisation, which he then started following. Inspired by this, my parents formed the 'Mataqara Healing Ministry'. It quickly grew in reputation and was soon officially recognised by the church as a lay-led ministry of healing. The primary means of this healing was through prayer and counselling.

On many occasions I would travel with my parents and the team and perform the healing prayers. This proved quite significant because within the brief period of time in which the association with the World Healing Crusade was forged, the use of traditional knowledge, methods and means of healing became overshadowed and overtaken by Christian-based prayers for healing.

Something puzzling then happened: there was deliberate denunciation of a number of the traditional medicinal plants and herbs my mother in particular used to cure illnesses, and every attempt was made to destroy these time-tested healing plant species. Their curative, healing and well-being elements became demonised. They became associated with harmful and malevolent spirits and spirit beings and therefore had to be eliminated! I was deeply troubled and questions of doubt and disbelief shrouded my rather young faith. It was with this sense of troubled faith that I went through high school and, by the time I reached university, I had pushed my early experiences and knowledge of God to my subconscious.

Yet there were parts of my past that could not easily be hidden away. I graduated from university in 1985 and it was almost a decade later that I began to reconnect with my formative theological experiences and knowledge. Then, in the 2000s, both my master's and doctoral research focused on the dynamic interactions between cultures and gospel, using land as the microcosm of this engagement. One of the themes I discussed in both levels of research was divine presence and perceived involvement in and through cultures and the stories handed down over generations. *Mana* and *malagigiri* are two Indigenous concepts that featured strongly in my research. Critical approaches to studying the Bible and alternative ways of studying and doing theology reawakened my subconscious and I started to interrogate some of the questions that had shaded my past. This phase of my life helped me to articulate in some theological fashion my formative experiences and knowledge of God. It also helped me understand stories of God's involvement with human beings and all beings. I thought of my own stories of becoming, particularly the story of how life and death wrestled within me when I was nine years old.

Life and death wrestled

It was February 1970 and I was a primary school pupil. The evening got dark quicker than usual because it was raining. I left our traditionally thatched kitchen, which was about fifty metres from our home, and I ran under the coconut palms towards the house. I stepped on a dead coconut frond on the ground and fell, got up and kept going until I got inside the house.

The next day I fell ill and within a rather short period of time I had gotten seriously sick. All kinds of explanations and interpretations about my sickness were made by many traditional authority figures. I could hardly turn in bed and I could not walk – as though I was completely paralysed. I was given medicine by the community nurse and church leaders came and prayed for me and over me, but my condition continued to deteriorate. I was then taken to the hospital for diagnosis and possible treatment, but the cause of my medical condition was never ascertained. Several months passed and my condition continued to get worse. Finally, I was sent back home because nothing more could be done for me. We all knew what this meant. That night was going to be my last night.

My family decided that I should stay near the community

clinic where my uncle was the nurse. Family members sat around the room filled with gloom and there was deathly silence. It was at that moment that someone entered. He said to my father, 'God sent me to come and heal your son.'

Heads turned and shock and disbelief were written on everyone's faces. What? This person was not a known member of the community. He was from another distant community and had approached my uncle to ask if he could stay with him, offering to keep the clinic surroundings clean. But there was more. He was known as someone who delved into the mysterious, into 'magic' and especially into the uses of natural medicine and cures, even to the point of being ostracised as a sorcerer.

He turned to my father and said, 'God wants the two of us to work together – you to say the prayer and me to do the ritual using the elements from the forest and sea.' In the nighttime quietness of the room his words were like a still small voice that rekindled the beliefs of my formative years, and in some mysterious ways reconnected my spirit with all that surrounded me.

My father had a son he could lose very soon so he did as he was asked – he prayed for the man and what he was about to do and he prayed for me. The man began to chant and continued to chant as he wove and shifted the tree leaves and sand all over and around me, creating a symbolic circle around me with his bodily movements. After a few minutes he stopped. Hearts raced and all eyes were pinned on me. Immediately, and I mean immediately, I stood up and started to walk around the living room, shouting, 'I can walk … I can walk … I can walk!' In that moment I felt an affinity with the sick person whom Peter and John healed, when he stood up and entered the temple, 'walking and leaping and praising God' (Acts 3:8). After several months of not being able to stand, let along walk, here I was, able to do both! A few days later, the man brought another friend of his – also known for his healing knowledge and skills – and together they brought me back to wholeness.

Understanding faith at the edges

Where does one begin to try to make sense of this? I asked my PhD research supervisor if it was okay for me to tell this personal story in my thesis and he said yes, so I did. At that time, I decided to leave the story open-ended, not attempting to provide any kind of rationalisation, and to let it speak to its readers and hearers. I do the same this time around. It is a personal story but one that I think would be useful for people to read and contemplate. My hope is that this story will inspire the reader to ponder deep and unasked questions of faith, especially the mysterious – the surprises and wonders that do not lend themselves too easily to neat and comfortable interpretations.

As a fisherman who romances theology, I close this article with the following musings.

Firstly, God is in the story – in the mega-stories such as the Christ Event, in the small stories such as the healing of Cliff and in the micro and silent, albeit invisible, stories such as oxygen emerging from green leaves, algae and phyto-planktons. This God in the story refuses to be domesticated. My most unlikely and ostracised healer spoke and extended God's word, God's breath and God's actions to me. My father spoke and breathed and acted. In her silence during the ordeal my mother laid her heart bare before God. Leaves of trees and sands from the shoreline became means of healing and wholeness for me. God is in my story – not just in one part, but in its entirety.

But then I also wonder: is this God in the stories of violence, wars, death and destruction? Is God in the stories of devastations caused by climate change and natural disasters? Is God in the stories heard through the cries, suffering, pain, longing, loneliness and silence of victims? These are real and existential questions to which there are neither simple nor straightforward answers. Down through the centuries, there have been many and various ways in which sojourners of faith have tried to respond to these complex questions about God: the despotic God, the immutable God, the suffering God, the liberating God, the loving God, the redeeming God, the journeying and accompanying God and so on. Knowing God on the edge can sometimes feel like an invitation to go beyond conventionality and orthodoxy, towards non-conformity and openness to the promptings of the Spirit of Jesus Christ and the human spirit.

Adopting a theological orientation that sees God in our stories has enriched my ministry, allowing me to listen to and hear people's stories, not only as a way to empathise with them in their situation but also as a pastoral pathway to offering support, help and guidance. For instance, in my current role as a Uniting Church Mission Catalyst in the Pacific Australia Labour Mobility (PALM) Scheme, I get to listen to many stories from the workers – good and heartening stories as well as those that are not as good and are disheartening. Discerning the intertwining of the grace and place of God with such human stories prompts and calls for a critical and creative pastoral response on my part and on the part of the mission team.

Secondly, God is in and with Creation. The central message proclaimed by Western missionaries was the great salvation of humanity through faith in Jesus Christ. This is primarily a redemption-centred theology – redemption not just from sin and death but also from this sinful world – in which we are invited to a heavenly home. This redemption-centred theology sees Earth as a temporary passing stage in the great drama of salvation. Alongside this theology, my early upbringing and my experience of healing provided the grounding to see and experience God in Creation, and to see that all life is interconnected and interwoven. I explored this further in my research that looks at the interweaving of culture, nature and theology. I find that a very helpful way of speaking about God in Creation is panentheism (not to be confused with pantheism). Marcus Borg points out that the Greek roots of the word panentheism indicate its meaning: 'Pan is the Greek word for "all" or "everything"; *theism* comes from the Greek word for "God", *theos*; and the middle syllable *en* is the Greek word for "in". Panentheism affirms that everything is *in* God, even as it also affirms that God is *more* than everything.'[3]

Yet again, questions arise: is God in the forces of nature – tropical cyclones, tornadoes, floods, earthquakes, tsunamis etc. – that destroy and kill? Or in the cultures that dehumanise, oppress and violate other human beings, especially the most vulnerable? Again there are no simple answers to such haunting questions and I will not pretend to know the answers. The wrestle between life and death and the healing that came about in my own story remains a mystery to me, and I am satisfied to keep it as such. The experience taught me never to take life for granted and to live it as worthy of someone who was brought back from the strangles of death.

Having an orientation of seeing God in and with Creation invites us to care for Creation and to have a posture of stewardship and guardianship. It creates opportunities and avenues to engage in ecological advocacy and speak truth to the powers that are causing and perpetuating anthropogenic climate change. This Creation-oriented theology and creation spirituality have provided leverage for the church and people of faith to engage in tangible and programmatic works of justice.

Thirdly, God comes to us from the most unexpected and unlikely places and in the most unexpected and unlikely ways. A casual look at some of the stories in the Bible shows this to be so. The man in the story of my healing was a stranger, on the edges of society, a practitioner of so-called magic – disliked, feared and ostracised. Yet God spoke to and through him and he became a channel through which healing and wholeness reached me again. He was a manifestation of both *mana* and *malagigiri*. This speaks volumes, especially when theologies and biblical interpretations can become so fundamentalistic and narrow that there is little or no room for the God of grace and surprises to move, work and bring healing and wholeness.

In my ministry across Pasifika, I have never ceased to be surprised by the ways in which so many people have nurtured and enriched my life and journey, including some that a community and church overlook. Openness to and expectation of God's movements and the Spirit's promptings and guidance have given churches and communities vision, relevance, currency and motivation in mission and ministry. For me this has also meant hearing the Spirit prompting me to realign with the land and seas and skies, and to once again consciously share breath and air with them and their constituents, just as my grandfather taught me when I was young, well before I attended science classes in high school. *Vari zino siai ikana meni qato* ('humans and plants breathe into each other' or 'humans and plants share the same breath'). I have told my story. This story is also part of the story of my parents, grandparents, siblings and community. It is a partial story of the place and role of my healer. It is a story of how my life interweaves with my surroundings – land, seas and skies and their constituents. It is a story of my encounter with death and how being healed has given me a new appreciation of and purpose in life. I am my story and yet it is a story that is not my own only – it is a story of interconnections and interweavings. In this way, it is a story that is bigger than me, for it is a story of and for many people and subjects. When will this story end? Perhaps this is a good question for readers to ask themselves! As for me, let me see how these interweavings can help to pave ways and paths ahead. I am more than happy to keep the answer as a mystery.

Making

Steve Taylor

Making and Aboriginal leader Aunty Ellen

In 2010 I arrived in Australia from Aotearoa New Zealand to serve as the inaugural Director of Missiology at the Uniting College for Leadership and Theology. An important moment in my making journey was when we, as a family, joined Uniting Church young people for a weekend with Aboriginal Christians from the Ngarrindjeri nation.

The Ngarrindjeri are the custodians of the lower Murray River, Coorong and the lakes in South Australia. Members of the Ngarrindjeri nation include writer and inventor David Unaipon (1872-1967), who featured on the Australian fifty dollar note. They also include Fingerbone Bill, made famous through *Storm Boy*, a book from 1964 by Colin Thiele, then a movie released in 1976 and remade in 2019. Fingerbone Bill is the custodian of the pelicans that soar the Coorong.

We watched pelicans swoop past as Ngarrindjeri elder Uncle Tom bent to dig in the sand. About thirty centimetres down, fresh drinking water seeped into the hole. Between the sea and the lake, Indigenous knowledge offered life. Later that day, Aunty Ellen taught us to make. We heard stories of the reeds that became fibre that became baskets. As we made mistakes, we built community. As we wove with our hands, we sensed connections with country that ran millennia deeper than European migration.

That weekend has stayed with me. Practically, it was a springboard to regular Walking on Country immersion experiences for candidates for ordained ministry at the College. Theologically, it invited me to deepen my experiential understanding of theology as a practice of making. I looked for unexpected sources, sought to increase my sensitivity to different ways of knowing and thought more deeply about sustainability in ministry.

French Jesuit Michel de Certeau researched the role of making in everyday life.[1] Certeau is considered 'one of the leading theorists of cultural dynamics'.[2] The key to Certeau's method is daily practices, including daily routines of cooking, walking and watching TV. Sociologist of religion Nancy Ammerman drew on Certeau's work in defining practices as 'a cluster of actions' that allow us to be attentive to social forces and creative possibilities.[3] Practical theologian Heather Walton drew on Certeau's work to describe how writing is a way of making that enables theological reflection on life and practice.[4]

I had drawn on Certeau's ideas for my doctoral research in contemporary religious innovation, arguing that Certeau's 'making do' is a methodology for practical theology.[5] It is one thing to analyse making intellectually. It is quite another to make with my hands while listening to an Indigenous Aunty describe her connection with country.

How might making as a practice inform our theology as

we work at the edges in mission? It is tempting to associate theology with books, but fresh expressions in Australia involves locating theology in new places. This is not an abstract intellectual exercise but a process of making and remaking.

For those who have migrated to Australia, there is a need to unravel the garments of faith we have brought with us. Once unravelled, there are opportunities to remake. This is not a deconstructing but a crafting of the threads of Scripture, the colours of the church year and the experiences of those who have gone before into garments suitable for this contemporary Australian context.

On the way to describing making in Australia today, let me detour through images of God as Maker, several making practices and a celebration of three theologians of making.

God the Maker

God as Maker of Heaven and Earth is woven through the Scriptures. In the accounts of creation in Genesis, God's Spirit hovers over acts of making and invites humans to tend and keep. Then in Genesis 3:21, God is described as making garments of skin for Adam and his wife. It is a practical and caring image of God working to restore human dignity.

God as Maker is a lyrical refrain scattered through Israel's hymnbook (as one example, see Psalms 115:15). The wisdom literature portrays God as a shaper of creation in Psalm 8:3 and delighting in acts of making in Proverbs 8:25.

The prophets provide further insights into God as a maker. Ezekiel 16:8 and 10-12 offer an amazing image of God:

> I gave you my solemn oath and entered into a covenant with you, declares the Sovereign LORD, and you became

> mine. ... I clothed you with an embroidered dress and put sandals of fine leather on you. I dressed you in fine linen and covered you with costly garments. I adorned you with jewelry: I put bracelets on your arms and a necklace around your neck, and I put a ring on your nose, earrings on your ears and a beautiful crown on your head. (NIV)

Jewish theologian Melissa Raphael writes of how, in Ezekiel 16:4-10, 'darning as practice and metaphor no longer connotes an antiquated inconsequential fireside chore or a tedious expedience of poverty. Nor is it merely a proper womanly skill once acquired by girls to equip them for marriage. It is what mends, renews and therefore ultimately *changes* the structure and fabric of very old things.'[6] Making offers transformation of everyday life.

In the Gospels, Jesus is described as a 'carpenter's son' in Matthew 13:5, suggesting he is raised and likely worked as a maker of furniture and farm implements. Perhaps this upbringing informs his use of metaphors of making; he explains the Kingdom of God as being like mending wineskins in Luke 5:36 and like spinning cloth in Luke 12:27-28. In the book of Acts, we glimpse makers in mission. New Testament scholar F. Scott Spencer describes the witness of three women 'of the cloth' in Acts – Tabitha, Lydia and Priscilla – and outlines how they drew on making skills in commercial ventures.[7] To use the words of Spencer, 'As the earthly Jesus announced to his disciples in the upper room —"I am among you as one who serves" — so the risen Jesus embodied in Tabitha might well have proclaimed in another upper room — "I am among you as one who *sews*".'[8] Making was woven into the early Christian witness.

The Practices in Making

Many more theologians work with images of making, but before considering their insights, it is worth rehearsing how making informs practice. Skills of visible mending, unravelling, embracing limits and side-by-side redeeming invite us to think in fresh ways about making theology at the edges.

Visible mending

Making at the edges includes visible mending. Visible mending is a practice of repairing textile items in ways that intentionally makes the repair visible.

As a society we tend to buy new rather than recycle and reuse. Yet something new and beautiful can be made from what is torn or worn. Machine-made jeans can be personalised, colourfully patterned with unique expressions of identity. Moth-eaten jerseys can be stitched with new threads in new colours. The results are clothes worn as badges of honour. Garments can be upcycled, saved from landfills and made into bespoke expressions of personal grace.

The processes are decorative, a way of celebrating clothes and people. The processes are also ecological, redeeming fabric from landfill. Visible mending can be applied to clothes. It can also be applied to individuals, communities and organisations.

Theologically, visible mending offers new ways of approaching church and mission. It can be tempting to throw out parts of the Christian tradition we think are beyond their use-by date. Yet the Resurrected Jesus has scars. There is a disturbing honesty as he offers Thomas his hands and side in John 20:27. The body of the Resurrected Jesus embodies Matthew 5:17, where Jesus announces: 'Do not think that I have come to abolish the Law or the Prophets; I have not come to abolish them but to fulfil them.' The Greek word *plerosia* can mean three different things in English. It can mean 'end', as in doing away with the Law. It can mean 'obey', as in serving the Law. It can also mean 'complete', as in fulfilling the Law. In this third meaning, Jesus is not doing away with the past. Instead, he is completing it. This makes sense of visible mending, which does not do away with a garment but creatively acts to remake it, often for different uses.

This week, I led the service at the local missional church plant I am involved in. We used *Lectio Divina* to explore John 21. One person pondered the abundance of fish cooking on a fire already lit by Jesus, as described in verse 9. Another person pondered how the disciples were invited in verse 10 to bring the fish they had caught. Together, those gathered asked what it meant for us to be like the disciples, bringing our work to serve a community in which God has already gone ahead of us. Where are the existing charcoal fires, fish and bread already cooking? In this scenario, we are not starting anew. Rather we are visible mending activists, adding the uniqueness of our colour and thread to what already is.

Unravelling

Making at the edges involves unravelling. Artist Lou Baker uses her knitting and stitching skills to make sculptures.[9] On what was then Twitter, she shared a short video of a jersey being unravelled into a ball of wool.[10] Once unravelled, the wool is a site of potential. New garments can be made.

We are part of the world and of a church experiencing enormous unravelling. At the edges, we are invited not to avoid unravelling but to find God amidst it.

In the grace of time, after unravelling comes the potential

to 're-ravel', to let God re-knit our theologies into garments fit for purpose. God is a weaver who invites us to share in remaking.

Through my ministry life I've sought to explore the edges. As a ministry student, I planted a church while training for pastoral ministry. As Senior Pastor, I worked with a team to plant a congregation in order to explore faith with seekers asking questions. As Director of Missiology at the Uniting College for Leadership and Theology, I developed a practitioner track to encourage pioneering. As Principal of Knox Centre for Ministry and Leadership, we implemented Seedlings, working with Presbyteries to develop new forms of Christian witness where candidates for ordination could be formed in mission.

In each of these situations, the work of making involved experiences of unravelling. Two practices were helpful. One practice was gratitude. The emotions around unravelling are valid and real. But those emotions are only one reality. Once, amid conflict with a church council, I found it important to make a list of each of the people there and reflect on the different ways they had blessed me. This helped me to appreciate each person and to find gratitude amid the unravelling of important things in my sense of call and identity. A second practice was to find new ways of reflective journaling. During one unravelling experience, I was journaling in an A5 journal. As I looked back, I realised that my handwriting had become smaller and smaller, tighter and tighter. I reravelled by purchasing a new A4 journal. I turned it 90 degrees to write in another direction. I used paint to provide new 'prompts' for reflection. Journalling in new ways was significant to a reravelling of my sense of call.

Embracing possibilities within limits

Recently I found myself making a manger for a new initiative. My small local church wanted to host a Christmas community worship service to express pastoral care for those in the community who had recently experienced loss. It's a small church with limited resources. Making mangers was not a skill I was taught in training for ministry. However, a search online threw up a video titled, 'Build a Manger In Less Than An Hour With Only An Old Pallet'. I had a wooden pallet I had found on the road a few years ago and a spare evening.

Channelling my inner Joseph, I worked to knock up a manger. The rough finish of the pallet seemed to speak of the humble setting of Jesus' birth. As I worked away, I realised the value of making within limits. The manger could be no larger than the timber I was working with, and the amount I could cut was guided by the nails holding the pallet together. The limits of a found object were a gift. Making in mission involves embracing constraints. Discernment becomes the art of finding God within the local communities we serve.

Side-by-side redeeming as stitches are dropped

My daughter taught me to knit. In 2019, I researched craftivists, people who knitted angels to gift to their communities at Christmas. I was on sabbatical and took the time to explore with my hands and head. I wanted to knit an angel and to research knitters. That required me to learn to knit. You don't learn to knit by reading books or watching YouTube how-to videos. You learn to knit through side-by-side mentoring.

Patiently, my daughter sat beside me. She cast on the first row. Then she held my hands as I made my first stitch. Finally, she patiently watched, full of encouraging noises and offers of repair as I dropped my first stitches.

There is something significant about learning from another and learning by doing. There is a humility in letting others knit the first row and hold our hands as we explore fresh expressions. The edges should not be places of lone endeavour but of side-by-side learning through hands-on experiments.

Making at the edges is full of dropped stitches. There are new skills to learn. What is needed are side-by-side guides. Somehow, those who themselves are at the edges provide the most encouragement. They might not have the answers. Yet they know what it's like to make mistakes, drop stitches and tangle balls of wool.

Theologies of Making

Early in my time in Australia, my supervisor gave me a poem they had written. It described the work of a plumber and the sense of work as craft. The poem resonated with the themes of Ephesians 2:10 and the idea of church as God's workmanship, made in Christ's image to creatively enact God's good purposes. The 'good words' are the church's craft, 'the consequence and outcome of the readers' new life in Christ'.[11] Arriving in Australia, burdened by definitions of theology as 'systematic', I began to see new possibilities in theology as participating in God's making and remaking of all things new (Revelation 21:5). Several theologians encouraged me as I explored making and remaking in theology and ministry practice. Two in particular stood out.

Making in ordinary time

First was the work of Amy Plantinga Pauw, who documents an ordinary times ecclesiology in which God's creative and sustaining grace is a making new and a making do. After writing a theological commentary on Proverbs and Ecclesiastes, Pauw wrote *Church in Ordinary Time*, arguing that ecclesiology had neglected the wisdom tradition.[12]

Creation, as presented in the books of Job, Proverbs and Ecclesiastes, offers distinct ways of thinking about the nature of God's participation in the world.[13] Amy Plantinga Pauw has worked with the Wisdom literature to develop a wisdom ecclesiology.

For Pauw, the Wisdom literature, as distinct from other creation theologies in the Old Testament, provides rich insight into the ambiguity of daily human life and the flourishing of all creation.[14] In ways different to the fall and redemption arc of the Genesis accounts, Job, Proverbs and Ecclesiastes envision a communal way of living in which God's gracious life is revealed in the ordinariness of human life.[15]

Pauw develops a doctrine of creation for ecclesiology in conversation with Jesus as cosmic Wisdom and Mary's child.[16] She crafts four arguments. First, making new in the Christian faith does not claim creation ex nihilo ('out of nothing'). Second, making is provisional and ad hoc because the story of the church is unfolding. 'Living in the shadow cast already by the resurrection, church is able by the power of the Spirit to repent of old sins and risk new patterns of communal life.'[17] Third, our making of theology occurs within creaturely limits. 'The bodily curriculum of the Spirit often proceeds at a slower pace than we would like.'[18] These ideas made sense as I learnt to knit, relying on others to teach me, realising the necessity of individual stitches to craft a whole and seeing my imperfections as markers of uniqueness in time and place rather than signs of failure.

Re-making amid tragedy

Melissa Raphael explored theologies of making in the tragedy of the Holocaust. In *The Female Face of God in Auschwitz*, Raphael explored the redemption of God in Auschwitz. She described the place of knitting in the death camps and how a woman called Sara knitted 'a gift from a worn-out stocking for her husband, still alive at that time in the men's camp'.[19] Raphael suggests that while making might not answer the 'why' of Auschwitz, it offers a 'practical mending of the world'.[20] Sara's making refuses to accept destruction as the only narrative that wins. Hence, Raphael suggests that personal making has theological value. There is a 'long history' of using craft and related terms to minimise making.[21] The acts of making embedded in craft are framed as less than art. Making is belittled as women's work, domestic, old-fashioned and pre-industrial. Raphael's attention to making in the most inhumane and tragic of human contexts dignifies making it as that practical mending of the world.

Pauw and Raphael have written theologically about the value of making for inhabiting the world. In Australia, Indigenous leader Brooke Prentis has acted theologically to weave making and justice.

Making and Aboriginal leader Brooke Prentis

Several years ago, Common Grace, an Australian faith-based organisation focused on social justice, launched a 'Knit for Climate Action' campaign. They invited knitters to make Climate Scarves to highlight 'the need for a bold and credible national plan to tackle the climate crisis'. The CEO of Common Grace was Wakka Wakka woman Brooke Prentis. She described the climate scarf as 'a very visual representation of what's happening each and every day'.[22] Each stripe of the scarf depicted one year in the history of global climate change. The graduation of colour showed the rise in average global temperatures from 1919 to 2019.

More than 600 knitters responded. The scarves were gifted to Senate leaders, MPs and church leaders in the winter of 2021. Scarves have since been gifted to world leaders, including Nicola Sturgeon, then the First Minister of Scotland, and Steven Guilbeault, Canada's Minister of Environment and Climate Change.[23]

Seeking to understand making at the edges, I interviewed knitters to get an insight into their motivations and to explore the theological connections they made as they knitted.[24] In making, these knitters experienced all five Marks of Mission. Making allowed ordinary people, particularly women, to participate in mission as telling, teaching, tending, transforming and treasuring. New ways of relating were evident, including side-by-side, prayerful engagement with local communities. Ordinary people, particularly women, found their voice as they shared their faith with politicians.

Making as a domain of Christian practice rarely features in theological accounts and mission thinking. Yet, in a contemporary culture saturated with words and cynical of deeds, the research has significance for how mission and theology are conceived in contemporary Australia and practised in local church contexts.

Making At the Edges

I thought back to Coorong and Aunty Ellen as I researched with these makers. Weaving invites different ways of relating. Mistakes are greeted with laughter and side-by-side offers of assistance. There is the creative search for new materials: reeds are less accessible now, so we visit Spotlight, Aunty Ellen observed. Making allows different ways of knowing to emerge. There is logic and there is also sensate knowing.

Making is spiritual practice. I knit as part of my Lenten and Advent experience. This involves making and praying using resources from the Facebook page of the Knitters at Victoria Methodist Church in Bristol. I experience embodied and Incarnational ways of being with God in the world. I draw insights from unexpected sources. I journal more carefully, seeking wisdom from my experiences 'within' the edges.

Making is practical ministry. My working with Scripture becomes an act of making. As I begin, I offer my hands to be guided by the Maker. I consider how the biblical text is unravelling me. I wonder what it means for images of God to be placed in side-by-side conversation with the hopes and dreams of my community.

Making is theology. The Maker of Heaven and Earth made, makes and remakes me. I follow a carpenter's son. The Spirit enlivens the processes of making, calling makers like Dorcas and tentmakers like Paul, Priscilla and Aquilla into mission. David Gauntlett, Canada Research Chair at The Creative School in Toronto, describes making as providing a 'sense of being alive with the process and the engagement with ideas, learning and knowledge which come not before or after but *within* the practice of making'.[25] I see the work of God's Spirit in the sense of being alive and the Incarnational pattern of Christ in the call to engage in mission and ministry *within* the practice of making at the edges. I share in the making of God, participating in the Divine work described in Revelation 21 as the making of a new heaven and new earth.

The psalmist tells me that I am wonderfully made. Ministry at the edges requires me to make. Practices of visible mending, unravelling, embracing limits and side-by-side experiential learning offer fresh ways to think about theology at the edges. Theology becomes a craft in community as I explore new ways of inhabiting spiritual practices. I encounter what David Gauntlett described as 'the beating heart of creativity' embedded in the processes of making theology at the edges.[26]

Eucharist

Karyl Davison

While trawling through a second-hand bookshop about fifteen years ago, I came across a little book by J.B. Phillips called *Your God is Too Small*. First published in 1952, it explores how we might find a God large enough to account for our current experience of life. Phillips also points to the spirit of 'churchiness' that pervades the church and that has captured, tamed and trained God to our own liking.[1] Phillips' observation confirmed my growing sense that our emphasis, both in practice and theology, needed to shift from a church-centred view to one that understood that *all* are the people of God and that prioritised participation in God's mission over church tradition. Over time, this shift led me to ask how the Lord's supper, through which participants might experience the presence of Christ, could be freed from the church's control and be used in missional settings. How did I get there? Let me share a bit of my journey.

More than just a meal

> On their return the apostles told Jesus all they had done. He took them with him and withdrew privately to a city called Bethsaida. When the crowds found out about it, they followed him; and he welcomed them, and spoke to them about the kingdom of God, and healed those who needed to be cured.
>
> The day was drawing to a close, and the twelve came to him and said, "Send the crowd away, so that they may go into the surrounding villages and countryside, to lodge and get provisions; for we are here in a deserted place". But he said to them, "You give them something to eat". They said, "We have no more than five loaves and two fish – unless we are to go and buy food for all these people". For there were about five thousand men. And he said to his disciples, "Make them sit down in groups of about fifty each". They did so and made them all sit down. And taking the five loaves and the two fish, he looked up to heaven, and blessed and broke them, and gave them to the disciples to set before the crowd. And all ate and were filled. What was left over was gathered up, twelve baskets of broken pieces. (Luke 9:10-17, NRSV)

There was a time when I thought this was a great story about a meal in which Jesus' ability to perform miracles was demonstrated. The power to perform miracles was the focus of the story rather than the meal itself. Now, after almost fifteen years working in the fresh expression space, I look at theology and practice not from the perspective of the church, but from the perspective of those on the margins of the church or those who have no connection to the church at all.[2] As a result, the focus of this story is no longer Jesus' power, but the meal itself – a eucharistic meal.

I have been an active member of the Uniting Church in Australia since its inception in 1977, and I spent much of that time in a relatively conservative congregation where, while I was encouraged to grow as a leader, I was not really encouraged to question my faith or grow theologically. That changed when I started working for the church in the area of lay Christian education and began theological studies so that I would know what I was talking about. It was life-changing. My faith came alive as I studied the Scriptures and the theology of the church, in particular the theology of the reformed tradition. The freedom to question aspects of the faith I had grown up with was intoxicating and life-giving. Feminist and liberation theologies further expanded and deepened my faith and eventually led me to question traditional interpretations of Scripture and church tradition. During the same period, I had many conversations with a colleague whose role was to encourage congregations to think and act missionally and who had previously worked with three congregations in setting up a café through which mission occurred.[3]

In late 2011, I was offered the opportunity to head up a fresh expression of church in the Wellington Regional Mission (WRM) of the Uniting Church in Western Australia. In seeking a minister, the WRM stated they were not looking to form a church in the way church has traditionally been practiced and understood, but instead were looking for a more flexible and open expression of church.[4] Their vision for what became the Eaton/Millbridge Community Project (Project) corresponded with my own conviction that if the Christian church genuinely wanted to share God's good news in the wider community in 21st century Australia, it needed to venture beyond traditional forms and get out into the communities in which we live, work and play.

And so the Project began by holding events for people in our local residential community, most often in the local parks. The first event was an Easter Egg Hunt. Our primary aims were to get people out of their houses, to meet their neighbours, to start making connections with us and one other and to experience some generous (incarnational) hospitality. Whilst providing an opportunity to gather as community and make neighbourly connections were of themselves important aims, I believed that hospitality was doubly significant because its practice conveys the gospel of Jesus.

Because the Project did not reflect the traditional forms of church, I was often asked, 'But is it church?' by people from outside the WRM. My 2014 paper 'But is it church?' addressed this question, concluding that yes, the Project was church.[5] In practicing incarnational mission, we didn't gather in a church building for worship, but understood worship as an everyday posture of faithful presence in our community. Instead of dispensing God's presence through a particular form of words or acts, we saw ourselves as a sacrament through which we offered a glimpse of God's realm in the communities of Eaton and Millbridge. Through studying the Scriptures from the edges, we came to understand that we were practicing the Lord's supper.

One of the key features of the Project was that at every community event we served food and drink free of charge – sometimes a sausage sandwich and soft drink, sometimes cupcakes and coffee. Our reasons for this hospitality, initially, were that it reflected the biblical injunction of hospitality, allowed us to demonstrate the values of Christ and showed that hospitality doesn't need to have strings attached. Over time I realised that these celebrations echoed Jesus' feeding of the multitude and, importantly, had the potential for transformation just as participating in the Lord's supper in its traditional setting does.

I began to wonder why, if the church truly believed that Jesus is made present in the eucharist, it is not used as a tool for mission, to awaken faith. That led me to ask why the church restricts participation in the eucharist to those already baptised. As a result of such questioning, together with a conviction that the church must share the gospel in fresh ways in our context, I began to see that serving food and drink at Project gatherings was itself a celebration of the Lord's supper, open to all.

Theology from the margins

At the heart of my claim for a radically inclusive communion table is the sense that for centuries the church has actively silenced and excluded voices from the margins. At different times, young people, women, people of colour and queer people have been silenced, as have those who are theologically unorthodox and those who have not been baptised. And for all the church's soul-searching as it tries to stem the decline in attendance, the church's own research rarely focuses on hearing from those who have either left the church or have never been part of it. While in socio-economic terms such people – like those who turned up at Project events – may not be considered marginalised, I would argue they are marginalised from the church's perspective. And so I began to critique the church's eucharistic theology and practice from the perspective of those on the margins of the church.

Eating and drinking in church

Scholars generally agree that by the second century the norm for eucharistic practice was that only those who had been baptised could be admitted to the Lord's supper. This norm has been generally supported by two interpretations of the sacraments: the objective reality of God's grace in and through the sacraments; and the importance of our faith response, which holds that the sacraments are only efficacious when they are received by faith. Where once I accepted this tension without question, I was forced to wrestle with what that tension meant for fresh expressions of church.

A look at the history of eucharistic theology and practice reveals some surprising variations of eucharistic boundaries that cannot be ignored. The Didache states, 'But let no one eat or drink of your Eucharist, unless they have been baptised into the name of the Lord'. Yet, as McGowan has observed, the very existence of this instruction indicates that some first-century Christian communities were giving communion to those who were not yet baptised.[6]

History also shows that there has been, and continues to be, diversity in understanding and practice of the Lord's supper.[7] Practices have changed over time, sometimes serendipitously, produced in a moment then going on to become unquestioned tradition, while others have slipped into obscurity due to misunderstanding or neglect. The very fact that aspects of eucharistic practice and theology in the church have been mired by controversy and inconsistency means claims of unchanging eucharistic practice since its so-called institution is nonsense.

The theological position on the eucharist I have come to is based on my understanding of Jesus as revealed in the gospels and experienced at Eaton/Millbridge Community Project events. Jesus consistently practiced the radical grace of God, most clearly demonstrated in his radically inclusive table practice. What else do the Scriptures reveal that might help us discern who may participate in the Lord's supper?

The biblical tradition

According to biblical tradition, the Lord's supper was instituted by Jesus during his last meal with his disciples. It is this meal theologians have traditionally focused on in developing their eucharistic theology.

The earliest account of this meal is found in Paul's first letter to the Corinthian church (1 Corinthians 11:23–26). Paul does not discuss the guest list at the meal. Rather, his purpose is to challenge the behaviour of the Corinthian Christians and to correct abuses that had emerged in their celebration of the communal meal.

The Synoptic Gospels identify Jesus' companions at his final meal as either the twelve or the apostles (Matthew 26:26–29, Mark 14:22–25, Luke 22:14–23), leading the church to insist that it was only Jesus' twelve male disciples, albeit fallible ones, present. But has reliance on a literal reading of this single meal distorted the intent of Jesus' ministry, and can we be confident that the New Testament's portrayal of the guest list is complete?

As I looked at the Scriptures from the context of the Eaton/Millbridge Community Project, I found other possibilities.

Eating and drinking the Gospels

The gospel narratives reveal that Jesus' most consistent social action was eating with those who were marginalised from the political and religious system of his day. Jesus' willingness to eat with all the wrong sorts of people was one of the things that shocked his contemporaries, raised the ire of religious authorities and ultimately contributed to his death. The table was, for Jesus, a sign of God's kingdom where all were welcome, even outsiders and those regarded as sinners or unclean, in sharp contrast to the meal practice of the religious elite who maintained rigid exclusion based on ritual purity.[8] Jesus welcomed those who could not, or did not, meet Pharisaic codes. In eating with those regarded as sinners, Jesus effectively practiced communion first, conversion second. In a world in which those considered sinners were condemned, Jesus' openness and inclusivity was irresistible to people on the margins. By placing limits on who may participate in the Lord's supper, I wonder if the church is excluding the very people with whom Jesus consistently shared the table.

As mentioned earlier, part of the reason for this distorted eucharistic theology and practice, with its emphasis on purity and exclusion, is the singular focus on the last supper as it is presented in traditional theology. Yet the last supper cannot be understood without reference to the meal ministry of Jesus that preceded it. Privileging the last supper over all other meals limits our understanding of both, and results in the impression that Jesus' last meal was distinctly different from all other meals. In contrast, when we view Jesus' meal practice as a whole, it leads to a greater understanding of Jesus' meal ministry, deepens our experience of the eucharist and encourages a more expansive and inclusive eucharistic practice and theology.

Jesus' radically inclusive meal practice is reported in all four canonical gospels (Matthew 22:1–14, Mark 6:30–44, Luke 5:29–33, John 12:1–8). Again and again, both in parable and practice, Jesus' welcome to the table, whether he was host or guest, is shown as being dependent on little more than a willingness to show up. Gospel narratives reveal that Jesus ate with all sorts of marginalised people: rejects of society and religion, people who were hungry, tax collectors and people who were regarded as sinners, as well as often hostile religious leaders and his own all-too-fallible disciples. Take, for instance, the parable of the wedding banquet in Matthew. When invited guests failed to attend, the king ordered his slaves to go into the streets and invite everyone they found to the banquet. They gathered, both good and bad, until the wedding hall was filled with guests (Matthew 22:9–10). This story posed a threat to the status quo of Jesus' time and calls the exclusionary practice of the church today into question.

But more than any other example of Jesus' meal ministry, his feeding of the multitude challenges us to question the church's exclusionary eucharistic theology and practice. The story is told in all four canonical gospels and is infused with eucharistic images. In Luke, the feeding narrative follows the twelve disciples' return from the missionary journeys Jesus has sent them on. Prior to their journey, Jesus told them that they were to take nothing on their journey, relying instead on God's providence and the hospitality of those among whom they would minister to sustain them. On their return, Jesus with the disciples slipped away to Bethsaida, but the crowds followed them (Luke 9:10). As the day was ending, the twelve asked Jesus to send the crowd away to find places to stay and food to eat. Instead, Jesus welcomed the crowd and challenged the disciples to give the gathered people something to eat (Luke 9:13).

Looking at this story from the margins, there are a number of aspects that stand against the church's eucharistic tradition. Firstly, this story is a visual or enacted parable that points to God's kingdom. It could well begin, as so many of Jesus' parables do, 'The kingdom of God is like a great picnic where everyone is included, and where Jesus takes five loaves and two fish and feeds thousands of people with heaps leftover'. Radical inclusivity is a key feature, in contrast to the exclusivity of the meal practiced in the church.

Second, the miraculous feeding prefigures the last supper both in the eucharistic language used and the way the story is told. It draws our attention to the last supper and points to the great banquet Jesus promised would occur when the world was reconciled with God. The gospel writers uniformly use four verbs to describe Jesus' actions: took, bless, broke, gave (Matthew 26:26–29). Those same verbs are used in all the gospel accounts of miraculous feedings, as well as in the last supper and Jesus' resurrection appearance on the Emmaus road. I believe the gospel writers deliberately linked this miraculous feeding story to accounts of the last supper, seeing both in much the same way. They are part of the long trajectory of the sacrament we call the Lord's supper.

The third aspect of the feeding narratives is its setting. While the particular location differs slightly between the gospels, in each case the meal occurs outdoors, not in a place of worship. To state the obvious, the last supper did not occur in a place of worship either.

The fourth aspect is who participates in this meal. Each gospel narrative refers to those gathered as 'a crowd'. Nowhere are they described as disciples or followers, yet no barriers are placed on their inclusion in this meal. There is no mention of anyone 'accepting' Jesus or being baptised. People were simply hungry, and Jesus fed them.

A final aspect is that this story, using the same four-fold pattern of take, bless, break and give, occurs six times in the New Testament, double that of the bread and wine ritual at Jesus' last meal. These multiple attestations are significant, suggesting that the story held great importance for those recalling the Jesus story.

These aspects led me to ask: why, if all of Jesus' other meals described in the gospels were shockingly inclusive, would his last meal be attended only by the twelve? Is it possible that centuries of exclusionary sacramental theology have been based on biblical silence rather than evidence? In a stunning example of radical hospitality, unlike the smaller group seemingly present at the last supper, when Jesus feeds the multitude some five thousand men plus women and children are fed, without regard to religious or any other status. Even those on the margins of religion and society were included, leaving us with the clear message - this miraculous meal is a far more compelling sign of the gospel than the church's closed table practice of the eucharist.

The Scriptures, when viewed in this light, support a move towards a radically inclusive participation in the Lord's supper.

From the margins to the church and back again

When the eucharist is experienced by outsiders, the result can be transformative. In her book, *Take this Bread*, Sara Miles describes how despite being indifferent to religion, she found herself walking into a church and receiving communion. 'In that shocking moment of communion, filled with a deep desire to reach for and become part of a body, I realised that what I'd been doing with my life all along was what I was meant to do: feed people.'[9] To her great astonishment the experience led her to faith and to the church, and she went on to become a priest at St Gregory of Nyssa Episcopal Church in San Francisco and start nearly a dozen food pantries in the poorest parts of the city.

Two experiences of the eucharist described by systematic theologian Jurgen Moltmann changed his understanding of the table. The first was among a group of people who had been participating in an anti-Vietnam War rally together. Moltmann writes how, sitting on the floor of an office, 'bread and wine passed from hand to hand in a small circle, and we felt the bodily presence of Jesus among us'.[10] A short time later he was at St Giles Church in Edinburgh where the eucharist was shared with those who had stayed behind after the sermon. Scattered here and there in the great church, Moltmann reflected that he felt no sense of community and left the church feeling depressed. He later stated that Jesus' supper is the feast of the crucified Christ whose hands are stretched out to everyone, inclusive of all, and that any attempt by the church to limit the openness of Christ's invitation to the table would be turning the Lord's supper into the Church's supper, thus spoiling the evangelical character of the meal.[11] Because Christ's invitation is prevenient and unconditional, the table must not be restricted to people who are 'faithful to the church' or to the 'inner circle' of the community. Rather, it is an invitation that reaches beyond the frontiers of Christianity to the whole world.

The contrast of Moltmann's two eucharistic experiences

echo my own contrasting experiences of the Lord's supper in the inherited church and in the park with the Eaton/Millbridge community. Far too often, participating in the eucharist in Sunday worship feels like 'going through the motions', something we do, the words repeated by rote. In contrast, eating and drinking at Eaton/Millbridge Community Project events were joyous and vibrant experiences of sharing in community and grace as we played, ate and drank together in the park.

The Uniting Church in Australia commits itself to keep all areas of its life under constant review for the sake of mission in the world. Empowered by this commitment, I will now set down my eucharistic theology.

My missional eucharistic theology

My theology is built on seven foundational assumptions. First, all human beings are created in God's image and likeness and are therefore God's people. This is in contrast to the notion that only those who are baptised into the Christian church are people of God. Second, both the Old and New Testaments exhort us to show hospitality, to both friend and stranger in our midst, as a hallmark of the kingdom community Jesus proclaimed. Surely the eucharist is the ultimate expression of hospitality in the life of the church. Third, the church exists not for its own purposes but for the sake of God's mission in the world, to bring about God's kingdom, proclaimed and embodied by Jesus. My fourth assumption is that the eucharist is a tangible enactment of the gospel in which Christ is made present. Fifth, Jesus died for all human beings without distinction. Sixth, the eucharist is a gift of grace, not earned but undeserved and freely given. Finally, the meal is made efficacious through the power of God's Spirit, which is not under the church's control.

With these theological assumptions in mind, together with my re-reading of the gospels, and encouraged by the Uniting Church's emphasis on reform and renewal for the sake of God's mission in the world, I found it difficult to justify the exclusion of anyone from the eucharistic table. For me, the Lord's supper can be *both* the meal that feeds Christ's baptised people for mission in the world *and* a tool for mission. Welcoming people who are not baptised into the meal of Jesus gives it an evangelical edge and seems to be an obvious move. With the help of God's Spirit, those who are fed might just meet Jesus and be transformed, and I believe that for the church to do otherwise amounts to a denial of the gospel.

My eucharistic theology can be summed up by Shirley Murray's communion hymn, the first verse of which reads:

> For ev'ryone born, a place at the table,
> for ev'ryone born, clean water and bread,
> a shelter, a space, a safe place for growing,
> for ev'ryone born, a star overhead.
> And God will delight when we are creators
> of justice and joy, compassion and peace:
> yes, God will delight when we are creators
> of justice, justice and joy.[12]

Murray's hymn reflects the vision of the church I believe God calls us to – a place that reflects God's kingdom, a place where *all* God's children may eat and drink together and meet the Christ.

It is this Christ we meet in the gospel stories. They reveal that Jesus' most consistent social action was eating with those who were marginalised from the political and religious system of his day. Jesus' willingness to eat with all the wrong sorts of people was one of the things that shocked his contemporaries, raised the ire of religious authorities and ultimately contributed to his death. In a world in which 'sinners' were condemned, Jesus' openness and inclusivity were irresistible to those on the margins. By placing limits on who may participate in the Lord's supper, is the church not excluding the very people with whom Jesus consistently shared the table?

Rachel Held Evans once said, 'God has a really bad habit of using people we don't approve of.'[13] Perhaps we could put it this way: God has a really bad habit of *including* people we don't approve of. Or as Darrell Guder puts it, 'When our table is less than the fullness of Christ's invitation, we eat and drink to our judgement.'[14] Welcoming people who are not baptised into the meal of Jesus gives it an evangelical edge and seems to be an obvious move if we are serious about participating in God's mission in the world. With the help of God's Spirit, they might just meet Jesus. To do otherwise amounts to a denial of the gospel.

Evangelism

Karina Kreminski

A beautiful awareness of God

When I was a little girl, I had the most beautiful awareness of God. I found God in nature, through my daily journalling and as I read stories – mostly fantasy and fairytales that ensconced me in wonder and mystery. I found God in rainy days as I sat by the window watching puddles form in our garden, and in the exuberance of our out-of-control Jack Russell. I wondered about who I was and why I was me and not someone else and what it would be like to be someone else. I made secret cubby holes inside and outside the house where I spoke to little critters and plants, and I knew that I was not alone. I sat in those cubby holes whenever I was sad or fearful and felt safe as I 'spoke' with that inner 'still small voice' that always sounded compassionate and kind. I had the most beautiful awareness of something that was greater, beyond me, and watching me with love.

I was also raised in a family that was religiously devout. We went to church – the Evangelical brand – every week. We participated in church events – choir, youth groups, progressive dinners, regressive dinners, fetes, festivals and conferences. I liked church – mostly. The music was sometimes so joyous and heavenly I wanted to cry. The stillness that happened during prayer gave me space to reflect and retreat inwards to find solace. These activities were a way for us to build connection and community as immigrants who longed for a home in the new land we had come to. But there were also rules in the church – explicit and implicit. The rules were about behaviour and what was seen as right and wrong. There was a connection in the church between appropriate behaviour and pleasing and finding acceptance from God. Some of it made sense to me but a lot of the time there was a dissonance between what I experienced in the garden, in my cubby hole, in my day-to-day life, and the message the church was communicating about God.

So I sometimes found God in church; but not always. And sometimes I found the antithesis of God there.

I also attended a Christian high school. Today it might be branded Fundamentalist but back then it simply seemed to me an extension of church – lots of rules that were attached to either pleasing God or falling out of favour with God. Lots of talk about sinning. Yet I found many moments of what I would now call grace there. Sometimes those moments came in doctrine classes. Other times grace came through our art teacher who was probably flying under the radar when she read to us from *Jonathan Livingston Seagull* for 'devotions' in the mornings. I'd catch the whispers of God's voice then.

At some stage quite early on in high school an evangelical tract fell into my hands. In the starkness of black and white visuals, it graphically depicted how lost humanity was and that the only way to find our way back home to God was to repent of our sins and accept Jesus as Lord and Saviour of the universe. I didn't particularly feel sinful, but being taught about sin through the church made me question my thinking and behaviour – enough to make me feel as though there *must* be something wrong with me. My innate lack of self-worth as a young person fused itself with this theology that claims we are depraved. It convinced me that I must be a sinner in need of repentance. Anyone who did not repent, the tract said, would be condemned to hell – a literal place of eternal fiery torment. I remember how utterly scared I was reading this, yet it seemed so authoritative and in line with what I was hearing at church and school. This must be what God is like, I thought. So I did the only reasonable thing a young person could do in such circumstances and got down on my knees, repented, gave my life to Jesus and ultimately became an evangeliser of this message. I remember a few of us at school getting our hands on dozens of these tracts and leaving them around cafés, shopping centres, public toilets and parks, praying they would find their way to the right people for their salvation.

This is how my view of evangelism and God were formed over many years. Even when I went to theological college much later in life and my faith became a little more nuanced and sophisticated, at its core it was still about believing in a God who wanted our obedience through correct behaviour. This included signing up to being devoted to the community of the faithful – the church – who would boldly share this message of the two ways to live: with God through Jesus or an eternity in hell.

A reductionistic theology

This view and practice of evangelism was undergirded by a particular theology. As I reflect on and interrogate this theological framework that shaped me, a few characteristics emerge.

The theology of the evangelism I believed and practiced when I was growing up, and even later when I was at theological college, was disembodied. The focus was on saving people's souls; the body and creation were marginalised. As long as people 'gave their lives to Jesus', their bodies didn't matter so much because they would be secondary in the new world ushered in at Christ's return. The care of creation was sidelined for the same reason – the new earth was coming. If our present world was destroyed through nuclear war or climate change, for instance, we could always rest our hope in the fact that another would appear. So life was separated between the spiritual on the one hand and the material or secular on the other – a view more in line with gnostic dualism than true Christianity.

Roger Helland and Leonard Hjalmarson, in their book *Missional Spirituality*, write about this separation of the spiritual and secular:

> Christians today regularly refer to their culture as the secular world. It's where one holds a secular job, attends a secular university, listens to secular music and watches secular movies and TV. Even though all cultures express religion and spirituality in one form or another, the so-called secular world is often wrongly perceived as a separate realm disenchanted from the sacred realm where the God way up there and Christian

faith reside. Some Christians place culture in one realm and place the institutional church, Christian faith and their personal spiritual life in another realm.[1]

Similarly, Paula Gooder, writing about the marginalisation of creation in Christian doctrine, notes:

> For many years ... Christians have displayed an ambivalence to creation and the environmental disaster that is approaching with ever-growing rapidity. This ambivalence emerges at least in part, out of an emphasis on the "good" of the spiritual to the exclusion of the physical. If we believe that our ultimate fate is a spiritual existence in heaven with God and that the physical world is coming to an end then it is much harder to feel motivated to act for the good of the planet.[2]

The view of evangelism I grew up with was also reductionistic. It simplified access to God, reducing connection to God to a formula and eliminating other perspectives that could enrich faith. This had its advantages in that it provided assurance of a relationship with God, but it led to a simplistic faith and potentially an arrogance that claimed the only way to God was the one prescribed way – that truth could only be found through this path and that other paths were not true at all. Theologian Barbara Brown Taylor wrestles with the Christian's relationship with other faiths in her book *Holy Envy*:

> The first time I heard the phrase "holy envy" I knew it was an improvement over the plain old envy I felt while

studying other faiths. When the Jewish Sabbath came up in class, I wanted it. Why did Christians ever let it go? When we watched a film of the God-intoxicated Sufis spinning, I wanted that too. The best my tradition could offer me during worship was kneeling to pray and standing to sing. My spiritual covetousness extended to the inclusiveness of Hinduism, the nonviolence of Buddhism, the prayer life of Islam, and the sacred debate of Judaism.[3]

Taylor's 'holy envy' of these other forms of religion emerged because her tradition of Christianity claimed that these other religions were devoid of truth and were even branded as 'evil'. Instead of finding truths within these religions, her tradition told her they were godless.

Along with this reductionism that preached Christianity as having a monopoly on truth, there was the conviction that to believe otherwise led to a falling away from God and to eternal punishment. Terms like 'backslider' or 'falling away from the faith' were used to keep the faithful believing in the one way to God. Followers felt fear and so stayed on the 'narrow' road to avoid the 'wide road that was easy'. Sadly, this was a punitive gospel – not a gospel of good news. In my book *Urban Spirituality*, I quote from Scot McKnight's book, *The King Jesus Gospel*, where he shares the experience of such a 'gospel' experienced by his student 'Craig'. Craig shares:

At its heart, I have to say that I was raised by the gospel of fear. ... Growing up as a child I was given basic ideas; you're a sinner. We need you to be with Jesus. And he saves us from hell. ... We always talked about how we are sinners and are drifting away from God and need to come to him before he "has" to send us to hell.[4]

I added:

> This indeed is a very punitive way to view the gospel that focuses on salvation but doesn't mention the broader context and good news of the gospel. When I think about my understanding of the gospel as a new Christian, this is what seemed to be missing, that is, a broader story or context that helped place my faith in the present and ground me in the unfolding story of our world as well as my role in it.[5]

Finally, the evangelism I grew up with seemed to view people as targets. There was always a sense of a hidden agenda in approaching people – it was not purely about friendship; the point was to make friends with people to get them saved and into church. This made followers feel pressured to try to save as many souls as possible, out of fear for their eternal destiny. This pressure sometimes led to comical practices like walking up to strangers in shopping centres and asking them if they wanted to be saved. But other times it could have disastrous consequences, as in the case of the missionary John Allen Chau who went to the Sentinelese. Chau was no novice; he was taught to believe and to practice the same type of evangelism I grew with. This led him to go to these isolated people who had never heard the gospel and attempt to preach to them. He died doing this, but more importantly he disrespected the wishes of the Sentinelese and potentially put their lives at risk with introduced diseases. An article about his story commented:

Chau's decision to contact the Sentinelese, who have made it clear over the years that they prefer to be left alone, was indefensibly reckless. But it was not a spontaneous act of recklessness by a dim-witted thrill-seeker; it was a premeditated act of recklessness by a fairly intelligent and thoughtful thrill-seeker who spent years preparing, understood the risks, including to his own life, and believed his purpose on Earth was to bring Christ to the island he considered "Satan's last stronghold".[6]

In the faith I previously held, Chau's actions and subsequent death would have been glorified as martyrdom for the sake of the gospel. Today I call it unnecessary and sad.

Moving into the neighbourhood: A transformation

In midlife I moved into an inner-city neighbourhood to 'plant a church'. I did a church planters' assessment and was assigned a coach by the denomination. I left my role as minister in a church in the suburbs, slightly burnt out and perplexed about what I felt was an inward focus in most churches. I felt as though over the decades the church had slowly become oriented towards itself and was therefore in danger of becoming redundant. This contrasted to the actual purpose of the church, at least according to the Chrisitan Scriptures, which is to be missional. The word 'missional' has been used for many decades now and has been contentious. For many it carries connotations of the reductive churched faith I grew up with – a way of sharing faith that is disembodied, truncated, punishment-based, self-righteous, unreciprocated and pressurised.[7] However, for me, missional simply means to orient the church outwards rather than being internally focused. It means the church prioritising the external community above itself, in the way that God prioritised the world and came (and continues to come) to us. In that sense you could say I have a low ecclesiology because the church for me is relative or marginal to the most important thing – God and God's relationship with the world.

When I moved into the neighbourhood, I envisioned starting up a church with a team and expected that people would be drawn to it. At the back of my mind I still had a reductionistic theology around evangelism. While I felt uncomfortable with this practice of evangelism, I didn't want to compromise being what I thought was a faithful Christian. It was how I was formed in church, school and theological college. Also, this way of faith felt neat and tidy, and my tendency towards finding comfort within certainty rather than embracing the messiness of life was satisfied by this clear-cut kind of theology.

However, that kind of thinking didn't last very long. Quite soon after moving into the neighbourhood and with no church emerging, I heard a very quiet small voice saying to me, 'Just love the community.' So, with nothing else to do, I did that. I showed up to community events, engaged with the local Neighbourhood Centre and hung out in all the places where our community gathered. I focused on getting to know my community and loving it. I ran workshops that centred around spirituality, meaning of life issues and faith, but without proselytising or focusing on Christianity. I was surprised when I realised I was enjoying myself. And the more I thought about it, the more I realised that at the back of my mind I was being reminded of something: that beautiful awareness of God all around me that I had had as a child, an awareness that was without hard and fast rules, behaviour correction, moralising or pressure. I began to see my whole neighbourhood as my 'church'. The church, in the sense of the gathered people of God, became one part of the ecology of the whole neighbourhood, working together for the flourishing of the community. Eventually my husband and I started up a gathering in our home. This gathering welcomes all people – Christian or not. We share food together and talk about matters of life, faith, spirituality and meaning. For us this is what a gathering or 'church' is – an open space where all are welcome.

Someone asked me recently about my shift in theology. They commented on how much I had changed regarding what I believe about God and faith. I told them that lots of things contributed to this shift – this process of deconstruction and re-emergence. However, a key factor was my experience of engaging in the neighbourhood – listening, loving and 'doing church' differently in my local context. This experience has shaped what I now believe and how I practice my faith. It's why, as difficult as the word 'missional' can be for some, I think there are helpful perspectives that can emerge when we see things through a missiological lens – that is, when we approach the world around us with an outward focus rather than inward focus. We learn to embody and share our mission – our values and purpose – contextually and authentically.

Shifts in my theology

When my focus shifted from starting a church in my neighbourhood to simply loving the people and place where I lived, I started seeing God at work outside the church. God was at work in my neighbourhood, not only in and through the church, but in and through a range of different people and groups. I started to see that God was bigger than the church and even bigger than the traditions and practices of my faith. I resonated with theologian Diana Butler Bass who, in her book *Freeing Jesus*, writes about her journey away from a stringent evangelicalism towards a more expansive faith. She writes about a time that a lecturer shared a Celtic poem in class and then said, 'This is the Celtic way. Everything is holy, every moment, everything and everyone. Christ came to reveal the sacredness of all things, to make clear what was hidden, the Light of the world.'[8] I too began to see things the 'Celtic way', viewing nature as expressive of the presence of God and my neighbourhood as a sacred rather than a 'secular' space. I no longer believed there were any secular spaces.

Along with this, I developed a theology of place, as I was beginning to see that place matters to God. God is restoring all things, not just saving souls. The Good News is good news for creation, too. I began to believe that working for the good of the neighbourhood is also a form of evangelism or mission. Walter Brueggemann writes beautifully about the importance of place:

> Place is space that has historical meanings, where some things have happened that are now remembered and that provide continuity and identity across generations. Place is space in which important words have been spoken that have established identity, defined vocation and envisioned destiny. Place is space in which vows have been exchanged, promised have been made and demands have been issued. Place is indeed a protest against the compromising pursuit of space. It is a declaration that our humanness cannot be found in

escape, detachment, absence of commitment and undefined freedom.[9]

I now see God present and moving in places – especially in neighbourhoods. The more I ground myself where I live, the more I develop relationships as I live out the values of God, the more it becomes a place where I see God at work, restoring all things that are broken. As mentioned earlier, church has become for me one part of the ecology of the neighbourhood. It is an important part, but one that must partner with people of all faiths and none – 'people of peace' (Luke 10:5-7, paraphrased) who have a desire to help the neighbourhood flourish. As Letty Russell writes, the church is a 'P.S. on God's love affair with the world'.[10] Evangelism, then, is about more than saving people's souls; it is about embodied engagement with and a grounding in our world.

Mutual transformation is something I inherently value now. I believe truth can be found in many places and that 'mission in reverse' is possible. We see many examples of this in the Christian and Jewish Scriptures. The example I love the most is that of the prophet Jonah in the Jewish Scriptures. You could say that the prophet was 'evangelised' by 'heathen' sailors on a boat that was about to capsize in a storm. They made an offering to Jonah's God on his behalf, since Jonah was running away from God! This story has convinced me of the mystery of God's ways rather than over-emphasising the certainties of faith. Evangelism means listening carefully to where I can hear God's voice, knowing that it might come from the most unlikely of persons and situations. It means trusting that God is at work in people's lives well before I show up.

Instead of a fear-based interaction with God and God's

world, I now engage with God and people with joy. I try to listen to people's stories and engage in authentic relationship with no agenda. There is an element of genuine conversation that emerges when I speak with people about faith, God and Jesus. We are searching together, knowing that we can learn from each other. Instead of proselytising, I simply share my faith when appropriate. God is still as magical to me as God was when I was that little girl in the garden and my hope is that people can be drawn to that God in me and in our world. I have stopped seeing people as targets – to get them into heaven or church – and now see myself as working *with* the community rather than *for* the community. We are in partnership together. In *Crossing Thresholds*, the authors write about the importance of authenticity in evangelism today: 'The activity of the church in mission will, therefore, not be focused on persuading new members to join per se ... but rather on creating relationships which participate in God's missionary love for the world.'[11] As a result of these shifts, I have changed my view and practice of evangelism to one that I believe is not reductionistic but rather expansive and inclusive.

Deconstructing evangelism?

As I reflect on the words I have written, I am left with a question: Should we still use the word 'evangelism'? I've had lots of conversations with people about this. Some people feel we should not use the word because it has negative connotations. It seems to imply the worst of our Christian faith – colonising, imperialistic, pressured, reductionistic, imposing. Unfortunately, we are in many ways shaped by the mistakes of the past and we carry them with us. But I was reminded by one of my students – a Pasifika woman who knows all about colonisation – that it might be more courageous to own the mistakes of the past than to try to hide from them. I resonated with her comment. We hide from the past when we change words and names to become something new and try to shake off the shackles that make us look guilty. But we always carry the past with us; it's unavoidable. Might it not be better, then, to carry those wounds that humbly remind us of what we are continually tempted to become if we are not watchful? I can also see the other side of the argument that invites us to courageously get rid of the old, reclaim the new and move forward – and never use the word 'evangelism' again. However, at the time of writing this chapter I sit in the former camp – using the word but qualifying it. I have been using the term 'soft evangelism', because I think it resonates with a culture today that is looking to walk more softly and gently on the earth.

What does this soft evangelism look like? Mostly it stems from my experience of doing church differently in my neighbourhood – non-proselytising, mutual, relational and joyful rather than fear-driven and punitive. A soft evangelism wrestles with the ethics of evangelism: What does it mean to share our faith appropriately? When is it inappropriate to share our faith? How do we share our faith without any agenda? How do we avoid the bait and switch of 'friendship evangelism'? As missiologist Leslie Newbigin asserts, we need to see evangelism as a joy, not as a 'mandate', which is militaristic fear-based talk.[12] In an age in the West where more people than ever are open to spirituality, I believe soft evangelism is needed as an approach to sharing our faith.[13]

We need denominations and churches to support us in this journey that is sometimes unhelpfully called 'deconstruction'.

Our journey is taking us to new places, new theologies and even new *Christianities* as we engage with our communities on the ground. We need to talk together about what is important to keep in our tradition and what needs to be jettisoned as irrelevant, reductive or unhealthy – the things that lead us into fear-based religion and the squashing of the childlike faith we may once have enjoyed. Certainly, re-imagining our faith, church and theology is our hope in these turbulent times.

Coda: Shifting perspectives of evangelism - a testimony
Pianissimo

Before my view on evangelism shifted, when I was still operating from a paradigm of fear, I encountered God in a mystical way that changed me forever. I was sitting in the food hall of a shopping centre in Sydney – the last place you'd expect to encounter God – and watching people buzz past me: couples window shopping; screaming kids latching onto their mothers, asking for the latest toys; bored husbands waiting for their wives to finish and go home; a posse of heavily made-up young women moving *en mass*, flicking their hair. And as I was sitting there, not thinking about God at all, I had a picture of me trying to reach up to God and, every time I did so, failing. Occasionally I would almost make it, getting closer to God because of a 'good' deed I had done. Other times I was thrust all the way down to the ground because of some 'bad' thing I had done – a rule I had broken. But then I saw God clearly reaching down to me and giving me a gift. I could not reach God; God had to reach me. And I took the gift – whatever it was. I glanced around me; people still looked the same, but I was very different. I was transformed from one who tried to catch God's favour to one who had freely received it. Fear evaporated and love gushed in. I have often wondered if this was the first step towards my shift in theology and evangelism that occurred much later. And now that I think about it, as I write this story, perhaps it was. That encounter convinced me that God is love; that there is a good God who eagerly initiates by reaching out to us and inviting us to participate in that love.

Conclusion / Threads

Creative work takes time. *Anchor Me* (2025), a recent documentary about New Zealand musician Don McGlashan, illuminated the demands of making music. Great music seldom falls from the sky. Rather, songs are crafted over time, through paying attention to life and persisting in struggle. *Anchor Me* captured McGlashan's daily practice of jotting down ideas and questions in journals. Footage revealed the importance of leisure in allowing the subconscious to rest and recreate. McGlashan spoke of waiting years for a single line to capture an experience and of the importance of work and exercise in allowing lyrical complexity to emerge. Working with words takes time.

As with songs, so also with books. *Edge-walkers* began with a Facebook post in August 2024. As Australian practitioners commented, a question emerged: 'How has our "at-the-edges" practice (of faith, church or theology) impacted our thinking and practice?' An idea was proposed: Let's reflect in writing. Let's invite edge-walkers to share their insights.

So we approached potential contributors. We suggested

a style: a single word and the use of 'memoir theology' as a way of bringing together the practical, emotional, spiritual and theological through recounting lived experiences. We gathered on Zoom, workshopped covers, read drafts and provided feedback.

But before the time of writing was the time of living. What you hold in your hands are years of lived experience and decades of immersion in ministry. What you have read is the courageous facing of deep questions, the vulnerability of listening to nagging doubts and the bravery of exploring the unknown. Each chapter is a singularity, the vulnerable sharing of a unique journey in exploring the unknown.

Yet amid the rich diversity of edge-walking, some threads seem to be present, weaving in and out of the seventeen chapters: expansiveness, togetherness, curiosity, creedal, truth-telling and playmaking. These threads reveal six characteristics of the lived experiences of edge-walkers.

Expansiveness: Beyond the known, the edge is a space of generative possibilities.

The edge is not a place as much as an experience beyond what was previously known. It is a 'sacred fringe' (Small) and a place of possibility (Pattenden), where 'God's transformative work becomes the most visible' (Kung). The edges are places of revelation, of an authentic life (Henderson) and of God at work in surprising ways. Meers described how walking to the edge 'saved' her faith. Hollier and Henderson describe new rhythms and a more expansive experience of God. Meers uses the word 'widening' in appreciation of what her community are finding as they walk the edge.

Togetherness: Edge-walkers seldom work alone, but rather share life in regular gatherings, pop-up spaces, digital experiences and life-changing encounters with their communities.

Let's 'start a church', said Hollier. 'What's the collective noun for a group of misfits?' asked Small. What does it mean to 'play with others'? reflected Pattenden. Meers describes the growth of 'Wild Church', Ingram the development of 'Table Church' and Woods the shape of Sonderverse.

Digital technologies play an important role in bringing people together. Edge-walking is occurring through podcasts (Small) and Facebook groups (Palmer). On digital platforms Woods describes how she is joining, rather than initiating, togetherness.

While many of these new forms of community are regular, others are 'pop-up' or spontaneous. Henderson creates art that, when exhibited, generates 'in-between-space' for deep conversations with visitors. Trevena hosts meals for people she meets on the streets and in parks. These experiences with others are momentary, yet lives are changed through shared encounters.

Encountering people brings changes. *Pakipaki* is an informal space. In sharing (*vahevahe*), giving (*foaki*) and receiving (*ma'u/tali*) between people, lives are changed (Taumoepeau, Mafaufau, Taufa and Taufa). Palmer, Trevena, Davison and Kreminski describe how meeting neighbours in local communities brings changes in their sense of self and understanding of God. Pattenden describes how play with others is 'person-forming and world-building'.

Hence, as Kung describes it, the edges are where the church together 'learns again what it means to truly live'.

Curiosity: A bigger God and a richer faith emerge from wrestling with questions, doubts and pain.

This is a deeply human book. The authors share strong emotions. Some, when writing, felt pushed to the edge, needing to be honest about nagging questions and feelings of not aligning with current patterns. Others felt pulled by a desire for more than what they were currently experiencing or an unmet sense of call. Stepping into the unknown required naming the full palette of human emotions (Small) and exploring new ways of knowing (Bird).

Palmer describes the integration, formation and reformation that results from curiosity. Kreminski, sitting in a crowded food court, experiences God's grace overwhelming the formulas of her faith. Bird writes of discernment and the critical and creative pastoral work required in listening for God's grace in human experience.

Creedal: Edge-walkers offer fresh images of God, names for Christ, relationships with creation and understandings of salvation.

The word 'creedal' describes the shape and form of Christian belief. It is a 'how' word focused on practice. In contrast, the word 'creed' is a 'what' word that describes a statement of religious belief. The practice of these edge-walkers, the 'how' of their particular moments in specific contexts, has resulted in fresh images for God and salvation and new phrases to describe relationships with Christ and creation.

God is everywhere, 'large enough to account for our current experience of life' (Davison). As a result, 'God made all materiality holy' (Moyle). God is experienced in creation: sunset, sea and magpies (Meers), and surf, seasons and wild places (Ingram). The edge is a place of Divine encounter, while streets, neighbourhoods and parks are places of transformation.

Jesus is on Country (Wolfe), an edge-walker across boundaries (Kung), a liberator among the traumatised (Hollier), the original misfit (Small) and the One 'coming alongside us' (Trevena).

The Incarnation is God's grace in human bodies (Pattenden), and resurrection is a 'story of scars' (Hollier). Salvation is the 'belonging' (Small) that comes when Jesus is present in our histories, wounds and hopes (Wolfe). Hollier and Bird experience salvation through healing in ways that invite new understandings of relating to pain and nature.

In describing their experiences, the edge-walkers are not suggesting that their words and phrases should be picked up as creeds to be repeated by other Christian communities. Rather, they can be shared as a way of encouraging future edge-walkers to remain alert to fresh creedal possibilities for faith, theology and church in their situations.

Truth-telling: 'Lest we forget' is a distinctive element in sanctification.

'Lest we forget' is often used on Anzac Day to encourage us to remember the sacrifices of the past. Several of the edge-walkers spoke of the importance of not forgetting aspects of life and faith in Australia that are often overlooked.

Walking in the lands now called Australia requires entering an old, old story. This includes learning from those who first walked on Country and 'the unsettling work of interrogating' our relationships, attitudes and privileges (Wolfe). The challenges of sanctification – a lifelong process of restoring the image of God in the life of the Jesus-follower – become particularly acute for organisations and institutions that have reaped benefits from colonisation. Hence, Wolfe's call to 'relinquishing: of ownership of ideas, of control of methods and of certainty about outcomes' resonates with Jesus' call to take up our cross (Matthew 16:24, Mark 8:34, Luke 9:23).

Another example of truth-telling as not forgetting appears in Kreminski's writing about evangelism. She resists the temptation to change or drop the word. Rather, she suggests that sharing faith in the lands now called Australia includes facing our mistakes. This allows our wounds to remind us of the ongoing work of finding God in unlikely places.

The New Testament describes Christians as people who follow Jesus, who grow in wisdom and favour (Luke 2:52) and who strive to mature in their faith (1 Peter 2:2). For these edge-walkers, this process of sanctification includes a commitment to 'Lest we forget' by truthfully naming the past.

Playmaking: Edge-walkers are formed through practices, experiments and adventures.

Pattenden describes the transforming experience of play. A willingness to improvise, individually and in communities brings new solutions and breathes life into change. Moyle reveals how shared practices allow communities to form and together face pressing contemporary concerns. Taumoepeau, Mafaufau, Taufa and Taufa offer insight into the blessing of informal spaces and the benefits of stories, songs and laughter. Woods describes the value of gaming not only as a digital experience but also as a way to deepen relationships. Taylor encounters experiences of making that value learning by doing.

These six threads provide rich insights into how being 'at the edges' has impacted the thinking about, and the practice of, faith, church and theology.

Outro

We end by returning to where I began: the documentary about the making of songs. In *Anchor Me* (2025), Don McGlashan describes how a song is his attempt to describe a moment in time. He reflects on the challenge of capturing life within a few verses and a single chorus. He concludes that his task is to be honest rather than comprehensive.

Edge-walkers is memoir. Each author has aimed for honesty. From many words, they have picked a single one. There are other words they could have selected, more stories they could have shared.

There are not only other words and other stories, but also other edge-walkers. There are as yet untold 'edge-sights' from those we are not yet aware of, those who said yes but for whom the realities of life had other ideas, and those who are yet to come.

We offer these edge-walking memoirs as a first word. We hope for more words, more stories from other edges and other walkers.

Edge-walkers are crucial for today's expression of Christianities. Our hope is that this book will encourage churches, denominations and leaders to amplify the voices of those edge-walkers in their communities and support and resource their initiatives.

Steve Taylor, with Armen Gakavian and Karina Kreminski

Endnotes

Mysticism – Carolyn Meers

1. Karl Rahner, 'The Spirituality of the Church of the Future', in *Concern for the Church*, Theological Investigations, Vol. 20 (Helicon Press, 1961), 143-153: 149.
2. Paula D'Arcy, quoted in Center for Action and Contemplation, 'Negative Capability', *Daily Meditations*, January 11, 2016, https://cac.org/daily-meditations/negative-capability-2016-01-11/.
3. Center for Action and Contemplation, 'Why Mysticism Matters', *Daily Meditations*, February 9, 2025, https://cac.org/daily-meditations/why-mysticism-matters/.
4. Cole Arthur Riley, *This Here Flesh: Spirituality, Liberation, and the Stories That Make Us* (Convergent Books, 2022), 41.
5. For a deeper exploration of centring prayer, see Thomas Keating, *Open Mind, Open Heart* (Continuum, 2006).
6. Rainer Maria Rilke, *Rilke's Book of Hours: Love Poems to God*, trans. Anita Barrows and Joanna Macy (Riverhead Books, 2005), 48.

Art – Michael Henderson

1. There are two aspects of prophecy: 'foretelling', or predicting the future; and 'forthtelling', or speaking truth or encouragement. I am using the word in the latter sense.

2. Krista Tippett, *Speaking of Faith: Why religion matters and how to talk about it* (Viking Penguin, 2007).

3. Miroslav Volf, *A Public Faith: How followers of Christ should serve the common good* (Brazos Press, Baker Publishing, 2011), 79.

4. Tippett, *Speaking of Faith*, 133.

Play – Rod Pattenden

1. Phil Porter and Cynthia Winton-Henry are the originators of Inter-Play. InterPlay offers an invitation to learn to play using a variety of expressive art forms that enhance a sense of creativity and liveliness. See https://interplayaus.com.au/.

2. Rod Pattenden and Susanna Pain, 'Play as a Spiritual Practice', interview by Meredith Lake, Soul Search, ABC Radio National, September 26, 2024, audio, https://www.abc.net.au/listen/programs/soul-search/the-spirituality-of-play/104295814.

3. Donald W. Winnicott, *Playing and Reality* (Routledge, 1971), 54.

4. 'Simeon Stylites', Wikimedia Foundation, last modified October 5, 2025, https://en.wikipedia.org/wiki/Simeon_Stylites.

5. Lisa Isherwood and Elizabeth Stuart, *Introducing Body Theology* (Bloomsbury Publishing, 1998), 33.

6. Elizabeth A. Johnson, *Women, Earth and Creator Spirit* (Paulist Press, 1993), 60.

Trauma – Joel Hollier

1. Joel Hollier, *The Shape of Religious Trauma*, 2024, www.joelhollier.com/religious-harm.

2. Mark McCrindle, *Faith and Belief in Australia: A National Survey on Religion, Spirituality, and Worldview Trends*, 2017, https://mccrindle.com.au/article/faith-and-belief-in-australia-2/.

3. McCrindle, *Faith and Belief in Australia*.

4. Richard Rhor, *Things Hidden: Scripture as Spirituality* (SPCK Publishing, 2016).

5. Heidi M. Ellis et al., 'Religious/Spiritual Abuse and Trauma: A Systematic Review of the Empirical Literature', *Spirituality in Clinical Practice* 9, no. 4 (2022): 213–231, https://doi.org/10.1037/scp0000301; Hollier, *The Shape of Religious Trauma*.

Earthy – Jono Ingram

1.   Shane Claiborne, *The Irresistible Revolution* (Zondervan Publishing, 2006), 10.

2.   Claiborne, *The Irresistible Revolution*, 105.

3.   Jonathan Wilson-Hartgrove, *The Rule of Saint Benedict: A Contemporary Paraphrase* (Paraclete Press, 2012).

4.   Shane Claiborne and Jonathan Wilson Hartgrove, *Becoming the Answers to Our Prayers* (Zondervan, 2008).

5.   Shane Claiborne, *The Irresistible Revolution 10th Anniversary Edition* (Zondervan Publishing 2006, ePub Edition 2015), 95, 97.

6.   Jono Ingram, 'A Prayer for Sitting Around a Fire', *Dirt Church Liturgy*, July 13, 2022, https://jcingram.wordpress.com/2022/07/13/a-prayer-for-sitting-around-a-fire/.

7.   An example of this type of Table Liturgy can be found at Jono Ingram, 'A Table Liturgy for Advent', *Dirt Church Liturgy*, November 27, 2024, https://jcingram.wordpress.com/2024/11/27/table-liturgy-for-advent/.

Misfits – Will Small

1.   Brian D. McLaren, *Faith After Doubt: Why Your Beliefs Stopped Working and What to Do About It* (St Martin's Essentials, 2021).

2.   Bradley Jersak, *A More Christlike God: A More Beautiful Gospel* (CWR Press, 2015); Rachel Held Evans, *Inspired: Slaying Giants, Walking on Water, and Loving the Bible Again* (Thomas Nelson, 2018); Pete Enns, *The Bible Tells Me So: Why Defending Scripture Has Made Us Unable to Read It* (HarperOne, 2014).

3.   Nadia Bolz-Weber, *Pastrix: The Cranky, Beautiful Faith of a Sinner & Saint* (Jericho Books, 2013); Brian Zahnd, *Sinners in the Hands of a Loving God* (Waterbrook Press, 2017).

4.   Kristin Kobes Du Mez, *Jesus and John Wayne: How White Evangelicals Corrupted a Faith and Fractured a Nation* (Liveright, 2020); David P. Gushee, *After Evangelicalism: The Path to a New Christianity* (Westminster John Knox Press, 2020).

5.   Phyllis Tickle, *The Great Emergence: How Christianity Is Changing and Why* (Baker Books, 2012); McLaren, *Faith After Doubt*.

6.   At the time I'm writing this the podcast has had around 126,000 downloads spanning 125 countries.

7.   Richard Rohr, *Everything Belongs: The Gift of Contemplative Prayer* (Crossroad Publishing Company, 2003).

8.   I interviewed the pastors of the church, Scott and Andrew, about the journey their church had been on here: https://www.spiritualmisfits. com.au/podcast/episode/7a3f5344/scott-higgins-and-andrew-dodd-how-hamilton-baptist-became-lgbtqi-affirming.

9.   This poem first appeared in my collection *Poems for When the World is Ending* (Lead by Story, 2023).

Pakipaki - Alimoni T. Taumoepeau, Uilisone Kiriona Mafaufau, Mosese Taufa and Seini Tokilupe Taufa

1.   *Talanoa* can also refer to the process of 'untying knots' in fishing. See Jione Havea, 'Bare Feet Welcome: Redeemer Xs Moses @ Enaim', in *Bible, Borders, Belonging(s): Engaging Readings from Oceania:* Semeia Studies 75, ed. Jione Havea, David J. Neville and Elaine M. Wainwright (SBL Press, 2004), 209-222: 210.

Neighbourhood - Christine Palmer

1.   Noel Castellanos, 'Incarnating the Good News of the Kingdom', in *Making Neighborhoods Whole: A Handbook for Christian Community Development*, by Wayne Gordon and John M. Perkins (Intervarsity Press, 2013), 166.

2.   Michael Moynagh, *Being Church, Doing Life: Creating Gospel Communities Where Life Happens* (Monarch Books, 2014), 122–125.

3.   John 1:14, Eugene Peterson, *The Message: The Bible in Contemporary Language* (Navpress, 2002), 1916.

4.   David Bosch, *Transforming Mission* (Orbis Books, 1991), 389–390.

5.   Jorge Acevedo, *Neighboring: Spiritual Practices for Building a Life of Faith* (Abingdon Press, 2019), 58.

6.   Lance Ford and Brad Briscoe, *The Missional Quest: Becoming A Church of the Long Run* (Intervarsity Press, 2013), 38–39.

7.   Moynagh, *Being Church, Doing Life*, 122–125.

8.   Moynagh, *Being Church, Doing Life*, 120.

9.   Ian Mobsby, 'The Overlooked and Underappreciated Text: Paul's Radical Vision of God's Mission', Contemplative Christian in a PostSecular Culture of Collapse, March 31, 2025, https://postsecularcontemplative.substack.com.

10. Karina Kreminski, Facebook, June 15, 2023, https://www.facebook.
    com/, reference lost.

11. Karina Kreminski, Facebook, June 15, 2023, https://www.facebook.
    com/, reference lost.

12. The Uniting Church in Australia Constitutions and Regulations
    (2018): 2.2.1 Duties of a Minister, https://www.nswact.uca.org.
    au/media/bfxnvj3h/constitutionandregulations-2018-updated-
    august-2019.pdf.

13. Tim Soerens, *Everywhere You Look: Discovering the Church Right Where
    You Are* (Intervarsity Press, 2020), 16.

Gathering - Simon Moyle

1. Anthony de Mello, *The Song of the Bird* (Image, 1984), 63; N.T. Wright,
   *The Day the Revolution Began: Reconsidering the Meaning of Jesus's
   Crucifixion* (HarperOne, 2016), 182.

2. John Howard Yoder, *Body Politics: Five Practices of the Christian
   Community Before the Watching World* (Discipleship Resources, 1994),
   17.

Kenosis – Jennifer Trevena

1. The term 'church planting' is an organic metaphor, drawn from
   nature, used to describe the process of starting a new church.
   However, it's important to acknowledge that it has sometimes
   become associated with a colonising approach, whereby a form
   of church is imposed from outside the context where it is being
   planted. Like all things, church planting can be done well or it can
   be abused. I believe that the Simple/Micro Church planting model of
   coming alongside people in their context makes it easier to avoid this
   problem. For a helpful introduction to the concept and practice of
   church planting, see Stuart Murray, *Planting Churches: A Framework
   for Practitioners* (Paternoster Press, 2008).

2. Someone who believes in and shares the evangel, i.e. the Good News.

3. Gen1K, 'A Blended Ecology A diversity of churches and leaders
   working together', n.d., https://www.gen1kmission.org.au/wp-content/
   uploads/2023/11/A-blended-ecology.pdf, 4. The Simple Church has
   been the primary model within Baptist contexts for over the past
   decade.

4.   Brian Saunders, 'Ecclesial Minimum', n.d., https://static1.squarespace.
     com/static/6710c30f1f08be1486d908fa/t/685d693b58f6c47633e2ea
     8e/1750952256924/Ecclesial+Minimum+Resource.pdf. See also Brian
     Saunders, 'Microchurches: A Smaller Way' (Underground Media,
     2019), 3, for a more detailed definition.
5.   Hak Joon Lee, 'Kingdom and Kenosis: The Mind of Christ in Paul's
     Ethics', n.d., https://fullerstudio.fuller.edu/kingdom-and-kenosis-the-
     mind-of-christ-in-pauls-ethics/.
6.   Mutuality is one of our core principles at BethanyHope. Our focus
     is on creating space where people experiencing homelessness can
     develop the confidence and skills to support one another rather than
     being positioned as dependents. We take power dynamics seriously
     and this is an ongoing area of reflection and discernment for us as a
     team.
7.   See, for example, Baptist Association of NSW and ACT, 'Our Shared
     Goal', https://www.gen1kmission.org.au/.
8.   See, for example, Eric Swanson, 'Build, Measure, Learn cycle
     for churches', February 15, 2021, https://www.youtube.com/
     watch?v=zSM_3ATI54k; Eric Swanson, 'Lean Start-Up (Part 1 of 2):
     Exponential Seven concepts of the lean start-up', December 22, 2016,
     https://exponential.org/lean-start-up-part-1-of-2/.
9.   From the outset, we communicate our metrics with the people we
     reach out to, by clearly explaining why we intentionally and regularly
     meet with them. When individuals start participating in BethanyHope
     worship, we share the metrics more specifically as we invite them to
     serve together with us.
10. Michael Adam Beck, Deep Roots, *Wild Branches: Revitalizing the
     Church in the Blended Ecology* (Seedbed Publishing, 2019), 18.

Digital - Kelly N. S. Woods

1.   Heidi A. Campbell and Stephen Garner, *Networked Theology:
     Negotiating Faith in Digital Culture* (Baker Academic, 2016), 119.
2.   Liberation Theology, with specific focus towards Migration Theology,
     highlights the issues and key language shifts needed.That my last
     name is Woods has not escaped me.
3.   Margaret Wertheim, *The Pearly Gates of Cyberspace. A History of Space
     from Dante to the Internet* (W. W. Norton & Company, 1999), 231.

4. Ilya Levin and Dan Mamlok, 'Culture and Society in the Digital Age', *Information* 12, no. 2 (2021), 9, https://doi.org/10.3390/info12020068.

5. I use *'faithing'* rather than *'faith'* to stress the praxis of belief, understanding faith as something we do together rather than simply something we hold. In this sense, faith emerges through shared practices of exploration and discernment, rather than existing as a settled or completed state.

6. OddRev is the online handle of Rev. Will Nicholas (https://oddrev. com/). See Zach Hope, 'Church members ditch board games, rescue nursing home residents', *The Age*, July 1, 2019, https://www.theage. com.au/national/victoria/church-members-ditch-board-games-rescue-nursing-home-residents-20190701-p522u6.html.

7. This was pre-COVID, so the idea of a Zoom Bible study seemed very far-fetched.

8. From 2019 to 2023 this community was known as SonderCloud – the digital region of The Sonder Collective. In 2023 The Sonder Collective made the move toward a solely digital community called Sonderverse.

9. Across socials our handle is @SonderverseCommunity. You can find us on twitch at www.twitch.tv/sonderversecommunity or you can check out https://www.sonderverse.org/.

10. A username that is part identity, part inside joke, part statement. There is a bigger story behind why this is my username. However, for this chapter all you need to know is that the Sonderverse community knows me by this name, not by Kelly.

11. Non-player character. This is a character in a game that is not controlled by a player.

12. https://www.dictionary.com/browse/sonder.www.twitch.tv/ sonderversecommunity. The game was called *Seven Days to Die*, where players are to gather resources, build a fortress and survive a world plagued by the undead.

13. Elizabeth Barrett Browning, *Aurora Leigh: A Poem, book seven* (J. Miller, 1864).

14. Guy Consolmagno, SJ and Paul Mueller, SJ, *Would You Baptize an Extraterrestrial? ... and Other Questions from the Astronomers' In-box at the Vatican Observatory* (Penguin, 2018).

Liminal – Cyrus Kung

1. Franciscan priest and author Richard Rohr, in Center for Action and Contemplation, 'Holy Transitions', *Daily Meditations*, May 3, 2023, https://cac.org/daily-meditations/holy-transitions-2023-05-03/. Rohr defines 'liminality' as follows: 'The Latin word *limen* means "threshold". Liminal space is an inner state and sometimes an outer situation where we can begin to think and act in new ways. It is where we are betwixt and between, in transition, having left one room or stage of life but not yet entered the next. We usually enter liminal space when our former way of being is challenged or changed – perhaps when we lose a job or a loved one, during illness, at the birth of a child, or a major relocation. It is a graced time, but often does not feel "graced" in any way. In such space, we are not certain or in control'.

2. Thomas Merton, *No Man Is an Island* (Shambhala Publications, 2005), 134.

3. Timothy Carson et al., *Crossing Thresholds* (The Lutterworth Press, 2021), 204.

4. Walter Brueggemann, *Hopeful Imagination: Prophetic Voices in Exile* (Ausburg Books, 1986), 34-35.

5. Brueggemann, *Hopeful Imagination*, 47.

6. Merton, *No Man Is an Island*, 135.

7. Merton, *No Man Is an Island*, 134.

8. Jung Young Lee, *Marginality: The Key to Multicultural Theology* (Fortress Press, 1995), 99.

9. Lee, *Marginality*, 98.

10. Sang Hyun Lee, *From a Liminal Place: An Asian American Theology* (Fortress Press, 2010), 5.

11. Cyrus Kung, 'Chapter 3: Locational Challenges for second generation Asian Australian Theology', *Location-Shaped Theologies: First Peoples and Second Generation Wisdom*, ed. Rosemary Dewerse (ATF Press, 2024), 102.

12. Grace Kwan Sik Tsoi and Philip Chia, *Chinese Church in Context: Voices from Downunder* (Wipf and Stock Publishers, 2025), 60.

13. Cindy S. Lee, *Our Unforming: De-Westernizing Spiritual Formation* (Fortress Press, 2022), 76.

Decolonisation – Naomi Wolfe

1. Letter from Hugh Jamieson to Bishop Perry, Mildura Station,
    River Murray, 10th October 1853. In Charles Joseph Latrobe and
    Thomas Francis Bride, eds., *Letters from Victorian pioneers: being a
    series of papers on the early occupation of the colony, the aborigines, etc.*
    (Published for the Trustees of the Public Library by Robt. S. Brain,
    Govt. Printer, 1898), 269 -275.

2. In Aboriginal contexts, storying (sometimes calling yarning or talkin'
    up) is grounded in relationship, responsibility and memory as a
    practice of truth-telling. In Christian theology this methodology
    functions as testimony and witness: a telling of truth that calls out
    what is otherwise normalised or made invisible. These stories are
    drawn from actual events, with identifying details changed for ethical
    reasons, and are given as testimony to experiences that are shared by
    many Aboriginal people and communities.

    You are encouraged to read the stories prophetically, as these stories
    name the everyday reoccurrence of colonial assumptions within
    Australian church life, institutional life and across the wider society.
    I'm using *prophetically* in the biblical and theological sense of naming
    injustice, exposing systems of power and calling communities to
    account. It does not mean prediction or abstraction, but a mode
    of truth-telling grounded in lived experience –particularly the
    experiences of those harmed by dominant systems. To read these
    stories *prophetically* is to hear them as theological truth-telling that
    confronts injustice and calls the church to account for the everyday
    practices it normalises.

    These stories are not exceptional moments of hostility, but ordinary
    interactions – across Sunday schools, seminaries, universities and
    collegial conversations in workplaces – through which Aboriginal
    people are corrected, silenced, appropriated or obliged to justify
    themselves. They are persistent and pervasive acts of casual and
    institutional bias and racism that occur even in spaces that are often
    viewed as reconciled, inclusive and benign.

    These stories are told with no animosity. They are told with
    deliberate generosity to the non-Indigenous peoples. There is no
    attribution of motive or spite. There is an acknowledgement of
    the complexity of humans, and there is an avoidance of labelling

individual as villain. This is a deliberate, theologically grounded act of generosity that reflects the Aboriginal way of relational accountability. However, prophetic generosity does not mean silence. Christian Scripture regularly witnesses that truth-telling is an act of love, and that repentance must begin with hearing rather than defensiveness.

As theological prompts, these examples confront the Church across Australia with questions that have been ignored or deferred: How does settler colonialism continues to shape the life of the Church, its epistemological practices and its moral imagination? Why are Aboriginal voices only received when they are comfortable and non-challenging? How can reconciliation be sought and expected without the practices of listening, confession, and healing? Storying functions as a decolonial practice that calls the Church to move past sentiment towards repentance, justice and transformation on these lands and with its peoples.

3. The Tommeginer peoples are the traditional owners of coastal land in northwest lutruwita/Tasmania, which includes the lands and waterways surrounding Table Cape and Wynyard.

4. In this context, 'a touch of the tar brush' is a colloquial saying that acknowledges that someone has Aboriginal ancestry. It was commonly used across lutruwita/Tasmania. Professor Bronwyn Carlson has an interesting article that discusses this term and others – see 'Who's counting? Identifying and acknowledging an Aboriginal lineage can be a complex and challenging process', March 8, 2016, https://insidestory.org.au/whos-counting/.

5. In the 1970s and 1980s there were no ordained female ministers, hence 'fraternity', though I would not use this word to describe these meetings or their sense of collegiality (or lack thereof) in contemporary times!

6. Garry J. Deverell, *Gondwana Theology: A Trawloolway Man Reflects on Christian Faith* (Morning Star Publishing, 2018), 42.

7. Lee Miena Skye, *Kerygmatics of the New Millennium: A Study of Australian Aboriginal Women's Christology*. No. 4 (ISPCK, 2007), 13.

8. Neville Naden and Jione Havea, 'Colonization has many names', in *Indigenous Australia and the Unfinished Business of Theology: Cross-Cultural Engagement*, ed. Jione Havea (Palgrave Macmillan US, 2014), 1.

9.   Chris Budden, 'Migration and Rudd's Apology: Whose Voices are Heard, and What Do They Mean for the Christian Community?' in Havea, *Indigenous Australia and the Unfinished Business of Theology*, 101.

10. Aileen Moreton-Robinson, ed., *Whitening race: Essays in social and cultural criticism*. No. 1 (Aboriginal Studies Press, 2004).

11. Marcia Langton and Rachel Perkins, eds. *First Australians* (Miegunyah Press, 2008).

12. Mark G. Brett, 'Redeeming Country: Indigenous Peoples under Empires and Nation States', in *Religion and Empire*, ed. Jione Havea (Lexington Books/Fortress Academic, 2018), 170.

13. Denise Champion and Rosemary Dewerse, *Anaditj* (Denise Champion, 2021), x.

14. Evelyn Parkin, 'The sources and resources of our Indigenous theology: An Australian Aboriginal perspective', *The Ecumenical Review* 62, no. 4 (2010): 390-398, 397.

15. Aunty Janet Turpie-Johnstone is an Aboriginal Elder and artist, retired Anglican priest and the first Aboriginal Council member of the University of Divinity.

16. There was a Memorandum of Understanding between Whitley College, NAIITS and the University of Divinity. See https://eternitynews.com.au/australia/breakthrough-on-teaching-theology-through-indigenous-eyes/. The partnership was successful, and eventually NAIITS would complete its coursework programs and join the Sydney College of Divinity (now Australian University College of Divinity) to become its own member college. See https://naiits.com/news/naiits-news-from-australia.

17. The University of Divinity School of Indigenous Studies was launched on December 13, 2021, with two foundational staff members: the Rev. Dr Garry Deverell and Ms Naomi Wolfe. See https://divinity.edu.au/university/school-of-indigenous-studies/.

Malagigiri - Cliff Bird

1.   Since the late nineteenth century, there have been dynamic debates between anthropologists and theologians who were in contact with Indigenous peoples as to what *mana* really means. The debate is long and interesting, but it boils down to whether *mana*, as it was used and understood in various Pasifika Indigenous contexts, was a noun or a

verb – a very Western framing. They tried to find a European verbal equivalent of *mana*. This proved to be very problematic, especially in the colonially designated geopolitical area known as 'Melanesia'. (Nothing could be more diverse as the overtly colonially demarcated Melanesia, Polynesia and Micronesia!) In Pasifika Indigenous episte-mologies, *mana* is a 'both/and' category, seen and understood both as a blessing beyond human and natural processes as well as effects and outcomes of natural processes.

2. Daniel L. Migliore, *Faith Seeking Understanding: An Introduction to Theology*, Second Edition (Wm. B Eerdmans Publishing Co., 2004), 4.

3. Marcus J. Borg, *Jesus: Uncovering the Life, Teachings, and Relevance of a Religious Revolutionary* (New York: HarperOne, 2006), 111.

Making - Steve Taylor

1. Michel de Certeau, *The Practice of Everyday Life*, trans. Steven Rendall (University of California Press, 1984).

2. Willem Frijhoff, 'Michel de Certeau 1925–1986', in *French Historians 1900–2000: New Historical Writing in Twentieth-Century France*, ed. P. Daileader and P. Walen (Wiley-Blackwell, 2010), 78.

3. Nancy Ammerman, *Sacred Stories, Spiritual Tribes: Finding Religion in Everyday Life* (Oxford University Press, 2014), 56.

4. Heather Walton, 'Seeking Wisdom in Practical Theology', *Practical Theology* 7, no. 1 (2014): 5–18, https://doi.org/10.1179/1756073X1 3Z.00000000028.

5. Steve Taylor, 'A New Way of Being Church: Approach to Cityside Baptist Church as Christian faith "Making Do" in a Postmodern World' (PhD diss., University of Otago, 2004), 192-199; Steve Taylor, *The Out of Bounds Church? Learning to Create a Community of Faith in a Culture of Change* (Zondervan, 2005).

6. Melissa Raphael, *The Female Face of God in Auschwitz: A Jewish Feminist Theology of the Holocaust* (Routledge, 2003), 142.

7. F. Scott Spencer, *Dancing Girls, Loose Ladies, and Women of the Cloth: The Women in Jesus' Life* (Continuum, 2004).

8. Spencer, *Dancing Girls*, 185.

9. See www.loubakerartist.co.uk and https://independent.academia.edu/ LouBaker.

10. @loubakerartist, January 20, 2021.

11. Ralph Martin, *Ephesians, Colossians, and Philemon* (Louisville, 1991), 29.

12. Amy Plantinga Pauw, *Proverbs and Ecclesiastes* (Westminster John Knox, 2015); Amy Plantinga Pauw, *Church in Ordinary Time: A Wisdom Ecclesiology* (Eerdmans, 2017).

13. David Kelsey, *Eccentric Existence: a theological anthropology* (Westminster John Knox, 2009), 345–354.

14. Pauw, *Church in Ordinary Time*, 23–33. See also Paul Fiddes, *Seeing the World and Knowing God: Hebrew Wisdom and Christian Doctrine in a Late-Modern Context* (Oxford University Press, 2013) and Ernest Lucas, *Proverbs* (Eerdmans: 2015).

15. Kelsey, *Eccentric Existence*, 161-162.

16. Pauw, *Church in Ordinary Time*, 55–67, 68–81.

17. Pauw, *Church in Ordinary Time*, 113.

18. Pauw, *Church in Ordinary Time*, 116.

19. Raphael, *The Female Face of God in Auschwitz*, 140.

20. Raphael, *The Female Face of God in Auschwitz*, 136.

21. Karl Chitham, Kolokesa U Māhina-Tuai and Damian Skinner, *Crafting Aotearoa: A Cultural History of Making in New Zealand and the Wider Moana Oceania* (Te Papa Press, 2019), 16.

22. Rebecca Abbott, 'Handknitted scarves tell story of a warming planet', *Eternity*, December 1, 2020, https://www.eternitynews.com.au/australia/handknitted-scarves-tell-story-of-a-warming-planet.

23. 'Mix your craft skills and passion for action on climate change', Common Grace, accessed April 20, 2025, https://www.commongrace.org.au/knit_for_climate_latest_action.

24. Steve Taylor, 'Making and Christian witness in Australia today', *Colloquium* 55, no. 2 (2025): 30-45. https://doi.org/10.2478/colloquium-2025-0004.

25. David Gauntlett, *Making is Connecting: The Social Power of Creativity, from Craft and Knitting to Digital Everything* (Polity Press, 2018), 32-33.

26. Gauntlett, *Making is Connecting*, 195.

Eucharist – Karyl Davison

1. J.B. Phillips, *Your God is Too Small*, 7th Edition (Epworth Press, 1954), 32.

2. I see fresh expressions as forms of church that seek to make

meaningful connections with people who have little or no connection to the inherited church. By proclaiming the gospel in actions of service and hospitality, those people may catch a glimpse of God's kingdom and begin a journey of discipleship.

3. I wish to acknowledge that I write on the lands of the Ngunnawal and Ngambri people. I also want to acknowledge difficulties with the language of 'mission', which for many First Peoples holds significant trauma. In the absence of more helpful language my chapter uses 'mission' language – for that I am sorry.

4. Eaton/Millbridge Community Project, 'Eaton Millbridge Guidelines', July 8, 2013.

5. Davison, Karyl, 'But is it Church?' in *We Are Pilgrims: Mission from, in and with the Margins of our Diverse World*, ed. Darren Cronshaw and Rosemary Dewerse (UNOH Publishing, 2015), 127–139.

6. Andrew McGowan, 'The Meals of Jesus and the Meals of the Church: Origins and Admission to Communion' (2003), https://repository. divinity.edu.au/entities/publication/0758a001-36eb-4595-9abd-b34d5f7e7707.

7. Karyl Davison, 'Sacramental Sausages: freeing the Lord's supper for mission', 2023, unpublished.

8. John Koenig, *New Testament Hospitality: Partnership with Strangers as Promise and Mission* (Fortress Press, 1985), 20.

9. Sara Miles, *Take This Bread: A Radical Conversion* (Ballantine Books, 2007), xi.

10. Jurgen Moltmann, *A Broad Place* (SCM Press, 2007), 164.

11. Jurgen Moltmann, *The Church in the Power of the Spirit: A Contribution to Messianic Ecclesiology* (SCM Press, 1977), 242–252.

12. Shirley Erena Murray, 'For everyone born a place at the table', Hope Publishing, https://www.hopepublishing.com/find-hymns-hw/ hw9159_16.aspx.

13. Rachel Held Evans, June 13, 2013, https://rachelheldevans.com/blog/ southern-baptist-boy-scouts-love-opens-door.

14. Darrell L. Guder (ed.), *Missional Church: A Vision for the Sending of the Church in North America* (William B. Eerdmans, 1998), 165.

Evangelism - Karina Kreminski

1. Roger Helland and Leonard Hjalmarson, *Embodying God's Love from*

the Inside Out (IVP Books, 2012), Loc. 331, Kindle.

2. Paula Gooder, *Body: Biblical Spirituality for the Whole Person* (SPCK Publishing, 2016), 4.

3. Barbara Brown Taylor, *Holy Envy: Finding God in the Faith of Others* (HarperOne, 2018), 64.

4. Scot McKnight, *The King Jesus Gospel: The Original Good News Revisited* (Zondervan, 2011), Loc. 330, Kindle, cited in Karina Kreminski, *Urban Spirituality: Embodying God's Mission in the Neighborhood* (Urban loft Publishers, 2018), 101.

5. Kreminski, *Urban Spirituality*, 101.

6. J. Oliver Conroy, 'The life and death of John Chau, the man who tried to convert his killers', February 3, 2019, https://www.theguardian.com/world/2019/feb/03/john-chau-christian-missionary-death-sentinelese.

7. I also want to acknowledge that the word 'mission' has a traumatic history for many Aboriginal and Torres Strait Islander peoples. While I continue to use the term, I do so cautiously, in the same way I use the term 'evangelism' – as a way of owning the mistakes of the past rather than trying to hide from them. See my discussion about the word 'evangelism' later in this chapter.

8. Diana Butler Bass, *Freeing Jesus: Rediscovering Jesus as Friend, Teacher, Savior, Lord, Way, and Presence* (HarperOne, 2021), 87.

9. Walter Brueggemann, *The Land: Place as Gift Promise and Challenge in Biblical Faith* (Augsberg, 2002), 4.

10. Quoted in Amy Plantinga Pauw, *Church in Ordinary Time: A Wisdom Ecclesiology* (Eerdmans Publishing, 2017), 28.

11. Timothy L Carson, Rosy Fairhurst, Nigel Rooms and Lisa Withrow, *Crossing Thresholds: A Practical Theology of Liminality* (Lutterworth Press, 2021), 107.

12. Leslie Newbigin, *The Gospel in a Pluralist Society* (William B. Eerdmans, 1989), 116.

13. See for example *Don't Forget We're Here Forever: A New Generation's Search for Religion* (Bloomsbury Circus, 2025) for an incredible journey of a young woman seeking faith in a secular society.

Contributors

Alimoni T. Taumoepeau is a minister of the Word and Intercultural Ministry and Climate Action Team Leader with the Uniting Church in Australia. He is passionate about leadership, with a commitment to flourishing faith and community service, motivated by an unwavering belief in the power of love and grace to transform lives and create positive change for the common good. Alimoni is passionate about social justice and actively addresses the needs of diverse congregations, fostering inclusivity and advocating for the marginalised. He seeks to integrate his Tongan cultural heritage and theological insights to promote understanding and unity among different communities. He is committed to inspiring future leaders and nurturing spiritual growth to make a meaningful impact in both local and broader contexts within the church and the broader community. Alimoni is married with two grown up children.

Carolyn Meers (Caro) lives and works on Dharawal country with her husband, their three kids and their dog Barney. Caro was the Pastor at Central Church Port Kembla for fifteen years and created a beautifully ordinary, creative community of faith. In late 2025 Central transitioned to a shared leadership structure and Caro remains part of the co-leadership team. She loves good food and wine, bushwalking, gardening, basketball and hanging out with friends and family. Caro is a qualified spiritual director and loves creating contemplative spaces, services and events that help connect people with the Divine.

Christine Palmer loves being part of her local community and looking for ways she can join in with what God is doing in her neighbourhood. She enjoys gardening and a good cup of tea. She was a primary school teacher, then a Pastoral Care Worker before being ordained in 2014 in the Uniting Church in Australia. Christine is currently in ministry at Suburban Seeds, a fresh expression initiative in Southwest Sydney, which is exploring how to grow a contextual worshipping congregation along with its other ways of being church in its community.

Cliff Bird is a fisherman who romances theology. He is also a theologian who is passionate about the intersectionalities of theology and faith with broader developmental issues and trends such as climate justice, socioeconomic justice and gender justice. He currently leads the Uniting Church in Australia's NSW/ACT Synod missional response to the Pacific Australian Labour Mobility (PALM) Scheme. Two of his most recent published works are *Reweaving the Ecological Mat* (2020), co-authored with Arnie Saiki and Meretui Ratunabuabua, and 'A Pasifika Approach to Alternative Epistemologies and Ecojustice' (2024), which was published in the *German Journal for Missiology and Intercultural Theology*.

Cyrus Kung is a second-generation Hong Kong Australian and an ordained minister in the Uniting Church in Australia. He works with the Mission Resourcing Team for the South Australia Synod and serves as Church Engagement Manager for Uniting World. Over the years, Cyrus has led second-generation English ministries and experimented with fresh expressions of church and church planting, including running a café that offered work experience to young people and refugees. He is passionate about helping people connect with their deeper selves while discovering the simplicity of Christ in our complicated modern world. Creativity, third spaces, liminality and hybridity are at the heart of how he approaches ministry and community life.

Jen Trevena is a Simple/Micro Church planter and practitioner who serves among low socioeconomic communities, including refugees and migrants and people experiencing homelessness. She is committed to innovative and contextualised missional church planting that empowers emerging leaders and enables multiplication. As a first-generation Korean immigrant,

Jen holds a deep passion for intercultural ministry and empowering non-English-speaking background leaders. With over a decade of missional community experience, she has spent the past four years supporting and championing Simple/Micro church planters and practitioners across Baptist Churches in NSW/ACT. She currently leads the Simple Church Network and works with the Church Multiplication Team at the Baptist Association NSW/ACT.

Joel Hollier is a writer, researcher, social worker and pastor who is passionate about creating safer spaces for people to build community and seek holistic wellbeing in fresh ways. He was a founding co-pastor of New City Church and currently holds a postdoctoral research fellowship at the University of Sydney. He is the author of two books exploring the LGBTQIA+ and religion intersection, and co-editor of *Understanding the Spirituality and the Sacred in Social Work: Spirited Conversations* (2025).

Jono Ingram lives on Wurundjerri Country (Melbourne), is a trained primary school teacher and has worked in Baptist Churches for ten years. He has spent the last eight years in the community not-for-profit sector as the Founding Director of an environmental non-profit, We Love Aintree. When he's not in the veggie garden, Jono might be running hills in Lerderderg training for an ultra-trail marathon, surfing on the Bellarine Peninsula or sitting around a fire pit with family and friends enjoying a nice home-brewed beer.

Karyl Davison is a pioneer minister within the Uniting Church in Australia. She is currently serving in the Kippax Uniting Church community, which includes a number of worshipping congregations, a community service organisation and missional engagement in a five-suburb housing development in the adjacent suburb. Prior to her move to Canberra, Karyl was, for five years, team leader of the Eaton/Millbridge Community Project, a fresh expression of church in a new housing development in Western Australia. Her DMin thesis, 'Sacramental Sausages: freeing the Lord's supper for mission', was focused on practising the Lord's supper within the life of the Project.

Kelly N. S. Woods is a religious practitioner and artist who cultivates sacred spaces on the edges of the expected, both online and offline. In digital spaces, she is known as PastoralHare. Formed through years of theological study, chaplaincy and creative practice, her writing explores how the sacred appears, plays and is shaped through shared belonging. Kelly writes from lived experience as a second-generation South African, gamer and creative and community curator. She is drawn to places where faith is questioned, remade and shared with care and abundant generosity.

Michael Henderson has worked as an artist and pastor for over twenty years. His work explores identity, lament and the divine through diverse mediums including painting, sculpture and writing. Career highlights include being a finalist in the 66th Blake Prize (2021), creating *Sculpture by the Sea* (1999) and displaying major installations like *Shorelines* on Tasmania's Parliament House Lawn (2018). His 2022 sculptural work, *How Lonely Lies This Land*, explored the relationship between Tasmanian Aboriginal and non-Indigenous communities, installed across three Hobart church venues. He lives with his family in lutruwita/Tasmania. His website is michaeljameshenderson.com.au.

Mosese Taufa was ordained as a Minister of the Word in the Uniting Church in Australia in 2008. He is a graduate of Sydney University with a Bachelor of Theology. He's had ministry placements in Wagga Wagga and is currently serving at Auburn Uniting Church. Mosese has a deep passion for the church, the preaching of God's Word and pastoral ministry. Prior to his studies at Sydney University and serving in the church, he graduated from Massey University, New Zealand, with a Bachelor of Science and subsequently became a high school teacher in Mathematics and Physics for many years. Mosese enjoys sports, gardening and spending time with family and friends.

Naomi Wolfe is a Trawlwoolway Aboriginal woman with Irish and Jewish German heritage. She lives and works on Wurundjeri Country (Melbourne) as a historian and theologian. Naomi teaches Indigenous and ancient histories at the Australian Catholic University and previously served as Academic Coordinator of the University's Jim-baa-yer Indigenous Higher

Education Unit. She is also a member of NAIITS: An Indigenous Learning Community and was one of the founding staff of the School of Indigenous Studies at the University of Divinity. Naomi is an adjunct at St Mark's National Theological Centre in Canberra and was recently appointed as a University Scholar by the University of Divinity. She is a follower of Jesus, a kinship carer, a history enthusiast and an unapologetic coffee tragic who loves to travel.

Rod Pattenden is a Uniting Church minister currently working as Mission Consultant in the Hunter Presbytery. He is an artist, writer and creative facilitator who has been involved in a number of creative projects working in the conversation between religion, spirituality and the arts. He is co-founder of InterPlay Australia and was for many years Chair of the Blake Prize, Australia's innovative visual art prize exploring religion and spirituality. He has curated a number of exhibitions exploring spirituality in Australia and is co-editor of the recent volume, *Imagination in an Age of Crisis* (2022).

Seini Siseliana Tokilupe Taufa is an Exit Candidate in the Uniting Church in Australia, seeking placement to serve as a Deacon. She was actively involved in the church for a long time and holds various leadership roles. She practices Spiritual Direction and running retreats. She is passionate about accompanying, developing, engaging and deepening the spiritual connection of others with God in a transformative way. She is a graduate of Sydney University and Charles Sturt University and recently obtained a Master of Theology. She enjoys gardening, music, crafts, community work, storytelling and spending time with family.

Simon Moyle has been Elder at GraceTree, a Baptist intentional community on Wurundjeri country near the Merri Creek, for more than twenty years. He is a Brother of the Holy Transfiguration Monastery and a nonviolence trainer and activist. He is married to Julie and dad to four wonderful people. If the wind is low, he'll often be found fishing from his kayak on Warn Marin (Westernport) or Naarm (Port Phillip Bay) (but leave him alone, he likes the quiet solitude).

Uilisone Kiriona Mafaufau has been Minister of the Word at The Lidcombe Samoan Congregation of the Uniting Church in Australia for ten years. He was formerly the Minister of the Word at Hawthorn Uniting Church. Uilisone has a Diploma from the Piula Theological College in Samoa and a Bachelor of Divinity and Master of Theology from the Pacific Theological College in Fiji. He was also enrolled in Doctoral studies at United Theological College in Bangalore, India, and at the Melbourne College of Divinity, and was a lecturer at Piula Theological College. Uilisone's passion is in translation, which is evident in his Master of Theology thesis: 'A Proposal for the Translation of the Greek New Testament into Samoan'.

Will Small is a poet, a speaker and the founder of Lead by Story. He is also the pastor of Meeting Ground Church, host of the Spiritual Misfits podcast and author of *All Things New* (2019) and *Poems for When the World is Ending* (2023). Will's work is often found at the intersection of the creative arts and social impact, using poetry, filmmaking, podcasting and other creative mediums to advocate for a more inclusive and just world.

Editors

Armen Gakavian is passionate about personal and community transformation and is a Pastoral Supervisor. His PhD was in Armenian cultural identity and longing for place. He has lectured in sociology, politics, social ethics, social change and leadership, and has worked as a researcher at Macquarie University and for NGOs in social inclusion, social policy, faith-based social services and multiculturalism. Armen co-founded the Centre for Comparative Genocide Studies at Macquarie University, the Leadership School in Armenia and several NGOs. He has co-led student faith groups and was a volunteer leader and mentor with The Salvation Army in a housing estate in Sydney. Armen is a freelance editor and for nine years was Coordinating Editor for Ethos: EA Centre for Christianity and Society. He is the co-founder of Neighbourhood Matters and At the Edges Publishing. He lives in Surry Hills on Gadigal land, where he connects with the local community.

Karina Kreminski has an Arts degree from Sydney University and worked in English teaching and journalism in Argentina. She has a doctorate in missional formation and was a Senior Minister at a church in Sydney. Karina was a Missiology Lecturer at a theological college and established a Master of Missional Leadership and a church-planting certificate there. In her role as Mission Catalyst with the Uniting Church, she speaks at churches, community groups and conferences on neighbourhood work. She is the author of *Urban Spirituality: Embodying God's Mission in the Neighbourhood* (2018) and writes about spirituality, theology and meaning-making. Karina lives in Surry Hills on Gadigal Land, where she is engaged in place-based community work, facilitating programs and events for community connection. She co-founded a storytelling project called Surry Hills and Valleys and is the co-founder of Neighbourhood Matters and At the Edges Publishing.

Steve Taylor is a public scholar working for AngelWings Ltd and an ordained minister. He serves organisations and seminaries in Australia, New Zealand and the United Kingdom, providing high-quality bespoke empirical research to communities experiencing change. Steve gained a PhD in practical theology from the University of Otago in 2004 for his empirical study of faith formation in new forms of church. He is the author of *The Out of Bounds Church?* (2005), *Built for Change* (2016) and *First Expressions* (2019), and co-editor of *Transforming Work* (2023). He has published over sixty academic outputs and over 285 public writing pieces. Steve is co-editor of the *Ecclesial Futures* journal and maintains academic accountability as Senior Lecturer, Flinders University, and Research Affiliate, Centre for Theology and Public Issues, University of Otago.